PHOENIX

PHOENIX

AMERICA'S SHINING ST★R

A Celebration of Phoenix' Enterprise
by Athia L. Hardt

Windsor Publications, Inc.—History Books Division
Managing Editor: Karen Story
Design Director: Alexander D'Anca

Staff for *Phoenix: America's Shining Star*
Manuscript Editor: Marilyn Horn
Photo Editor: William A. Matthews
Production Editor: Amy Adelstein
Editor, Corporate Profiles: Judith Hunter
Production Editor, Corporate Profiles: Phyllis Gray
Editorial Assistants: Kim Kievman, Michael Nugwynne,
 Kathy B. Peyser, Priscilla Solis, Theresa J. Solis
Publisher's Representatives, Corporate Profiles:
 Beverly Cornell, Richard Fry, Walker Whitley
Layout Artist: Thomas McTighe
Production Assistant: Deena Tucker
Layout Artist, Corporate Profiles: Dan Irwin
Designer: Bradford Boston
Art Director: Ellen Ifrah

Library of Congress Cataloging-in-Publication Data
Hardt, Athia L.
Phoenix: America's shining star.
Bibliography: p. 353
Includes index.
1. Phoenix (Ariz.)—History. 2. Phoenix (Ariz.)—
Description—Views. 3. Phoenix (Ariz.)—Industries.
I. Title.
F819.P57H37 1989 979.1'73 88-20839
ISBN 0-89781-287-5

Windsor Publications, Inc.
Elliot Martin, Chairman of the Board
James L. Fish, III, Chief Operating Office
Michele Sylvestro, Vice President Sales/Marketing

This is dedicated to
Bill and Athia Hardt, who had the
vision to choose Arizona as a place
to raise a family.

Contents

Phoenicians of today pave the way to the future in a place where ancient civilizations found prosperity and promise.

A unique labor force, transportation mode, and media give Phoenix its distinctive vitality.

Careful management of energy sources, water resources, and land development is crucial to Phoenix's growth.

The importance of services and trade in the city's economy characterizes Phoenix's reputation for friendliness.

Chapter Fourteen
Building Greater Phoenix

From concept to completion, Phoenix' building industry shapes tomorrow's skyline.

Chapter Fifteen
The Marketplace

The area's retail establishments, service industries, products, and sporting events are enjoyed by residents and visitors to the area.

Foreword

Phoenix, located in the Valley of the Sun, is a modern city founded on the traditions of the Old West. Photo by Don Stevenson

For decades, perhaps since Gable and Lombard honeymooned here, Phoenix existed as the ideal resort—the desert getaway, the sleepy, charming not-so-far-off hideaway.

Today its myriad of four- and five-star resorts and convention centers maintain that reputation. But Phoenix has grown into something much more. Aided by an abundance of natural resources, skilled human resources, and a growth-oriented economic climate, Phoenix is also one of the nation's fastest-growing business meccas.

Even now Phoenix is established as a stronghold of the burgeoning electronics and semiconductor industries in the United States. Its fast-growing financial and professional service sectors are catapulting Phoenix into a major office center and commercial hub for the Southwest.

Backstopping this development and laying the foundation for future growth is Sky Harbor International Airport. As the gateway to Phoenix, Sky Harbor is one of the nation's most efficient airports—with an aggressive construction program already underway that will carry the city beyond the 1990s.

Evoking the spirit and drive that founded the city, Phoenix has emerged as an entrepreneurial hotbed that has given rise to companies helping to shape the city's future. In fact, a national business publication ranked Phoenix third among all American cities in employment growth, entrepreneurship, and new business start-ups in 1987.

Complimenting this activity is a Southwestern life-style that makes Phoenix attractive to business and family. A sun-filled climate, moderate cost of living, and endless hours of outdoor recreational opportunities make for an inviting place to live and work.

These are the dynamics that are presented in this exciting book on the city of Phoenix. Sponsored by the Phoenix Economic Growth Corporation, the book describes one of the nation's most vibrant urban economies and highlights a corporate community that has greatly contributed to Phoenix's emergence as one of the country's leading cities. We hope you will enjoy *Phoenix: America's Shining Star*

and visit our city to see firsthand why the promise of Phoenix shines as brightly as its Western sun.

A Partnership for the Future of Phoenix

The Phoenix Economic Growth Corporation (PEGC) is the economic development partnership between Phoenix city government and the private sector. Together, these two vital segments of the Phoenix community share a paramount goal: to define, achieve, and maintain the best possible quality of life for our city.

PEGC is a not-for-profit corporation governed by a Board of Directors, consisting of chief executive officers and business representatives from all major sectors of the Phoenix economy, and elected and appointed officials from the city government.

PEGC combines the resources of government and business to promote economic development on a citywide basis. It is the only such group in Phoenix with a public charter sanctioned by city government.

The Phoenix Economic Growth Corporation offers professional assistance, at no charge, to help a company relocate or expand in the Phoenix marketplace. Services include:

MARKETPLACE ANALYSIS

Market data, including socioeconomic demographics, business community and industrial composition, development activity and trends, and profiles of Phoenix in the national marketplace.

FINANCIAL SERVICES

PEGC links companies to private lenders.

PEGC guides businesses to appropriate government-sponsored financial programs.

SITE SEARCH ASSISTANCE

PEGC helps companies locate a property or building to meet their facility requirements.

START-UP INFORMATION AND ASSISTANCE

PEGC expedites permits and cuts red tape.

PEGC provides zoning and licensing information.

PEGC provides companies with state and local regulatory information.

WORKFORCE AND EMPLOYEE TRAINING COORDINATION

PEGC links employers with recruitment assistance services.

PEGC helps to identify employee training programs to meet the individual requirements of companies.

EXPORT AND IMPORT ASSISTANCE

PEGC guides companies through services and facilities available through the Arizona Department of Commerce and Phoenix Foreign Trade Zone.

BUSINESS COUNSELING AND ADVOCACY

PEGC counsels companies on the local business structure, utilities, taxes, transportation, housing, education, human services, cultural activities, etc.

PEGC acts as an advocate for individual business interests to city decision-makers.

PEGC tailors presentations and market orientations on Phoenix as a place to live and do business.

PEGC arranges custom briefings and tours to introduce companies to Phoenix.

For more information on PEGC programs and services, contact PEGC at:

Phoenix Economic Growth Corporation
Two North Central
Mezzanine 210
Phoenix, Arizona 85004
(602) 253-9747

Acknowledgments

Many thanks to Chuck, Nancy, and Jessica Case and to Anne Stephenson and Katie Orcutt for their assistance and support.

The author also wishes to acknowledge the many community, business, and government leaders who gave of their time and thoughts through personal interviews.

Bustling metropolitan Phoenix is balanced by nearby desert serenity. Photos by Susan I. Davison (left) and Nyle Leatham (above)

PART

ONE

A Model
of American
Enterprise

CHAPTER ONE

Heart of the Southwest

Phoenix. Even the name conveys potential. Land of opportunities. Desert oasis. Young city with a past as rich as the Old West, and with—even more vital—a bright future as one of America's great cities.

Like the bird in the mythical legend from which its name derives, Phoenix was reborn on the ashes of a colorful historical past. Arising literally upon the foundation of an ancient Indian civilization, the city of Phoenix took root in the 1860s nearly 100 years after the American Revolution. Almost immediately the population doubled. It is a trend the city has repeated ever since. Rapid growth, and the excitement that comes with it, is what Phoenix is all about.

Phoenix, located in the Valley of the Sun, is a modern city founded on the traditions of the Old West. Photo by Don Stevenson

The Past

When travelers today enter Phoenix, they unknowingly pass over an ancient Indian village, one of hundreds of such villages built by the Hohokam Indians sometime between 300 B.C. and A.D. 200. More than a thousand years before Columbus sailed to the New World, long before a single colony was founded by the Pilgrims on this continent, the Hohokam Indians had developed an intricate society in what would later become known as the Valley of the Sun. Many of the ruins of that society have been preserved today.

Where the Hohokam came from no one can be sure, just as no one is sure where they eventually went. There are those who believe they emigrated from Mexico to the Valley to create their complex urban civilization of towns and houses, cultivated fields of maize, squash, and beans, and—most remarkably—hundreds of miles of irrigation ditches and canals. Others believe the Hohokam developed from earlier groups known as Southwestern Archaic cultures—nomads who traveled throughout the desert. During the height of the Hohokam period, historians believe, there were from 50,000 to 100,000 people living in the Valley.

When they arrived in what was later to become Phoenix, the Hohokam found a valley bounded on the north and south by majestic mountains, a valley 40 miles long by 10 miles wide and bisected by a river, the Salt River. The irrigation system they created with only Stone Age tools has been compared, in the enormity of the undertaking, to the pyramids of Egypt. Tons of dirt must have been transported to create canals that ranged from 6 feet wide to 64 feet wide. The canals, which provided water for drinking, cooking, and all the other needs of life as well as crop irrigating, were rediscovered and used by the settlers who came to the area in the 1860s. In fact, these canals were the ancient forerunner of

Today's recreations of southwestern architecture have drawn inspiration from structures like this Phoenix area church. Photo by Carol Toplain

the irrigation system that traverses the Valley today.

Though the Hohokam ruled the Valley of the Sun for more than a thousand years, they disappeared sometime in the fifteenth century. Historians speculate that some natural disaster may have occurred—an earthquake or drought, for instance—that marauders may have intruded, that declining fertility may have caused the Hohokam to dwindle in numbers, that even the irrigation system itself may have been responsible if the Hohokam irrigated beyond the capacities of the soil. Some believe that the Salado Indians, a Mogollon people from central Arizona, migrated into the area and that the Hohokam culture simply blended with theirs to create today's descendants, the Pima Indians. The name Hohokam means "the departed" in the Pima language, and, for whatever reason, that is what the Hohokam did.

By the time the first Spanish explorers arrived in the Arizona area about 1650, the Hohokam villages had been in ruins for 200

Left: Arizona's rich historic background has brought many cultures together in a modern-day melting pot. Here, an Apache Indian is dressed in ceremonial garb. Photo by Nyle Leatham

Facing page: The tiny carved animals in this Indian fetish are made of shell, turquoise, and other stones. Indian art is plentiful, both in museums and shops in the Phoenix area. Photo by Matt Bradley

years and what remained, besides the legends of their existence, were their canals. Though all evidence indicates that the Spanish expeditions concentrated on areas south of the Valley, the foundation of the Mexican heritage that has played such an important role in the Valley was laid when the Spanish confronted, then blended with, the Indian peoples of central Mexico.

Though there had been a Mexican presence in the Salt River Valley before, the first significant group of Mexican-Americans came in response to a call for agricultural and mining labor in the 1860s. When the U.S. army established a post at Fort McDowell (30 miles northeast of what is Phoenix today), a group of Mexican teamsters and packers were among the pioneers. Put into perspective, it was about the time that the American Civil War was drawing to an end that the potential for the Valley, outlined by the canals of the Hohokam, was recognized by the new settlers, among them the Mexican descendants of those early Spanish visitors.

Above: The domes of St. Mary's Church in downtown Phoenix are a lovely reminder of the city's Southwestern heritage. St. Mary's was constructed a century ago under the guidance of a German priest, Father Novatus Benzing, in the tradition of the Spanish architecture. Photo by Carol Topalian

24

The first Anglo settlers came into the Arizona Territory led by their love of adventure or their search for fortune. Many of them stopped en route to California's rumored treasures, but, intrigued by the beauty of the area, never went on. One of them, John Y.T. Smith, set up haying camps on the banks of the Salt River to feed the cavalry horses at Fort McDowell and drew upon Mexican laborers from Sonora and Tucson. Another early pioneer, a former Confederate soldier named Jack Swilling, looked at the Hohokam canals that had passed the test of time and saw the future of Phoenix. With Mexican workers, he began to retrench the canals in the 1860s. Wheat and barley were planted, 30 farms were started, a steam flour mill was built, and Phoenix' history of rapid growth began.

Photos this page: The Pioneer Arizona Living History Museum preserves the city's Old West traditions. Photos by Mark E. Gibson

Phoenix pioneer Jack Swilling's life reads like a Hollywood script. It's hardly a role for Robert Redford, though—this protagonist's life reveals too many villainous episodes!

Born in 1830 in South Carolina, the son of a cotton plantation owner and a Southern belle, Swilling, by most accounts, was reasonably well educated. One historian has even dubbed him, along with Darrell Duppa (who is widely credited with naming Phoenix), "classical scholars." The term is probably an exaggeration, but at least the two were somewhat acquainted with Greek mythology.

Whether Swilling, who retrenched old Hohokam irrigation canals and dug new ones with a company formed from 12 investors and $10,000 in capital—the Swilling Irrigation and Canal Company—is a hero or a scoundrel is open to debate. Probably the truth falls somewhere in between.

Clearly, Swilling was an unusual individual. By the time he was in his mid-forties, this red-headed pioneer, who stood more than six feet tall, had been a teamster, a prospector, a miner, a flour-mill manager, a gambling house operator, an Indian fighter, a guide, a farmer, a Confederate sol-

Pioneer Jack Swilling was crucial to Phoenix' development. Courtesy, Arizona Department of Library, Archives and Public Records

dier who deserted to the Union side, and Phoenix's justice of the peace and first postmaster.

Swilling died at the age of 48 in an Arizona jail cell, accused—he said unjustly—of having participated in a stagecoach robbery. His body had been racked by previous injuries as well as by the morphine and alcohol he used to soothe the pain of the old wounds.

Historical accounts describe him as generous and kind when he was not drinking, but often cruel, particularly to his Mexican wife, Trinidad Escalante, when he was. He may have killed a man, or more than one. Although it is said Swilling made a fortune from a rich gold mining pros-

pect near Prescott in 1863, he just may have been broke enough to need the proceeds from a stagecoach robbery by 1878.

Whatever is true about his character—whether he was the hero some believed or the villain some suggested—Swilling played a crucial part in the development of Phoenix. While others saw the Valley of the Sun as a dry, valueless place—a sort of adobe ghost town—Swilling must have recognized its potential. Perhaps he suspected that the area had once been one of the largest population centers of the world, home to some 20,000 Hohokam Indians, and dreamed that it would be again.

Drawn to Arizona in the late 1850s, Swilling organized his Phoenix area irrigation company in 1867. Soon the water his canals brought from the Salt River was causing the Valley of the Sun to bloom. Swilling himself began to farm wheat, barley, and corn.

The effort he initiated expanded. And expanded again. And again and again.

Just before his death, Swilling wrote to an Arizona newspaper, "I will be remembered long after the names of my persecutors have been forgotten."

And he was right.

In 1867 there were 60 people in the Valley, according to historical accounts. By 1870, according to the federal census, that number had increased four times.

It was left to an English immigrant, "Lord" Darrell Duppa, whose nobility credentials are

Above: Beginning in the 1860s, Americans began to retrench the canals built by the ancient Hohokam Indians. Courtesy, Arizona Department of Library, Archives and Public Records

Right: The base of Camelback Mountain remains today as prosperous farmland. Courtesy, Arizona Department of Library, Archives and Public Records

questionable, to name the new community. Having observed the town grow so rapidly once the Hohokam's ancient irrigation system was unearthed, it is said that Duppa, a well-read man, chose a symbol that seemed appropriate and called the new town "Phoenix."

"A new civilization will rise from the ashes of an older one, just as the Phoenix bird rises from its own ashes," he is quoted as saying.

Historical accounts of the establishment of Phoenix—first as a town, then as a county seat, and eventually as the state capital—talk about rapid expansion, building booms, and the proliferation of free enterprise. The same words are descriptive of Phoenix today. Attracted to the Valley for its sunshine and its beauty, the people and the businesses they brought with them have created an atmosphere where growth is the byword and opportunity is taken for granted.

"Phoenix was pioneered by those who never recognized impossibilities," is the way former Phoenix mayor Jack Williams, who later served as governor of the state, put it.

Phoenix in the late 1800s was a colorful Western town, not unlike the variety Hollywood portrayed in many Western movies. Agriculture played an important role in its financial base, and it had its share of saloons and gambling halls, shops and one-room schools. By 1880, 1,708 people lived in Phoenix.

Until 1887, when the Maricopa and Phoenix Railway linked it with the main line of the Southern Pacific Railroad, access was by stagecoach or horse-drawn wagon. Not until 1895 did the Santa Fe Railroad arrive in Phoenix, but that didn't stop the prospectors, the ranchers, and the farmers from coming. It is said that the winter-visitor syndrome (Phoenicians today use the term "Snowbirds" to describe the numerous visitors from the Midwest and East who flock to the city in winter) began in 1895. That is when Whitelaw Reid, owner and editor of the *New York Tribune*, came to the Valley for respiratory problems.

By the turn of the century, Phoenix was no longer a provincial little town. A newspaper, the *Salt River Herald*, had begun publishing in 1878, and Arizona's first ice plant had started operating a year later. The first theater had opened in 1877. The city's first real swimming pool—how those pioneers would marvel at the thousands of pools that dot the Phoenix landscape today!—had been constructed at Eastside Park in 1887. Frame and brick had replaced adobe as the dominant construction material.

Below: The advent and availability of the automobile made the wide open spaces of the desert much more hospitable. Courtesy, Arizona Department of Library, Archives and Public Records

Above and right: The Salt River Project and Central Arizona Project increased irrigation in the Phoenix area. Courtesy, Arizona Department of Library, Archives and Public Records

Below: Water has always been the city's most revered resource. This water main was installed in 1905. Courtesy, Arizona Department of Library, Archives and Public Records

Linked to both coasts by railway, the city continued to grow. With growth came prosperity—paved streets, tall buildings, parks, resorts, and automobiles. According to one historian, the attraction of the automobile in the wide open spaces was already so great that between 1913 and 1920 the number of cars in Maricopa County, where Phoenix was (and is) the major population center, rose from 646 to 11,539.

Above: By 1900 Phoenix was beginning to flourish as a city with schools, farms, and businesses. Pictured is an art class in a Phoenix Indian school.

It was in the early 1900s that a movement, born in the prolonged drought that had plagued the West in the 1890s, bore results, and one of the first water projects authorized under the federal Reclamation Act began in the Phoenix area. It was an effort crucial to the future of Phoenix. Valley farmers organized themselves in 1903 as the Salt River Valley Water Users' Association and pledged the lands of the members of the association as collateral to guarantee repayment of a federal construction loan. A dam was to be built on the Salt River, where water could be stored and reclaimed.

On March 18, 1911, President Theodore Roosevelt dedicated Roosevelt Dam, the world's tallest masonry dam, east of Phoenix, and the Salt River Project was virtually complete. The result of the vision of these pioneers was a storage dam to feed the existing canal system, a permanent water supply for Phoenix and the surrounding areas. Today, for most of the year, except during floods, the Salt River is an empty bed where it winds through Phoenix. The project serves central Arizona and the Salt River Valley as both a public utility and a successful multipurpose water reclamation project, distributing annually about one million acre-feet of water.

By 1936, 66 years after the name "Phoenix" was adopted, 55

years after the city was incorporated, and 47 years after it became the state capital, Phoenix already was developing as a business center. It ranked 13th nationally in per capita retail sales, having survived the Depression with few scars. The population exceeded 48,000, and prosperity led to the growth of a number of department stores, including Goldwaters, established in Phoenix in the late 1880s. According to historians, the store boasted a number of firsts—the first passenger elevator in Arizona, the first cashier station in a central system, and the first automatic-opening door.

Operated today by a national chain, Goldwaters was begun by the father and uncle of one of Phoenix's most famous residents, Barry Goldwater. Former U.S. Senator Goldwater, who ran unsuccess-

Below: Roosevelt Dam was constructed as part of the Salt River Project. Courtesy, Arizona Department of Library, Archives and Public Records

Left: An intricate canal system, based on the canals dug by the Hohokam Indians a thousand years ago, has helped to create an oasis in the desert. The reservoir and canal system is operated by the Salt River Project. Photo by Nyle Leatham

Facing page: The beauty of the surrounding area, matched with Phoenix' unbeatable weather and life-style, draws thousands of new residents every year. This sunset showcases the Salt river east of Phoenix. Photo by Nyle Leatham

fully for president in 1964 and became known as "Mr. Conservative," got his political start in 1949 when he was elected to the Phoenix City Council.

The growth spurred by the irrigation waters of the Salt River Project was phenomenal. Though additional dams on the Salt and Verde rivers increased the availability of surface water and pumping of groundwater further expanded farm irrigation, political leaders began to realize the Valley of the Sun would need to bring additional water from the Colorado River into central Arizona in the future, if the growth was to continue. In the mid-1940s the Central Arizona Project plan was presented to Congress for authorization by two Arizona senators—Ernest McFarland and Carl Hayden. The water was to be delivered only for farm irrigation in Maricopa and Pinal counties. It was the beginning of a long fight, both in Congress and in the courts, where the State of California contested Arizona's right to the water.

In 1968, 22 years after the battle began, Congress authorized con-

struction of the Central Arizona Project (CAP). By then it was estimated that about one-third of the water the CAP would bring would be used for municipal and industrial purposes. By 1980 that figure had grown to one-half. The $3.6-billion project, which will be extended to the Tucson area by 1991, began delivering 1.5 million acre-feet of water per year to Maricopa, Pinal, and Pima counties in 1985.

The Present

In the past 20 years, Phoenix has experienced an 80 percent increase in population, growing to nearly one million residents, and a 50

Affordable and attractive housing persuades many to relocate to the Phoenix area. Photo by Nyle Leatham

percent increase in land area, to an area of 386 square miles—larger than many counties in the Eastern United States.

The little Western town has grown up. Tenth-largest city in the United States in population and third-largest in land area, Phoenix was ranked third among the country's fastest growing U.S. cities by *Inc.* magazine when job generation, rate of significant new business start-ups, and the percent of young companies enjoying high-growth rates were calculated. *Inc.* also ranked the state of Arizona first in the country for its favorable business climate.

"Economic growth and diversity have been helped along by the 'favorable regulatory climate' that is a favorite of state boosters everywhere—but that, in Arizona's case, seems more than just a cliche," the magazine wrote.

Community promoters are fond of pointing to the "spirit of cooperation" that exists between government and free enterprise in Phoenix and the state as a whole. Among the advantages they cite are the right-to-work status of Arizona and a state tax structure that is designed to attract business.

Another source, *Forecast '87*, ranked the Phoenix metropolitan area as the leading Western city in business activity. The publication, sponsored by Western Savings and Loan Association, annually surveys business climates in selected Western metropolitan areas: Phoenix, Denver, Portland, Sacramento, Salt Lake City, San Antonio, and Seattle. In all but one of seven business indicators looked at in the 1987 study, Phoenix was first.

Within a relatively short period of time, Arizona has exchanged an economy based on the "Four C's"—copper, cattle, cotton, and citrus—for a more diversified economic base that includes an emphasis on "high tech," but which is also strong in growth in construction, finance, tourism, the service industries, insurance, and real estate. And Phoenix, the population base of the state, has been at the heart of the activity, diversification, and growth.

Well located to serve as a regional business hub for Nevada, Utah, Southern Colorado, New Mexico, and Southern California, Phoenix is fast earning a reputation as a business metropolis.

Attractive to high-tech industry because of relatively low operating costs, ample labor, and an alluring life-style, Phoenix has become the third-largest electronic center in the country. Executive living costs in the area are far below the U.S. average and fall below those of other Western cities such as Denver, Dallas, Houston, and Los

This bird's-eye view shows Grady Gammage Audiorium and Arizona State University, particularly known for its engineering and business colleges. Photo by Nyle Leatham

Angeles. Phoenix also has been a consistent leader in job availability. Employment growth in the city more than doubled over a recent 14-year period, expanding at a higher rate in the Phoenix metropolitan area than anywhere in the U.S. And it enjoys the proximity of Arizona State University (ASU), the sixth-largest campus in the nation and fast becoming a major research institution. ASU currently is expanding, with campuses in downtown Phoenix and on the west side of the city.

Growth continues to be the name of the game in Phoenix.

Pages 38-39: A summer thunderstorm threatens the Valley, creating a spectacular view. Photo by Susan I. Davison

Facing page: Sailing is a popular sport at nearby Lake Pleasant. The man-made lake also attracts windsurfers, skiers, and fishermen. Photo by Nyle Leatham

Projections show the city will continue to increase in population by more than 3 percent each year, topping one million by 1990. Phoenix was the fastest-growing metropolitan area in the entire nation in a six-year period that ended July 1, 1986, according to the U.S. Census Bureau. The U.S. Commerce Department's Bureau of Economic Development predicted Phoenix will be the second fastest-growing metropolitan area in the nation for the next 15 years.

"The influx has made Phoenix and the Valley of the Sun the second fastest-growing market in the fastest-growing region in the U.S.—the Sun Belt," wrote the Phoenix Economic Growth Corporation in a recent publication. "But it isn't only phenomenal growth that makes Phoenix unique. It's a combination of factors, including an enterprising, hands-on spirit that extends to all aspects of life, from business to government, culture, and recreation. The steady flow of energetic, well-educated newcomers creates an open, receptive environment that welcomes opportunity and new ideas. Phoenix is a young city, determined to avoid the mistakes of older urban centers."

Phoenix is a young city not only in its own age, but also in the age of its residents. Though its attraction to retirees is known worldwide, what may not be so well known is that the median adult age in the Phoenix metro area is 31.1 years. Drawn by employment opportunities, thousands of newcomers settle in the Phoenix metro area each month. More than 28 percent of the city's residents are college educated, a statistic far above the 16 percent national average.

The third-warmest city in the United States, with the lowest annual precipitation and highest percentage of days of sunshine, Phoenix has long been known as a location attractive to tourists. Annual average temperature is 72 degrees, and annual average rainfall is about seven inches. Its purple mountains, gorgeous sunsets, picturesque palm trees, and easy life-style have all contributed to its reputation as a vacationer's paradise, particularly in the months when the rest of the country is fighting snowstorms, sleet, and—at best—gray, dismal skies.

Located in the heart of the Sonoran Desert, Phoenix is encircled by the Phoenix Mountain Preserve, a visual monument to the success of efforts to maintain the beauty of the area. Several lakes border the Valley to the east, as do the Superstition Mountains. Long the romantic symbol of rich Western lore, it is said that the Superstitions still contain the wealth of the "Lost Dutchman's Mine," a lost gold mine

Golf is a popular year-round pastime in the Valley of the Sun. This photo shows the 1988 Phoenix Open. Photo by Susan I. Davison

that has lured many an adventurer into the mountains since 1880.

All of this is part of what leads the tourism industry in the Phoenix metro area to expand at an annual increase of nearly 7 percent. Over 6 million visitors come to Phoenix annually, spending more than $2 billion. Some of them attend conventions at the downtown Phoenix Civic Plaza, where the convention center has bookings through the year 2000.

But what also has become clear in the 1980s is that Phoenix is more than a mecca for tourists. What is alluring to travelers is all the more attractive to the businesses and residents who call Phoenix home.

Phoenix offers the good life. With 111 golf courses and more than 1,200 tennis courts, with its wide open spaces and a plethora of swimming pools, Phoenix has an environment that encourages recreation. Site of the nation's largest municipally owned park, South Mountain Park, the city contains three regional parks with over 16,000 acres, and hundreds of smaller-acreage parks. Winter sports enthusiasts find snow and skiing available only a two-hour drive away. Boating and fishing fans enjoy the proximity of six lakes—yes, there are lakes in the desert—and mountain streams. Spectator sports abound. The National Basketball Association's Phoenix Suns, professional baseball (the Phoenix Firebirds) and major league baseball spring training, the ASU Sun Devils (1986 PAC football champions), the fifth-largest college football bowl game in the country (the Sunkist Fiesta Bowl), and—of course—a large selection of professional rodeo events, provide a wide choice of indoor and outdoor excitement. In 1988 the St. Louis Cardinals of the NFL chose to relocate and become the Phoenix Cardinals. Negotiations are under way to build a domed sports stadium.

Spiraling red rock scenery, the gorgeous valleys and spires of the Grand Canyon, the unbelievable cliff dwellings and mesa homes of various Indian tribes, the romance of the historic Spanish missions of Tucson, fishing and hunting territory, the lure of the Mexican border—all of this is within easy driving distance of the centrally located capital.

That cultural development goes hand in hand with economic development is a relatively new concept for Phoenix, but it is one Phoenicians are embracing with enthusiasm. Once struggling to support a part-time symphony, the city now proudly enjoys the fully professional Phoenix Symphony, one of the finest in the country. City officials' commitment to the arts was demonstrated by the creation of the Phoenix

Arts Commission in 1985, and by the adoption of a Percent for Art Program (assuring that funding for public art will be available as new construction takes place) and by a successful bond election with a major art component in 1988. In two years' time—1986 to 1988—Phoenix went from having no funding for public art to having one of the largest budgets—more than $2 million—in the nation.

Cultural opportunities range from the unique Phoenix Zoo, with its African savannah and the Desert Botanical Garden, to the Phoenix Public Library and its 10 branches, the Phoenix Art Museum, the Heard Museum, the Arizona Theater Company, the Arizona Opera Company, and the Phoenix Children's Theater. The list goes on and on.

The hospitality business is a thriving and growing part of the city's life-style. Long known for an abundance of quality Mexican restaurants and steak houses, Phoenix now can brag that its wide variety of gourmet and ethnic restaurants rivals that of any city in the nation. And there are more five-star resorts in the surrounding Valley of the Sun than in any other city in the U.S.

Phoenix has come a long way from the days when Jack Swilling stumbled over the Hohokam canals and wondered if they could be used to further the city's future. Though it has been challenged by the problems that come with rapid expansion, it has not been hampered by the road stops that accompany a no-growth phase or a population decline. Phoenix continues to grow, and city officials say they are committed to nurturing an environment that assures economic vitality as well.

The Future

"The key to the future of Phoenix will be to manage, control, and structure the growth so the life-style of those who already live here

will still prevail," wrote a Phoenix business consultant.

"Today we face the compound challenge of developing, protecting, and enhancing our city's environment," Phoenix Mayor Terry Goddard said in a 1987 State of the City address.

Are the two factors—burgeoning growth and a continued, even bettered, quality of life—compatible? Phoenix political and business leaders say a resounding "Yes!" But they are also aware that the danger of falling prey to the growth-related problems of traffic congestion and air pollution exists, a pitfall to be avoided.

Among the projects currently under way or in the planning stages that city leaders agree will enhance the quality of life in Phoenix are these:

Downtown. Like many major cities, Phoenix has faced the specter of a stagnant downtown. Both public and private efforts are under way to stimulate development. In the last 15 years, Phoenix has constructed a new and spacious Civic Plaza, spurred the construction of two major hotels and a 170-unit residential complex, and opened Heritage Square, a unique area of preservation for some of the area's early Victorian-style homes and a popular outdoor gathering spot.

Dozens of other projects are under way, including the $19-million Herberger Theater Center, and several new highrises. Patriots' Square, a downtown park, is being transformed into a shaded grass-and-brick amphitheater that will feature fountains and a variety of food and entertainment year-round. Private funding efforts are adding a laser lighting and projection system that would be visible throughout the Valley. A "solar oasis," a demonstration project that shows

Facing page: This donkey is among the live exhibits at the Pioneer Arizona Living History Museum, a popular attraction for tourists as well as native Phoenicians. Photo by Steve Weiss

Below: A remarkable display of cacti and other succulent plants, trees, and flowers from all the deserts of the world grows naturally in an outdoor setting at the Desert Botanical Garden in Phoenix' Papago Park. Photo by Matt Bradley

how solar energy can be used to provide cool air, is being constructed at the Civic Plaza, a first of its kind in the world.

Transportation. Plans to expand the existing bus system, improve streets, add freeways, and enlarge Sky Harbor Airport are all in the works. By the year 2005 a total of 320 miles of freeway will be available in the city. A unique feature of the Papago Freeway, which currently is under construction, is its design, which tunnels underground at the heart of the city. This design will permit a park to be con-

At the Desert Botanical Garden, cacti come in all shapes and sizes. Photo by Mark E. Gibson

structed on the surface, over the freeway.

Phoenix' 10-year transportation funding plan includes more than $300 million for public transit. The city's six-year major street program calls for construction of 105 miles of major streets at a cost of $283 million.

A $160-million fourth passenger terminal is being added to Sky Harbor Airport, which has experienced the highest increase in use of any airport in the nation. The eighth-largest airport in the world,

Facing page and right: Heard Museum offers fine displays of both prehistoric and contemporary native American arts. Photos by Matt Bradley

measured by the number of operations, Sky Harbor is serviced by 22 airlines and is used by 15 million passengers a year.

Education. Though the city itself has no direct funding responsibility for schools, the Phoenix City Council—cognizant that enriched educational opportunities are a vital component in future development—formed the Phoenix Commission on Excellence in Public Education.

"Traditionally, education has been left exclusively to our school districts and the state," the document forming the commission stated. "However, an increasing number of cities are recognizing that when the educational needs of their residents are not addressed, the city suffers significant economic problems and out-migration."

The 21-member blue-ribbon panel, which includes business representatives and educators, was given charge to report to the council on the status of education in Phoenix, educational initiatives currently at work in Phoenix and other cities, and the outlook and recommendations for education in the city.

At a higher educational level, officials point to Arizona State University's branch campuses on the west side of Phoenix and downtown (the ASU campus is located in Tempe, just east of Phoenix, about a 20-minute ride from downtown). The ASU College of Engineering is engaged in an on-going effort to develop high-level programs in computer and communication sciences, solid-state electronics, computer-aided processes, thermo sciences, energy sciences, and transportation systems.

Water. Water will continue to be a critical resource in this city, as it has been in the past, but Phoenix is committed to a water supply ample to meet industrial and personal needs. Phoenix residents have not been conservative water-users, feeling free to create green-lawned oasis life in an environment suited to desert vegetation. But water experts say that an existing Phoenix conservation program that emphasizes public awareness and education has reduced water demand greatly, and that careful management and further efforts to reduce consumption, coupled with the CAP waters, will mean the city has sufficient water to meet projected growth demands.

Land-Use Planning. Phoenix has adopted an "urban village" plan that is hailed by city planners nationwide as a pioneering effort. The plan is aimed at breaking a big city into village-like clusters, where residents can shop, work, and live, and is designed to help solve traffic and pollution problems. The Phoenix general plan encourages mixed uses of land in nine individual villages within the city. The core of each is designed as a mini-downtown, with more density and higher buildings than on the outer fringes of the village.

Arts and Libraries. The City of Phoenix plans to enlarge both its existing art museum and library in the foreseeable future. Both facilities currently have large portions of their collections in storage, and the council and the voters of Phoenix have indicated a commitment to make

Runners enjoy a morning jog along the Arizona Canal. Photo by Susan I. Davison

the needed improvements. The council has approved yearly increases in operating funds for both areas.

Business Development. More than 20 organizations are working to stimulate the Phoenix economy. One of the relatively new players in the field is the Phoenix Economic Growth Corporation (PEGC), formed in 1985. PEGC has published a five-year strategic plan for business development, encouraging an increased partnership between the private and public sectors. PEGC grew out of the Mayor's Ad Hoc Committee for Economic Development.

"Money and sun may bring people to Phoenix," a futurist predicted in 1986, "but it's the quality of life that will keep them."

It's a thought that underlines the philosophies of all those concerned about the city's future.

"We've gone through an awkward maturing process the last 10 years, sort of coming from being a large small town to being a small large city. And that's been an important transition. It's resulted in a simultaneous growth and maturing of cultural institutions and recreational opportunities," said Mayor Goddard. "I think the quality of life is unquestionably better than it was 10 years ago, and it's unquestionably getting better still."

CHAPTER TWO

Dynamic City in the Sun

The Biltmore Golf
Course offers a striking
view of the city skyline.
Photo by Nyle Leatham

Every month, thousands of people move to Phoenix, making the city and its suburbs one of the fastest-growing metropolitan areas in the country, according to the U.S. Census Bureau.

In many ways, it is that continuous, consistent growth that has been the area's main "industry," as important to Phoenix as the automotive industry has been to Detroit. Drawn to the desert oasis because of its climate, natural beauty, life-style, and attractive labor market, the newcomers have contributed to what one promotional brochure describes accurately as the city's "self-perpetuating dynamics."

"New residents, attracted by plentiful jobs, stimulate the economy with their income, while their needs create still more jobs, attracting additional newcomers," explains the brochure. "This situation is reflected in the steady and striking growth of both personal income and retail sales. By 1990, the average household income is projected to reach $36,610. And since 1960 areawide retail sales have risen an incredible 1,000 percent."

That the job market has kept up with the tremendous growth is remarkable, given the fact that the population has grown as rapidly as it has.

Phoenix' central location in the Southwest and its easy access to the West Coast have contributed to making the city the heart of one of the most dynamic markets in the country. In effect, the city has become a twentieth-century melting pot of second- and third-generation Americans relocating in search of a better life. Today more than 1.9 million people live in the Phoenix metropolitan area, the great majority of them within the boundaries of the city of Phoenix.

What does this mean for Phoenix' future? Now the 10th-largest city in the nation, the city is expected to continue to grow substan-

tially. Though there are some who believe the rate of growth may slow a little in the future, the U.S. Department of Commerce has predicted that, if the current rate of growth continues, Phoenix soon will be the fifth-largest city in the U.S. And though growth brings unique challenges, they are challenges that most of the country—faced with declining

Facing page: Phoenix is a melting pot of Southwestern cultures and of visitors from other states. Photo by Matt Bradley

Below: The modern architecture found in many of the new buildings stands out in the desert setting. Photo by Nyle Leatham

California
1983
PHOENIX
HYDROFORCE

populations and high unemployment rates—would gladly face. The bottom line is that all the rapid migration into the area has fueled prosperity in the Valley of the Sun, and it is expected to continue to do so.

Change is part of daily life in the Phoenix metro area. From one month to the next, a vacant lot becomes a tall building. A two-lane street becomes a four-lane road. This pattern of change has fueled a willingness to try new approaches, to experiment—attitudes that simply could not exist in a less mobile city.

Above: The rate of construction in Phoenix is phenomenal, with high rises sprouting throughout the city. Photo by Matt Bradley

Facing page: The construction industry has been a major source of employment in Phoenix, where rapid growth has called for expansive building. Photo by Matt Bradley

In such a dynamic market, the availability of an adequate labor force, a convenient transportation mode, and a growing media market play a vital role. This chapter examines those aspects of the Phoenix community.

A Young, Technically Trained Labor Force

The steady flow of newcomers to the Phoenix metro area creates a large work force that is unique for its age, educational level, and motivation.

The median adult age of the newcomers is 31.1 years, while 28 percent are college graduates (compared to a national average of 16 percent). A large number come equipped with technical and managerial training, according to the Phoenix Economic Growth Corporation.

"In general, the labor force is younger and more technically oriented because of the mix of jobs we have here," said one labor statistician.

In the last decade, Phoenix—and the state of Arizona—has moved from an economy that was highly dependent on its natural resource base, particularly agriculture and tourism, to an economy that is diversified. The city has led the state in its rapid transition from an economy that in the 1950s was based on the "Four C's" —copper, cattle, cotton, and citrus—to one that is stimulated by a range of factors. Economists point to the balanced character of the economies of both Phoenix and the state as big assets.

Studies have shown that employment growth in the Phoenix metropolitan area has occurred in three main areas: regional and/or national administrative headquarters; high-tech manufacturing; and retirement/tourism, making the city increasingly important as a center of business activity in the Southwest.

Phoenix is a young and growing city, and this is reflected in its residents. Newcomers to Phoenix have a median age of 31.1 years. Photo by Nyle Leatham

Just as the nation has experienced a rapid growth in the service economy, so, too, has the Phoenix area. In fact, personal service employment in Arizona as a whole has grown greatly. As the state capital and largest urban area in a state that is increasingly urbanized (75 percent of the population of Arizona lives in one of two urban areas—Phoenix or the much smaller community of Tucson), Phoenix has a large number of jobs in government, business, and financial services. Because of the building activity generated by the growth trend, construction is a strong source of employment.

Manufacturing—particularly aerospace, electronic, and semiconductor manufacturing—plays a major role in the Phoenix economy, although national slowdown trends in this area have been felt in Phoenix, too, leading local industry to work towards diversifying the high-tech base in recent years. Efforts have been made to broaden the extent of the high-technology products manufactured, providing an integration of components instead of specializing in the manufacturing of chips. From 1975 to 1984, high-tech manufacturing grew an average of 7 percent a year, compared to a national rate of 4 percent a year. High-tech industries comprise 49 percent of all Arizona manufacturing.

Mountain West, a Phoenix-based research firm, found in a recent study that, in addition to the large labor force, industries also were attracted to the city by the availability of land, the general absence of trade unions, and the reasonable cost of building and maintaining real property. "Labor, on the other hand, is attracted by the availability of jobs and the reasonable cost of living compared to other major metropolitan areas," the research firm concluded.

While tourism has remained an important part of the city's economic base, it has become much more convention oriented. The Phoenix Civic Plaza has expanded to keep up with convention demands,

The Phoenix Civic Plaza fountain becomes a gathering spot on warm spring evenings. The Civic Plaza is a national convention center in part due to expansion efforts. Photo by Susan I. Davison

emerging as a major national convention center.

The affluence of the area has kept Phoenix' unemployment rate consistently lower than the national average, and that is expected to continue in the future, despite the phenomenal growth projections. From 1978 until recently, Phoenix' unemployment rate, averaging 5.7 percent, has remained beneath the national average of 7.5 percent while the population has continued to climb. Job expansion has sim-

Above: Phoenix, easily accessible by major highways, is located off Interstates 10 and 17. Photo by Nyle Leatham

Pages 66-67: Along with mass transit, expansion of the roads and freeways in metropolitan Phoenix have become priorities. Photo by Tom Stack ply kept up with the growth rate. Though that slowed down somewhat recently, partially because of the international impact on the whole high-tech industry, Phoenix is expected to continue to have an unemployment rate far below the national average in the future.

From Stagecoach Stop to Transportation Hub

In a relatively short span of time, Phoenix has transformed a reputation as a landlocked and, therefore, somewhat isolated city to an image as a transportation hub for the Southwest. Only 100 years ago stagecoaches were the main mode of access to the frontier town.

It was in 1887 that the arrival of the railroad first made apparent the fact that Phoenix would not remain an isolated community for long. The Maricopa and Phoenix Railway was completed, linking Phoenix with the main line of the Southern Pacific. The Santa Fe Railroad arrived in Phoenix in 1895, and the Southern Pacific main line in 1926.

Today, when Phoenix is easily accessible by air, rail, and highway, the impact that the arrival of the railroad had in those times is difficult to grasp. Historians say the railroad was greeted with "a jubilee celebration," an event that forever put an end to days when the only connection to the transcontinental line was a six-hour stagecoach ride.

"The inaccessibility to a main-line system meant Phoenix was considered 'off the beaten path' by locals and visitors alike," writes G. Wesley Johnson, Jr., in his book *Phoenix: Valley of the Sun*.

The railroad was the first of the new transportation systems that would place the city squarely in the middle of the beaten path.

Today the city's location (ideally located to serve Mexico, Nevada, Utah, Southern California, New Mexico, and Southern Colorado, as well as all of Arizona) has become one of its major assets.

Phoenix is conveniently located to offer fast and direct service to other key markets in the Sunbelt, all areas of the nation, and the world.

"The advent of air conditioning, aviation, and computers meant you could live in Phoenix and take care of your corporate activities anywhere in the world within a day. Why live anywhere else?" asks N.A. "Dutch" Bertholf, Jr., the head of Phoenix's Sky Harbor International Airport, himself a relocated Easterner.

Phoenix is a city of close to 400 square miles, the third-largest city in land area in the country, larger than many entire counties in the Eastern United States. As a result, Phoenicians continue to rate highly the importance of the independence associated with driving one's own car. For that reason, among others, much of the city's future transportation agenda is geared toward providing a better network of roads and freeways within metro boundaries.

Following nearly a decade in which the city's voters wrestled with indecision about whether to build more freeways, Phoenix has made an ambitious commitment to creating a balanced transportation system. More than 200 new freeway miles will be interwoven with an employer-based ride-sharing program, increased bus service, and a planned rapid transit system.

Facing page: Located in the middle of Phoenix, Sky Harbor International Airport is the eighth-largest airport in the world in terms of operation. Photo by Nyle Leatham

Below: Passenger facilities have been expanded at Sky Harbor International to accommodate the increasing air traffic. Photo by Nyle Leatham

The city that for so long was perceived as a tourist destination is growing up. Now an economic center, with major financial and business services and an always-growing population, Phoenix is making a commitment to implement the transportation system needed to support its expanded role.

The Airport

Sky Harbor International Airport has surpassed even the incredible growth experience of the Phoenix metro area. In 1982, 7.4 million passengers used the airport. Since that year the number of passengers flowing through the airport has increased by about 15 percent annually, to a total in 1987 of 15 million passengers. The airport served more passengers in the first half of the 1980s than it did throughout the entire 1970s.

No other airport in the nation—perhaps in the world—has experienced such consistent, rapid growth, and projections are that the airport will become one of the busiest in the nation within a few years. According to a study reported by the Economic Outlook Center in the College of Business at Arizona State University, about one-

half of the visitors at the airport are departing Arizona and the other half are arriving from elsewhere. Of the arriving passengers, about one-half are returning Arizonans and the other half are visitors. And of the visitors, about one-half are business travelers.

The 2,200-acre Sky Harbor has expanded its facilities to keep up with use and will continue to do so in the future. A $160-million fourth terminal with 32 new gates and the capacity to expand to 76 is under construction and will be operable in late 1990. The terminal project also will add two concourses, 2,600 parking spaces, a major north-south taxiway, an additional east-west taxiway, and a dual-level terminal roadway system. Terminal 3, which opened in 1979, is an attractive facility that features convenient access to shops and restaurants and an outstanding display of Southwestern art.

Twenty-two airline carriers use the airport—about a dozen of them are major airlines—providing Phoenix with one of the best patterns of air service to the Southwest and with good service to the rest of the country. One growing airline, America West, recently made Phoenix headquarters for its operations.

Among its chief attractions, Sky Harbor, which is 21st in number of passengers and 8th in total operations in the nation,

claims its convenient location and the efficiency associated with the Phoenix climate.

The airport is located "right smack in the middle of Phoenix," making access to freeways and rail lines unsurpassed, points out Bertholf, the aviation director. Sky Harbor also has "the benefit of climatic conditions that other airports don't have," he added. The airport annually experiences only about eight hours during which it is not fully functional, the highest percentage of operational time of any airport in the U.S.

Sky Harbor has come a long way since the city of Phoenix purchased it from a private company for $35,300 cash and a $64,700 mortgage in 1935. The city also operates two smaller airports in the Valley that are heavily used by businesses in the area. The Phoenix-Goodyear Municipal Airport on the west side of the Valley of the Sun was purchased in 1968 from the U.S. Navy and has one of the highest growth potentials of Arizona's general aviation airports. Only 200 of its 800 acres have been developed. The Phoenix-Deer Valley Municipal Airport, purchased in 1971, is one of the busiest airports in Arizona, averaging 250,000 takeoffs and landings per year.

Access by Truck and by Rail

Five high-speed U.S. Interstate highways and a growing system of state roads cross Arizona, making truck-line overnight delivery possible to San Diego, Los Angeles, Las Vegas, Albuquerque, and El Paso. Markets in San Francisco, Salt Lake City, and west-central Texas can be reached by the second morning.

The city is served by the Santa Fe and Southern Pacific railroads. The two lines connect for reciprocal switching in Phoenix. Fast freight access is available by connecting lines from either coast, from Canada to Mexico, and into the interior of Mexico.

Roads and Freeways—Phoenix on Wheels

Phoenix transportation administrators use the words "balanced transportation system" to describe the interwoven maze of transportational services they expect to see in operation in the city by the end of the decade. They envision a system that includes an effective rapid transit system, but they are frank about the fact that the majority of the transportation burden will continue to be carried on the city's roads and freeways. Therefore, the city has committed itself to creating an efficient blending of freeways, parkways, bus routes, mass transit corridors, on-demand services, commuter lanes, and other services such as park-and-ride lots.

Phoenix is a city in which it is easy to find one's way around, thanks to a grid-road system that is logical and can be quickly learned. The great majority of the Valley is served by a single freeway, a combination of Interstate 17 and Interstate 10.

In the last five years, the city has made an ambitious commitment to improving its arterial roads. Annually, Phoenix has devoted about $25 million to maintenance and $60 million to reconstruction as well as construction of streets in the 4,000-

mile street system. Another 105 miles of major streets will be completed at a cost of $283 million in the next couple of years.

In the next decade, the character of the road system will change dramatically. Work is under way to add 231 new miles of freeway in the area, a response to voter approval in 1985 of a $5-billion funding package for freeways and public transit. By the year 2005 a total of 320 miles of freeway will allow Phoenix to carry about 35 percent of its traffic on the freeway system. Among projects slated for completion in the next few years are the Papago Freeway extension into nearby Tempe, home of Arizona State University, the Squaw Peak Parkway within the city, and a stretch of an outer-loop freeway in northwest Phoenix and Glendale.

Facing page: An aerial view exemplifies the area's grid-road system. Photo by Mark E. Gibson

Below: The Papago Freeway expansion is one of the efforts Phoenix has taken to keep pace with population and traffic growth. Photo by Don Stevenson

At the present rate of growth, in just 12 years the number of cars in the Phoenix area on the road during rush hour will increase by another quarter of a million—a rise of 30 percent.

That's the kind of statistic that could defeat someone less optimistic than Larry Miller, executive director of the Regional Public Transportation Authority (RPTA). But Miller, who was a key transit planner in Vancouver, British Columbia, before he was hired to head the Valley RPTA, has a plan to deal with the rapid growth. It's a plan that calls for mass transit, better freeways and roads, more carpooling, and more buses.

"It's not pie in the sky," Miller says. "When people say, 'Can this happen?' my best response is, 'Can we afford for it not to happen?'"

Though the freeways currently planned or under construction in Maricopa County are designed to improve the flow of traffic, transit planners say that in the long run, growth catches up with freeways. Los Angeles is a good example.

Thus, Miller has been charged with creating a comprehensive, balanced transportation system that will integrate

Surface street and freeway expansions are part of Phoenix' plan to accomodate population growth. Photos by Jim Marshall (above) and Susan I. Davison (facing page)

a variety of transport modes, including the automobile. "I'm optimistic because I see the public and their leaders being cognizant of the issues," says Miller, who won the job over 90 applicants in 1986 after a group of Valley mayors who went to Vancouver to tour its rapid transit system met him. Miller then was general manager of B.C. Transit in Vancouver.

A key portion of the system envisioned by RPTA planners involves the creation of a multibillion-dollar regional mass transit system. This will probably be a light-rail system that includes automated elevated guideway transit for the more heavily traveled corridors.

In 1985, Maricopa

County voters authorized funding for construction of 233 miles of freeways and expressways as well as authorizing creation of the RPTA to begin long-range transportation planning, including strategies for mass transit. Over the next three years, RPTA was also responsible for increasing bus service in the metropolitan Phoenix area by 15 percent, adding 15 new routes and expanding route lengths by over 5,000 miles. Improvements included rush-hour-only service to many parts of the county, all-day connections east-to-west and north-to-south, increased bus frequency in some regional corridors, and new buses to ensure these services.

RPTA also expanded dial-a-ride services in Sun City in a test program to determine whether flexible, on-demand bus service could better meet the needs of the area's residents. Sun Cities Area Transit, a private, non-profit contractor, uses wheelchair-accessible nine-passenger vans in the test program to collect riders from their homes in the retirement community and drive them to a nearby transit terminal. It also began managing the Maricopa Association of Government's Regional Ridesharing

Program, an effort to offer employees carpooling, vanpooling, and public transit alternatives.

The next step in the creation of the coordinated system is expected to be taken in 1989, when voters will be asked to approve funding for the RPTA's finalized plan. Miller claims the Valley needs financial commitment. "If you don't spend the dollars on this, you are going to spend the dollars somewhere else," he says. "Growth fuels the economic machine here more than anything else. It's not going to continue at the pace it has been if we don't solve the pollution and transportation problems."

He adds that Phoenix can avoid following in the footsteps of Los Angeles by encouraging growth along transportation corridors. "The Los Angeles transit people have this advice: Get started today," he says.

Larry Miller and the RPTA are committed to making that start.

Rapid Transit—A Dream Becoming Reality

History, as well as modern examples elsewhere, conclusively proves that transportation or the quality of access is one of the key determinants of the extent, nature, and location of development. To continue to simply build highways or widen streets or synchronize traffic lights to accommodate the future would be costly, if not prohibitive in financial and environmental terms. A balanced transportation system is called for, and the Regional Public Transportation Authority is moving forward to provide the missing portion.

The speaker is Larry E. Miller, executive director of the Regional Public Transportation Authority (RPTA), and if he has a little of the missionary's zeal in proclaiming his message, perhaps he can be forgiven. Miller, who was responsible for the planning and construction of an $834-million, 12-mile rapid transit system in Vancouver, is heading up an organization that has been fully operational since September 1986, and he is working under a tough deadline. In 1989 he and his organization must present to the voters a plan—a balanced transportational plan with a strong mass transit component—so attractive that they will agree to boost sales taxes to up to half a cent to put it into effect. The Phoenix system is expected to cost billions of dollars and take 20 years to complete.

In its infancy, the RPTA has fo-

Phoenix residents daily see sunsets like this over their backyard fences. It's all an attractive part of the good life in the bustling Southwestern hub. Photo by Susan I. Davison

cused on managing a regional ride-sharing program, working with employees to set up computer-match vanpool programs, coordinating specialized transportation for the handicapped, and expanding routes and adding hours to the city's bus system. But to many, the most exciting potential is its work in planning for a 100-mile rail system to speed commuters to and from work. It is this component, advocates say, that will keep Phoenix from following in the footsteps of its overcrowded, congested neighbor, Los Angeles.

"Voters in 1985 gave us the mandate to develop the missing part of the transportation system in the Valley," Miller said. Without it, he added, "we may find ourselves choked out of existence."

Already, the RPTA has been responsible for continuing improvements in the city's bus system. Owned by a private company until the mid-1970s, when the city purchased it, the bus system has steadily improved service ever since, growing from a system of 200 buses to more than 300. Recently, under RPTA planning, it lengthened weekend and evening service.

Severo Esquivel, surface transportation manager for the city, called the bus system "the backbone of any rapid transit system in the future," and said, "We really have the skeleton of the system now."

Bus ridership has increased 50 percent in the last three years, he said. "The car always will be the principal mode, especially in the West. But a balanced system helps by making it easy to mix and match—to mix the transportation systems and provide options to the people."

The Media—Like Phoenix, Prosperous and Growing

Like most new towns, frontier Phoenix was hungry for news—news from the outside, and news of what was happening within its own borders. The city's first newspaper, the weekly *Salt River Herald*, began publishing in 1878 and became the daily *Phoenix Herald* a year later, still more than a year before the city's incorporation. The tiny publication was the forerunner of what has become today the state's largest and most powerful newspaper, the morning daily, the *Arizona Republic*. Though for several years the city had a competitive environment of three or four daily newspapers operating most of the time, by 1914 the number had been reduced to two—the *Arizona Republic*, derived from the earlier *Herald*, and the *Arizona Gazette*, which has evolved into the sister paper to the *Republic*, the afternoon newspaper, the *Phoenix Gazette*.

Facing page: The beauty of Phoenix is illustrated in magazines throughout the nation. Photo by Susan I. Davison

Below: The Arizona Republic and the Phoenix Gazette have played important roles in the shaping of the city's future. They are among the most dominant players in a varied media scene. Photo by Susan I. Davison

These scarlet buglers add splashes of color to the Boyce Thompson Arboretum. Photo by Nyle Leatham

The two newspapers were to exert a growing impact on the way the city developed, particularly after they were purchased in 1946 for $4 million by Eugene C. Pulliam, owner and publisher of the *Indianapolis Star*. Like other strong publishers of his time, Pulliam exerted great personal influence over his newspapers and took an active role in determining the political character of the city in which they operated. According to his biographer, Pulliam, who died in 1975, called the purchase of the two newspapers "the best buy I ever made." No wonder! Today, media executives from other entities guesstimate the newspapers' gross revenues at somewhere between $200 million

and $350 million annually. The *Republic* has a daily circulation of 331,000 and a Sunday circulation of 508,000. The *Gazette*, which does not publish on Sunday, has a daily circulation of 113,000.

Though the *Republic* and *Gazette* continue to wield considerable clout as the largest print media voice in the Valley, they are joined today by a wide variety of media, including 19 AM and 17 FM radio stations, 9 television stations (4 major), and a growing number of cable television systems. The largest of the latter is Dimension Cable, with 172,000 subscribers and the greatest number of plant miles—5,300 miles—of any system in the country. Times Mirror Cable is the parent company.

USA Today came into the market in 1984, putting $12 million into the construction of a printing plant in a Phoenix suburb. Newspaper administrators claim the paper has experienced wide acceptance, partly because of the large number of winter visitors who are seeking news from their hometowns.

Two weekly newspaper entities have gained a strong share of the market in the Valley. Independent Newspapers, which publishes in eight Valley markets, has a total combined circulation of more than 214,000. *New Times,* a lively tabloid that began in 1970 as a 12-page underground publication at Arizona State University, distributes 128,000 copies a week and has published as much as 160 pages in an issue.

Phoenix also has three city-oriented magazines, *Phoenix Metro, Phoenix Home/Garden,* and *Arizona Living,* as well as the internationally distributed *Arizona Highways,* which probably has introduced more foreigners, Midwesterners, and Easterners to the extraordinary beauty of Arizona's deserts and mountain lands than any other single source.

Furthermore, the entrepreneurial atmosphere of the city has spawned the creation of three thriving business publications: two weeklies, the *Arizona Business Gazette* and the *Business Journal;* and a monthly magazine, *Arizona Trend.* The *Business Journal* chose Phoenix for the headquarters of its Western region, which includes Hawaii, San Diego, Los Angeles, San Jose, Sacramento, Portland, and Seattle.

"Phoenix is where I wanted to live," explained publisher Armon Mills, vice president for the Western region. Mills came to Phoenix as president of the newspaper's parent company, American City Business Journals, in search of a publisher for the Phoenix publication, looked it over, and decided to take the job himself.

Zinnias form a colorful entrance to the Mountain Bell Building, which reflects the Abacus office building across the street. Photo by Matt Bradley

"I came here and thought, 'This is too good to be true,'" he said.

The city has worked well as a hub for his newspaper's Western region, he added. "It has direct flights to all the markets I cover. I was in San Jose for a couple of days last week and San Diego three weeks ago. I go to Kansas City for meetings of the board of directors."

All the fast-paced growth of the area has created increased demands for information gathering, and five daily newspapers in Phoenix' suburbs are helping to fill the need. As the editor of one of them put it, "We all have our hands full keeping up with the growth of the market."

"The fact of the matter is that Phoenix is a growing, enormously pluralistic town," summarized Phoenix pollster Earl de Berge. "A lot of different media—electronic and print—are finding a place in the market."

CHAPTER THREE

City of Foresight

ocated in a valley
between mountain ranges, Phoenix is
a growing metropolis that combines
its roles as desert oasis and bustling business center, still rich in land available for development despite its relent-
less expansion. It is a city whose
appearance and environment belies
its location on the northern edge of
the Sonoran Desert. Seen from an airplane, the city is covered with green
lawns and dotted with swimming
pools. Though Phoenix experiences
an average rainfall of only seven
inches per year, the city's water supply is adequate to accommodate foreseeable personal and business
growth, particularly under the plan-

*Although located in the
Sonoran desert, Phoenix is
dotted with swimming pools
and lawns, thanks to early development of the canal system
and water management pro-
grams. Photo by Nyle Leatham*

ning mechanisms that resulted from the adoption of the Arizona Groundwater Code in the mid-1980s. And the energy picture for the metropolitan area remains bright, as it does for the rest of the state.

The phenomenal growth of the area has encouraged a favorable commercial real estate market. At a time when cities nationwide are experiencing rising vacancy rates, Phoenix is the second-leading U.S. city in the rate it is absorbing new office space, following only Los Angeles. Though the market has slowed somewhat from its record-setting pace of the early 1980s, real estate construction continues to do well in Phoenix, in no small part because land prices generally are lower than in other areas in the Sunbelt.

Careful management will be the key to the continued efficient development of Phoenix's natural resources in the future. It will determine whether, for example, sufficient development occurs in now-vacant areas to support the mass transit system contemplated. It will decide if water supplies can continue to meet water demands. Finally, city planners say, it will settle the question of whether the Phoenix of tomorrow will be not merely bigger, but also better.

Land, availability of water, and an adequate source of energy will play crucial roles in determining the path of future growth.

Planning for the Future—Land

Like most Southwestern cities, Phoenix has plenty of land. Its physical boundaries constantly are expanding; it has grown from 246 square miles in 1965 to its current size of close to 400 square miles.

With all that space (and still growing through annexation), Phoenix is the third-largest city in land area in the United States.

Metropolitan Phoenix has a total of more than 36 million square feet of office space, and the majority—about 70 percent—is within the city's boundaries. The city has come through a record-

Phoenix is a city with no shortage of space, having enough square miles to rank as the third largest city in land area in the United States. Photo by Don Stevenson

establishing building spurt and is entering a phase of less building as industry works to fill existing new space. During 1985 the Valley's commercial real estate industry experienced one of its most active years in leasing, lending, and building ever recorded. Building permits were issued for more than 7 million square feet of office space and 6.5 million square feet of industrial space. Brokers leased more than 3.2 million square feet for office space alone. But the easy availability of financing for office construction added even more space than could be filled, despite the fact that the diversity of Phoenix's economic base creates a large office space tenant base. In 1986 a record 3.7 million square feet were absorbed.

The natural result of the rapid building cycle has been a slow-down in building permits, at least when compared to the mid-1980s.

Conscious of the problems of urban sprawl that can accompany the great advantages of land availability, city leaders have undertaken to ensure careful developmental planning with adoption of the "General Plan for Phoenix, 1985-2000." Among the key components of the plan, adopted by the Phoenix City Council in 1986, is its urban-village concept, the outgrowth of an extensive citizen-based planning process that began in the early 1970s.

The plan is intended to break the city into clusters where residents can shop, work, and live, allowing urban, suburban, and even rural life-styles to coexist within one "village." A blueprint for balanced growth, the urban-village concept has been hailed as a pioneering effort to provide for orderly growth and to retain "a humane city." Even critics of the plan applaud the concept, though they

Facing page: An urban village concept adopted by the Phoenix City Council will develop the city into clusters of residential and commercial districts. Photo by Don Stevenson

Below: Expansion and development in downtown Phoenix has created more than 36 million square feet of office space. Photo by Don Stevenson

Above: Central Avenue is slated for continued development to facilitate commercial expansion downtown. Photo by Nyle Leatham

Facing page: Residential neighborhoods are close by to downtown Phoenix. Photo by Matt Bradley

argue over whether the city will maintain the vision.

Richard Louv, a California futurist, who once criticized Phoenix as a city that was growing too quickly, told a newspaper reporter after the council adopted the plan that Phoenix is "a pioneering city" in the urban-village approach, and said Phoenix had broken from the pack of Sunbelt cities that "had that knee-jerk mentality of not planning the city."

"I think Phoenix has more consciousness of the need for more urban-style planning, the need to keep it a humane city," Louv told the *Arizona Republic*. "It remains to be seen whether in reality it will develop humanely."

Phoenix leaders are determined to see that it does. And they believe the mixed-use plan, in conjunction with mass transit and freeways, will go a long way in helping to solve traffic and pollution problems associated with growth.

Under the general plan, nine village clusters are designated; each contains a mini-downtown and a high-density core, surrounded by decreasing density uses. Areas that already are high in density are singled out as village cores, with development projected up to the year 2000. The policy emphasizes the importance of infill and higher-density urban development. In addition, the plan provides for continued development of the city's principal street, Central Avenue, concentrating the maximum intensity of commercial use downtown and allowing for highrise waivers to be granted as appropriate.

Thirty percent of the land in the urban villages is vacant and suitable for development. (An additional 18 percent is not developed, but unavailable, due to floodplains, mountain preserves, canals, and transportation corridors.) As a result of the Arizona legislature's passage of the Urban Lands Act in 1981, about 7,000 acres of state land within the urban villages also is suitable for urban planning under a sale, lease, or exchange arrangement with the state. Another 50,000 acres of state land that falls under the purview of the Urban Lands Act is located in four peripheral study areas that are not completely within city limits.

The act permits the orderly development of the designated urban lands under agreements negotiated between the state, private developers, and municipalities. For the most part, the land deals that have been negotiated thus far under the act have been characterized by the various parties as beneficial to all of them, providing developers with a chance to lease or buy land that otherwise was vacant, improving the value of adjoining state lands that were not a part of the deal or, in the case of lease arrangements, bringing more dollars into the state fund, and giving cities added amenities such as golf courses and parks.

Planners say that equally as important as the land that is available for development is the land that is not—the majestic acreage that falls within the Phoenix Mountain Preserve, the largest municipal park in the U.S. More than 24,000 acres of mountain land in the Phoenix area will remain forever unscarred, providing a scenic backdrop for the busy city, thanks to action taken by city leaders in the early 1970s. Because most of Phoenix lies in a valley between mountain ranges on the north and south, the impact of the creation of the preserve is felt daily in the picturesque view provided by the unaltered slopes.

The area surrounding Phoenix is being rapidly developed, enabling the city to realize its urban village plan. Photo by Nyle Leatham

Left: A new development with a Spanish-style look nestles at the base of Camelback Mountain. On the left of the mountain is a rock formation known as the Praying Monk. The slopes of Camelback are part of the Phoenix Mountain Preserve. Photo by Matt Bradley

In the late 1960s the future of the mountains was not so secure. Residents moving to the foothills of Squaw Peak, Camelback Mountain, and other mountainous areas were encroaching on the mountain slopes. City leaders worked to set aside the mountains not yet built upon as municipal lands, acquiring the lands with funds approved by city voters in a special bond election and through federal revenue sharing. They created the Phoenix Mountain Preserve to forever ensure for future Phoenicians the mountainous vistas that exist today.

Water in the Desert

Thanks to the foresight of a group of pioneers who followed the clues left behind by early Indian settlers and established an intricate system of irrigating waterways and storage dam facilities, modern-day Phoenicians have always had an adequate water supply. Phoenicians, for example, have never experienced the kind of summer water shortages and penalties for excessive use that some cities such as New York City regularly encounter. To ensure that its water supply will continue to meet the growing demands that accompany population growth in the future, Phoenix has created a water management program that promises an ample supply of that precious natural resource to meet industrial and personal needs. With the additional waters of the $3.6-billion Central Arizona Project—and given careful management—water experts say the water supply will continue to keep up with the phenomenal growth rate in the future.

Without the capacity for water storage, Phoenix simply could not have become what it has. It took a group of persistent farmers who foresaw the need to convince Phoenicians and federal officials of the possibilities at the turn of the century. In a very real way, what oil meant to Texas, what gold did for California, the precious

Above: Shadows overtake the banks of the Salt River, east of Phoenix, as the sun sets. Photo by Steve Weiss

resource of water contributed to the Valley of the Sun.

The stereotypical picture of an oasis—a space of greenery fighting to survive in a parched, encroaching desert—does not apply to Phoenix. In large part, this is because the Salt River Project (SRP), born in the prolonged drought of the 1890s, was created to service an agricultural demand that increasingly is changing to an urban focus. The SRP water, which comes from reservoirs on the Salt and Verde rivers, supplies most of Phoenix.

One of the first five federal reclamation projects approved in 1903, the project began as an effort by farmers who organized themselves as the Salt River Valley Water Users' Association and worked for federal approval in an effort to secure irrigation for their fields. But the Salt River Project is being urbanized at the rate of 3,500 to 7,000 acres a year, resulting in decreasing water demand by agricul-

Above and facing page: A network of irrigation systems has made the Phoenix area bloom with prosperity. Photos by John Cancalosi (above) and Dick George (facing page) ture and increasing demand by municipal and industrial users. Ironically, SRP managers say, the changeover from agriculture to urban use does not "free up" more water for the future, even though urban use demand is less than agricultural demand.

"While it is true that per-acre water demands are greater for agricultural lands than urban lands, the realities are that SRP area farmers typically have supplemented SRP allocations with additional groundwater from other sources," explains an SRP brochure.

The efforts of those early farmers to secure Arizona's water future were built upon in more recent history by state and community leaders who worked to ensure that the Central Arizona Project (CAP) would become a reality. At the forefront was the late U.S. Senator Carl Hayden, one of the most powerful leaders in the Senate, who used his influence to work for the CAP. The idea of bringing water

Arizona's innovative groundwater law strives to protect water quantity. This irrigation system lies outside Phoenix. Photo by Dick George

from the Colorado River into Arizona was born about the time Arizona became a state in 1912, but it took three more decades before the plan was presented for the first time to Congress for authorization. It took more than another 20 years for Arizona to win court battles over its claim for water rights and resume the congressional battle, which finally culminated with passage of the CAP bill in 1968. Over the years the goal of the project did not change, though the purpose for bringing the water to Arizona did. In 1968 it was estimated that about a third of the 1.2 million acre-feet of Colorado River water to be delivered to the state would be used for municipal and industrial purposes, as compared to the 12,000 acre-feet intended for those purposes in the original plan. By 1980 the estimate of the proportion of municipal and industrial use of the CAP water had grown to one-half, and that percentage continues to increase.

Today the CAP is delivering water to the Valley of the Sun, fulfilling the promise of an earlier generation.

Faced with a dwindling groundwater table and a burgeoning population, the state undertook in 1980 to put into effect what the *Los Angeles Times* called "one of the nation's toughest laws" to protect water quantity and followed it a few years later with another unprecedented action aimed at protecting water quality. The new groundwater law, named by the Ford Foundation as one of the 10 most innovative programs in state and local government, established water conservation goals for Phoenix and other areas of the state and was a unique compromise effort. It is widely considered the most comprehensive groundwater law in the nation.

Representatives of government, agriculture, the mines, the cities, and others with particular interests in the state's water future met together under the guidance of former Governor Bruce Babbitt to draft an agreement that could be sold to the Arizona legislature for approval. It was nearly the same technique that the governor used to press for a tough water-quality program in 1986. A committee of representatives of all the vested interests involved met to write landmark legislation to protect Arizona's precious water supplies from pollution by mining, farming, industrial, and municipal use. The consensus law was seen as a crucial development in the effort to secure Arizona's water future.

Phoenicians, unused to thinking about water in terms of conservation, already have made major voluntary strides towards meeting requirements of the groundwater law, and city leaders say there is every reason to believe the city will have no difficulty continuing to do so. Without creating any mandatory restrictions on water use, Phoenix had complied with—and exceeded—its per-capita conservation goal of 251 gallons per day by 1986. Voluntary techniques used included a public awareness program, water structure revisions, and other conservation-oriented techniques. In fact, Phoenicians reduced use from 267 gallons per day in 1980 to 241 gallons per day by 1986, a decrease in water demand of 22,000 acre-feet per year.

Future conservation efforts will include zoning ordinance changes to restrict turf and lawn sizes, an aggressive secondary school water-conservation program, adoption of very low-flow device plumbing codes, implementation of a program designed to inform industry and commerce of the best available technology in conservation, and continued emphasis on water rates to discourage high water consumption. The conservation program is expected to save more than 107,000 acre-feet per year, enough water for a city of nearly 500,000 people.

In 1986 the Arizona legislature passed the final piece of the water-legislation picture, limiting the use of drinkable water in lakes for new developments. The new law, once again, was a compromise measure. It restricts most new artificial lakes in Phoenix and three other areas of the state to the size of any Olympic-size swimming

Facing page: Developments create artificial lakes by use of storm-water runoff of ground water in effort to conserve water. Photo by Susan I. Davison

Pages 102-103: Efficient use of water has allowed the construction of artificial lakes in the Phoneix area. Photo by Nyle Leatham

pool unless they are filled with effluent, storm-water runoff, poor-quality water, or water pumped from the ground as part of programs to correct waterlogging and water-contamination problems. Exemptions were made for lakes in which a substantial capital investment had been made by January 1, 1987, and for golf-course lakes, public-recreation lakes, one-acre "centerpiece" pools at resorts, and lakes expected to be filled with effluent within five years after construction.

Ancient man worshiped the sun. Modern man seeks to harness it.

Given that dynamic and the climate in the Valley of the Sun, it is no accident that Arizona State University's School of Architecture has chosen to make bioclimatic design—design to meet biological needs in respect to the climate—a major focus of its program.

Ask Professor Jeffrey Cook about the nearby university's growing national reputation in the world of architecture, and you'll get a quick response: "We're talking international, not national." What he means by that, he says, is that the Tempe campus is "one of the few places that students from abroad can come to study in a place that's sensitive to climate in building and land use."

The school, opening a new architecture building, has "strong ambitions," Cook explains. "We want to develop ourselves as a regional center for energy use in the hot, dry Southwest," he says.

The local climate makes such a specialty a natural, a fact which has spawned similar research and development programs in the College of Engineering and

The Salt River Project and Arizona Public Service provide electricity to Phoenix. Photo by Kevin Cruff

Applied Sciences at ASU.

In 1982, that college created the Center for Energy Systems research, a 40-faculty research arm that contains 15 laboratories focusing on areas that range from biomass fuels to solar thermal conversion. Working in partnership with the energy industry, the facility is proposing to the National Science Foundation the development of a Center of Excellence for Electric Power Technologies (new kinds of electric industry materials). The Center for Energy Systems also has

set as priorities gas energy research, new strategies for managing energy in the environment, and space energy technology. Robert L. Sears, research analyst for the center, notes that ASU has recognized energy as one of its five priority develment areas and is constructing a new Goldwater Engineering and Science Center, scheduled to open in 1990 with the latest in research capabilities.

The city of Phoenix efforts to develop a solar oasis in its downtown also is "a very important idea" for future energy progress, the architecture school's Cook adds. The city project grew out of a summer pilot project that demonstrated the use of air, water, and plants to increase human comfort without wasting precious energy resources. Support for the summer project was so widespread that the city moved to establish a more permanent structure.

All these proposals require—and have—a partnership between the public and private sectors. That kind of symbiotic cooperation has helped both the architecture school and the engineering college in the past, resulting in benefits to the private sector as well. .

In the meantime, city water managers have begun efforts to increase the supply by working to maximize water yields of the CAP and related facilities, by importing water from outside city boundaries, and by reusing wastewater for turf, irrigation, and agricultural exchange water.

"Good water management can help to preserve the life-style which makes Phoenix an attractive city in which to live and work," George Britton, Phoenix environmental services manager, wrote recently. He added that the city's conservation and augmentation plans are designed "to serve the projected population of the city through 2035, as well as providing a margin of safety during drought or loss of supply from water-quality problems." ·

Energy

Three major utility companies supply most of the electricity and natural gas consumed by city users at rates competitive with other areas in the United States. Salt River Project and Arizona Public Service provide the electricity, while Southwest Gas Corporation provides natural gas to metropolitan Phoenix.

The major source of energy generation in Arizona is hydroelectric. Nine hydroelectric generating stations operate throughout the state, providing about 43 percent of the state's electrical needs. Coal-fired power plants are close behind, providing about 42 percent. Arizona has far less reliance on petroleum-based energy than the national average, securing .6 percent of its electricity from that fuel, compared to a national average of 5.1 percent.

Probably the most controversial aspect of the energy picture is also seen by its proponents as the aspect with the most potential—nuclear energy. Though nuclear electricity accounts for only 4.8 percent of overall energy generation, that percentage is expected to grow. The first and second units at the Palo Verde Nuclear Generating Station, located 50 miles outside Phoenix, are on line, developing yet another power source. The third of the 1,270-megawatt units was scheduled to go commercial as this book went to press. When it is fully operational, Palo Verde will become the largest nuclear plant installation in the United States.

Needless to say, the nuclear plant is not without its critics—those who oppose nuclear energy as well as those who contend it is expensive and overbuilt for Arizona's energy needs. However, Arizona Public Service (APS), which owns the largest share of the nuclear power plant and is the construction and managing partner, believes the plant will provide efficient, low-cost power to meet growth needs in the not-so-distant future. Though APS has announced it will consider selling the output of the plant's Unit 3, APS managers predict that the output will be needed in the 1990s.

Given Phoenix annual average of 329 days of sunshine, it is not surprising that solar energy is emerging as a player in the energy game. By the end of 1986, 100,000 solar units were operating in the state of Arizona, the majority of them in the Phoenix area. The nation's largest process heat plant is operating in nearby Chandler, a half-hour drive from downtown Phoenix. State, university, and utility company research is under way.

Arizona Public Service has developed the Solar Test and Research (STAR) center in neighboring Tempe to test how well various types of solar equipment perform in the Valley's weather and environment. APS also operates a five-megawatt, solar-powered test generating station at Sky Harbor International Airport and a solar-powered home in Yuma. Arizona State University, which has developed some of the broadest experience in photovoltaics of any university in the country, also will be involved in the STAR project.

Civic Plaza is the site of the planned "solar oasis," where air, water, and plant life will be used to create an environment with temperatures averaging 20 degrees lower than those around it. Photo by Susan I. Davison

"Everybody knows how to heat water with solar, but the important thing is to make electricity," Keith Turley, president of APS's holding company, Pinnacle West Capital Corporation, said recently. "The technology is there, but a lot of improvement needs to be made. The real problem is you've got to be able to make it cheaper than you can with nuclear and coal. We're a ways from that, but we're continuing to concentrate on solar research."

The Arizona Department of Commerce estimates that annual energy savings due to solar units in Arizona from 1978 through 1986 was $34 million. Demonstrating its interest in further development of the technology, the state is devoting $1.9 million to support the demonstration of advanced community solar planning and design techniques, including a "solar oasis" that is being constructed in downtown Phoenix and large-scale photovoltaic applications for electrical power generation.

Though the contribution of solar to the total energy picture is negligible when compared to that made by coal, hydroelectric, or even nuclear, solar energy researchers are working to improve that statistic in the future.

CHAPTER FOUR

Hospitality and Growth

If there are two key words that can be associated with the service and trade industries that dominate the economy of Phoenix, they are hospitality and growth.

Hospitality fits because a large portion of the two industries is related to tourism and to eating, drinking, and food-supply establishments. Hospitality fits also because it is a characteristic the visitor often ascribes to the people of Phoenix.

And growth—well, growth fits just about everything in the area. But it particularly applies to services and trade, two industries that have bustled with growth and vitality in recent decades.

Service and trade industries add to the diversity of Arizona's capital city. Photo by Nyle Leatham

Whether services or trade was Arizona's largest industry in the 1980s is somewhat open to debate. The first half of the 1980s belonged clearly to trade, but services took the lead about midway through the decade. Recent indicators hint that the lead might return to trade, as the rapid growth of the service industry has slowed in the wake of the slowdown of the construction industry.

But whatever economic indicator is right, one thing is clear for the entire decade: Between them, the trade and service industries employ nearly half the state's work force and will continue to dominate the economic scene in the future.

The growing importance of services in Phoenix reflects the nationwide swing away from goods-producing industries and toward service jobs.

Above: Retail and service industries are fast-growing sectors of the ecomony in Phoenix.. Photo by Don Stevenson

Facing page: Hospitality has contributed to the growth of tourism in Phoenix. Photo by Don Stevenson

Just as the post-World War II era has seen a dramatic change in the nation's economy to a more service-oriented structure, employment in Arizona's service industries also has been increasing faster than in any other sector. Phoenix has surpassed national trends due to its rapidly growing population base and support from the tourism industry. The increase has not been accompanied by the decline in manufacturing employment that has occurred nationally. That spells diversification to economists, and that's good news for Phoenix.

"Phoenix is the most and best-diversified economy in the country. I've studied every major city west of the Mississippi, and another Phoenix doesn't exist," economist Elliott D. Pollack told an Arizona magazine in 1987.

Metropolitan Phoenix, which accounts for nearly two-thirds of Arizona's economic activity, experienced a 65 percent increase in its service industry over a 10-year period beginning in the mid-1970s. That rate was 2.5 times as fast as population growth. Business services were responsible for well over half of the increase.

Today, Phoenix is emerging as a business and financial hub for the Southwestern United States. Between 1981 and 1986 the number of businesses in metro Phoenix increased by 12,017—35.5 percent. Approximately one-third of the businesses existing in Phoenix today were not there five years ago. About 40 percent of the new businesses are in the service industry—ranging from advertising and data processing to garment and repair services.

Wholesale and retail trade in metropolitan Phoenix also has experienced major growth, though something short of the phenomenal statistics for the service industry. From 1981 to 1986 the trade industry grew 16.2 percent in the metro area, and accounted for 22.7 percent of all new employment in the area.

According to 1985 employment statistics, wholesale and retail trade was the number-two industry in both the state and the metropolitan area, placing it ahead of government, manufacturing, finance, insurance and real estate, construction, transportation, communications and public utilities, agriculture, and mining.

Statistics like these led *Inc.* magazine to choose Arizona as the hottest state in the Union for entrepreneurial activity and economic expansion both in 1986 and 1987. The magazine also picked Phoenix as the third most dynamic city in the nation in terms of job generation, rate of significant new business start-ups, and percent of young companies enjoying high-growth rates.

"The obvious lesson in all this," *Inc.* wrote in its article ranking the 50 fastest-growing U.S. cities, "is that it is easier for a city to come from nowhere than to reverse a steep decline. Because smaller companies cluster in the service and retail sectors, it is difficult to start and grow them when corporate customers in town are closing down operations and thousands of potential retail customers are losing their jobs."

As one urban-studies expert defined the growth phenomena for the magazine, "For older cities with heavy manufacturing bases, it's going to be a much harder transition to a more entrepreneurial economy."

Services
The Phoenix metropolitan area, with a large and rapidly expanding economic base, functions as a regional service center for Arizona and other

parts of the Southwest. Specifically, the metropolitan area provides a wide variety of relatively sophisticated producer, distributive, social and personal services to businesses and individual consumers far beyond its legal boundaries. It is already home to a large number of regional offices and warehouses of national corporations and to a growing number of companies with primary headquarters in Arizona.

—Douglas Kukino, Arizona Department of Commerce, *Arizona's Changing Economy*

Although traditional economists sometimes argue that growth in the service industry cannot support long-term economic growth, there is a new school of economic thought that disagrees.

As the Arizona State University (ASU) Center for Business Research puts it, those economists who reject services growth as having long-term payoffs have adopted a stereotypical view of services as menial and low-paying support to primary industries such as mining, agriculture, and manufacturing. Instead, the ASU Center says, the service industry has grown to focus on information-centered businesses and firms that perform technologically sophisticated functions. In Arizona nearly one-half of service employment can be classified as professional, including health, legal, engineering, and architectural services, and some business services (data processing and software producers, for example).

In its publication *Arizona Business*, the ASU Center for Business Research contends:

As society has evolved, some services have become essential rather than merely a secondary product. Information, for example, is beginning to be perceived as a necessary good. It is an almost infinitely expandable resource, on which significant economic growth can be based for an indefinite period of time. Similarly, constantly improving health services are now viewed as in-dispensable. This sector alone provides one-third of the total personal income of Arizona's services industry.

Furthermore, in Arizona, according to the State Department of Economic Security, many services "import" dollars in as real a manner as the export of manufactured products does, because of tourism.

Employment in the service industry has grown impressively since 1960, when less than 15 percent of jobs in the state were service-related. As recently as the early 1980s, the service industry was ranked the number-two industry in Arizona, following on the heels of trade. But as expansion of services and finance, insurance, and real estate outpaced other industries in the economy, services took over the number-one spot.

Based on 1985 figures for employment, personal income, and gross product, the service industry was number one, both in the Phoenix metropolitan area and in Arizona, while finance, insurance, and real estate together ranked number five. Government ranked third in Arizona and fourth in the Phoenix area. Trade was ranked

Facing page: A helicopter lands on the pad at Good Samaritan Hospital. Thireeen acute-care hospitals in the area provide 5,000 beds and a wide variety of specialties. Photo by Susan I. Davison

Below: Metro Phoenix is becoming a regional health center, and 59 percent of the 80,000 people who work in the health-care industry in Arizona are employed by hospitals. Pictured is Good Samaritan Hospital. Photo by Susan I. Davison

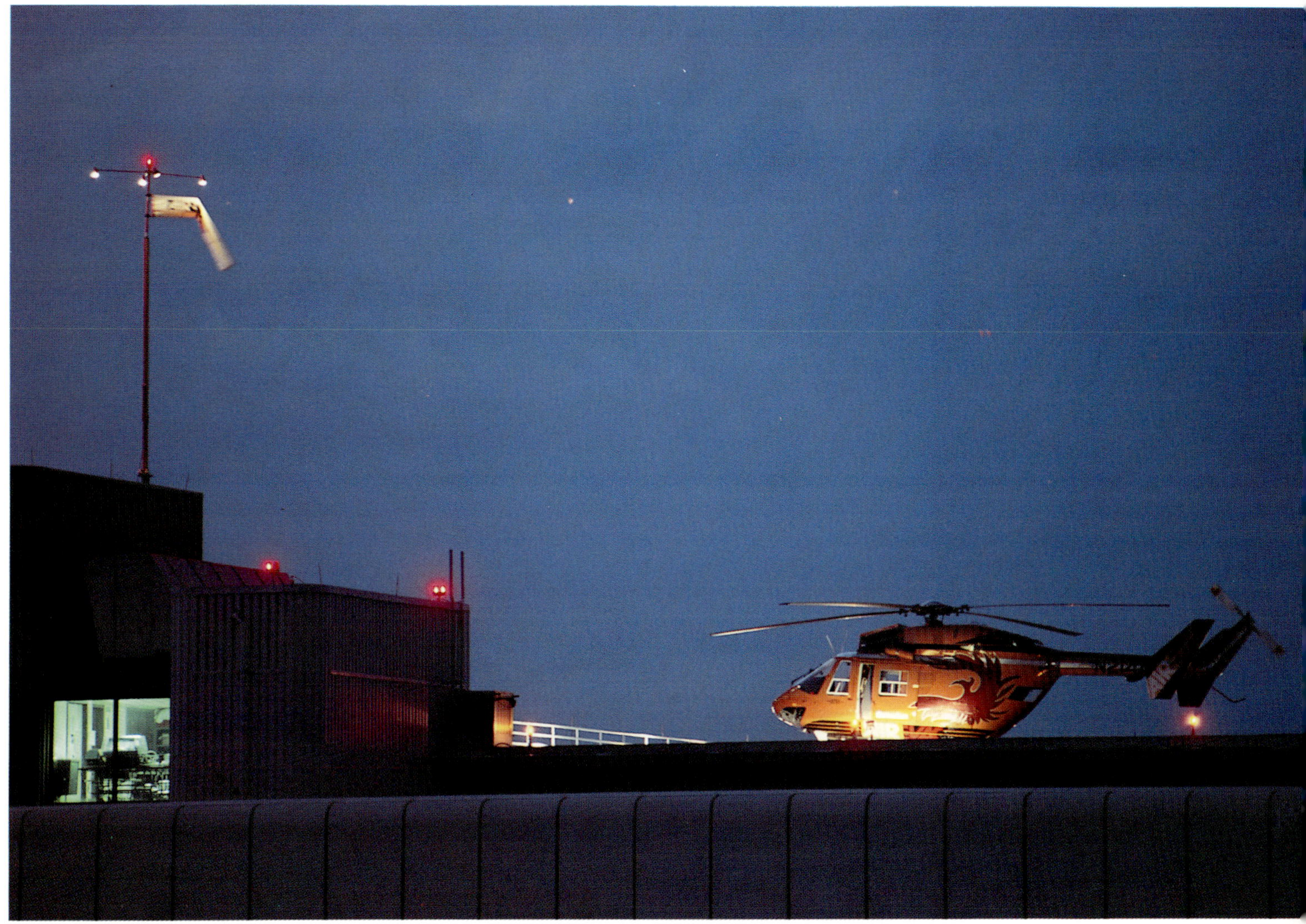

second, both for the state and the city, while manufacturing was ranked third for the city and fourth for the state. In 1986, the last year for which statistics were available, the service industry grew another 8 percent.

The service industry expansion reflects changing times, including the fact that women are playing a greater role in the workplace in Arizona, as they are throughout the nation. This has meant more demand for consumer and social services such as day-care, and has resulted in increases in family incomes that enable families to pay for more services.

Metro Phoenix is becoming a regional health-care center. The health sector, a growing industry in the Phoenix metro area in particular, is responsible for 29 percent of all service employment within Arizona. About 80,000 people in Arizona are employed by firms rendering health services. Most employees (59 percent) work in hospitals, with physicians' and dentists' offices and nursing and outpatient-care facilities providing jobs for the rest.

Business services account for 22 percent of employment, or about 60,000 people. Computer and data-processing services, manpower pools, and modeling services are in this category.

Other important employers in the service industry are social services (8 percent or about 22,000 people) and hotels, motels, and lodging (responsible for 10 percent or about 28,000 people). In the lodging industry, more large corporations and chain organizations have become players in the Phoenix-area marketplace.

Facing page: Lodging accounts for the employment of nearly 28,000 people in the Phoenix area. Photo by Don Stevenson

Below: The Veterans Administration Medical Center stands in the center of the city. Photo by Matt Bradley

By some accounts, tourism should be listed as the number-two industry in metropolitan Phoenix because a large portion of the service industry can be related to it. Most economists do not consider tourism as a separate industry in compiling statistical reports. However, the service most clearly related to tourism, the lodging industry, has experienced long-term, continual growth. The Arizona Department of Economic Security has forecast a 21 percent rate of growth for lodging services through 1991, a forecast surpassed only by the 27 percent expected for business services and 26 percent anticipated for "other" services.

The Pointe in Tyme features award-winning entrees from the nation's finest restaurants. Photo by Charlene Faris

An Arizona State University College of Business study of new businesses launched in 1986 found that eating establishments predominated, followed by auto-repair shops and hairstyling salons. More than one-half the new businesses, which were organized at a rate of about 300 a month, were in the service or retailing sectors. The typical founder of a new business was a 40-year-old male Caucasian who had some post-high school education and was employed the previous year.

In the area of professional services, the Phoenix metropolitan

area has more than 5,900 architects and environmental designers, 120 landscape architects, 500 mechanical engineers and 1,500 civil engineers, and 5,900 lawyers.

It is interesting to note that of 60,000 firms doing business in Arizona, 20,000 provide services. (Trade accounts for about 13,000.) Small firms predominate in the service industry. Most have fewer than 10 employees.

Trade

Wholesale trade—sales to retailers or business users—and retail trade—sales for personal or household consumption—employ about a quarter of the city's work force. Buoyed by tourism and a growing population, trade plays a stronger role in the city's economy than it does in the nation's.

It is not surprising, then, that retail sales in the Phoenix metropolitan area climb significantly each year. From about $8 billion in 1982 to more than $12 billion in 1987, retail sales have sustained consistently strong growth. In fact, since 1960 areawide retail sales have risen a whopping 1,000 percent.

Members of the tourism industry accredit anywhere from about $2 billion to $5 billion a year to the tourism industry. Though the amount is open to dispute, no one disputes that tourism—particularly convention-oriented tourism—is an important part of the metro area's present and future. Of 13 Mobile Five Star resorts in the United States, four are located in metropolitan Phoenix and two are in the heart of the city. The city's eight-block-square, 312,000-square-foot Civic Plaza has bookings 15 years ahead.

One survey conducted by the Phoenix and Valley of the Sun Convention and Visitor's Bureau concluded that the average visitor to metropolitan Phoenix spends $98 a day, 47 percent of it

It took the Phoenix and Valley of the Sun Convention and Visitors Bureau 22 single-spaced pages just to talk about the new hotels and resorts being opened, constructed, or planned in the near future in the area. That fact alone is indicative of the importance tourism plays in the economy.

According to the bureau, the Valley had 25,000 hotel and resort rooms in 1986, 27,415 in 1987, and nearly 31,000 in 1988. At the last count (and the count is changing every day), there were 128 hotels and resorts, 74 of them with meeting facilities.

Add to those statistics the fact that a 1987 bureau study found that the average Phoenix area tourist spends $95: 34 percent on lodging, 30 percent on shopping, 26 percent on food and beverages, 6 percent on attractions, and 4 percent on transportation. Pretty soon, to paraphrase Everett Dirksen, you're talking real money.

The survey also found that the average visitor was 49 years old, had an annual income of $50,400, and stayed 7.4 nights in the Valley.

And . . . what area has more Mobil Travel Guide Five-

A sunny indoor atrium offers an attractive environment for guests at the Embassy Suites. Photo by Matt Bradley

Star Award-winning resorts than any other area of the country? That's right—Phoenix and the Valley of the Sun. The Valley boasts 3 of America's 12 resorts that have received the rating. They are the historic Arizona Biltmore, Marriott's Camelback Inn, and The Pointe at Squaw Peak.

The Arizona Biltmore, a resort built in 1929, lays claim to the most history of any resort in the Valley. It is here that John Kennedy bounced across the lobby as a child, and that Clark Gable and Carole Lombard chose to hide away. The 502-room Biltmore, designed by Albert McArthur, a protégé of architect Frank Lloyd Wright, has 17 tennis courts, 3 swimming pools, 2 PGA-rated golf courses, and lawn games ranging from lawn chess to croquet.

The 423-room Camelback Inn, opened in 1936, has also

been given the AAA Five Diamond Award. The resort has a 30,000-square-foot European-style spa, 2 PGA-rated 18-hole golf courses with desert mountain views, 10 lighted tennis courts, 2 swimming pools, walking and jogging trails, bicycling, and shuffleboard.

The Pointe at Squaw Peak is a newer, Mediterranean-styled resort that also offers a mountain view, lush landscaping, and 600 suites. In addition to its swimming pools and tennis courts, the Pointe offers the opportunity to horseback ride or take haywagons to outdoor cookouts in the 2,700-acre North Mountain Park.

One of the largest resorts in the Valley of the Sun, The Phoenician Golf and Tennis Resort, has just opened with 620 rooms and 60,000 square feet of meeting space at the base of Camelback Mountain. The resort combines recreational facilities—a spa and fitness center, indoor racquetball and squash courts, a golf course, 13 tennis courts, and jogging and bicycle paths, with 60,000 square feet of high-tech meeting space, including a 22,400-square-foot ballroom.

It all adds up to a multi-million-dollar business.

Above: Swimming pools abound in backyards and at resorts in the Valley of the Sun. Here, swimmers cool off at the Hyatt Regency in Gainey Ranch, a resort in nearby Scottsdale. Photo by Matt Bradley

Right: The holiday season comes to the Borgata, an elegant shopping center offering 50 luxury boutiques in nearby Scottsdale. Photo by Susan I. Davison

for lodging, 23 percent for food and drink, 18 percent for shopping, 8 percent for transportation, and 4 percent for recreation.

As a part of the economy, retail sales date back to Phoenix' earliest inhabitants. There is evidence that the Hohokam somehow obtained seashells, probably by trading agricultural products.

Though for many years Phoenix remained primarily an agricultural city and secondarily a commercial city, it continued to grow and prosper. By 1936 Phoenix ranked 13th nationally in per capita retail sales. Names like Boston Store, Korrick's, and Goldwaters played a major role in the retail industry.

It was 1957 when Park Central, the city's first shopping mall, opened its doors. Both Diamond's and Goldwater's department stores immediately moved to the new location from their downtown sites. It was the beginning of a 30-year bleak period for the downtown as shoppers in the automobile-dominated city showed their preference for the convenient parking and close proximity of stores in the mall.

Today Phoenix has 13 shopping centers with more than 1,000 retail stores and a downtown that is making a comeback. Another half-dozen shopping malls are scattered in adjoining metropolitan areas. The

Sculptor John Waddell's
Dancers *welcome visitors to
the Civic Plaza. Photo by
Mark E. Gibson*

Right: The Greenhouse Restaurant offers outdoor dining. Photo by Mark E. Gibson largest of them all is Metrocenter, a 265-store enclosed two-story mall that also houses a skating rink, movie theater, and scores of restaurants.

Most employment in Arizona's trade industry is in retail sales, primarily in eating and drinking establishments. Second in employment are food stores, and third, general merchandise stores. Trade employment is concentrated in the state's two major metro areas; Maricopa County has 67 percent of the industry's workers.

In wholesale trade, wholesalers of machinery, equipment, and supplies lead the industry in Arizona, while those wholesaling food and related products are next in numbers of employment. Because the Phoenix metropolitan area is at the hub of the state's highway system, employment in wholesale trade in the state is concentrated in the capital city and surrounding areas.

Projections for the entire trade industry call for more growth over the next 25 years. Trade employment is expected to continue to outpace the national trend as population continues to spur growth in Phoenix industries.

Economic observers say eating and drinking places will continue to lead the retail industry to accommodate demands of a growing population and the continually growing number of two-wage-earner families.

Though housing construction already has slowed in the Phoenix area, the boom that occurred in the mid-1980s will necessitate development of neighborhood shopping centers and other retail establishments, according to the Arizona Department of Economic Security.

Overall the prescription for the future is more growth. It may be perhaps a bit slower than Phoenicians are used to, but the growth of the city's service and trade industries will still outstrip what is seen in most of the country. The hospitality industry—and the hospitable character of the city's inhabitants—will continue to play important roles in Phoenix' future.

One of the city's many shopping malls is the luxurious Biltmore Fashion Park, located at Camelback Road and 24 Street. Restaurants and shops ranging from Saks Fifth Avenue to the Sharper Image are housed there. Photo by Matt Bradley

CHAPTER FIVE

Industry in the Valley of the Sun

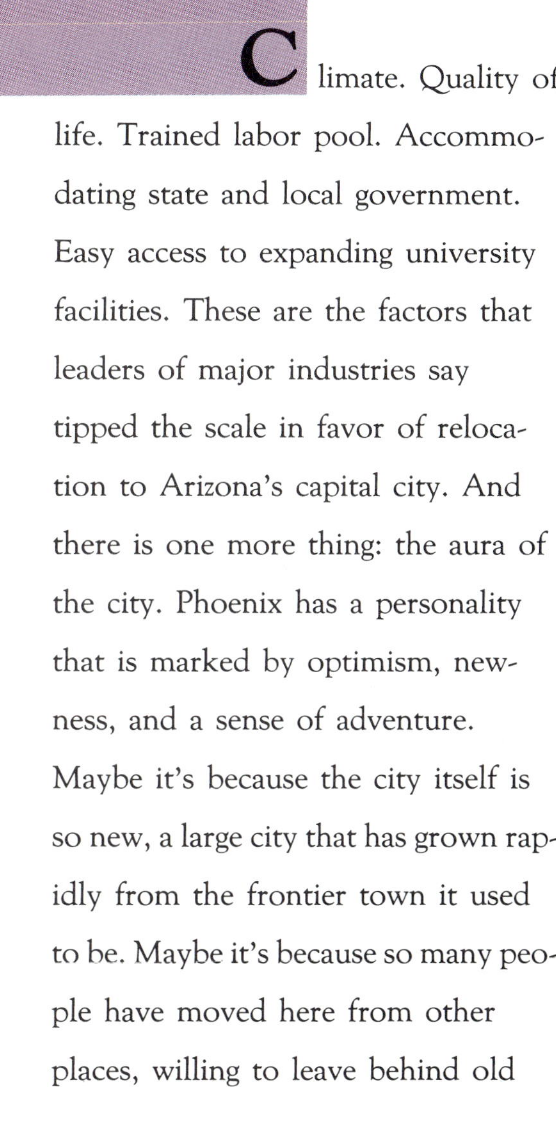

Climate. Quality of life. Trained labor pool. Accommodating state and local government. Easy access to expanding university facilities. These are the factors that leaders of major industries say tipped the scale in favor of relocation to Arizona's capital city. And there is one more thing: the aura of the city. Phoenix has a personality that is marked by optimism, newness, and a sense of adventure. Maybe it's because the city itself is so new, a large city that has grown rapidly from the frontier town it used to be. Maybe it's because so many people have moved here from other places, willing to leave behind old

Optimism, newness, and a sense of adventure exemplify the personality of Phoenix. Photo by Nyle Leatham

lives in favor of new approaches. Maybe it's, quite simply, the sunshine. Whatever is responsible, Phoenix is undeniably a city of great opportunity.

Phoenicians "in general have a more positive attitude," said Joseph J. Campanella, former head of Honeywell, Inc.'s Avionics Systems Business in Phoenix. "I don't know if it's the sunshine or what."

The proliferation of industries in the Valley of the Sun has been

aided by the increased flexibility of companies and the products they handle. In the past, companies looking to relocate may have been tied to an area by something as basic as the availability of raw materials. But with modern transportation systems and the growing number of products that are small, light, and easy to transport, many more companies are able to choose locations because they want to be there.

Gone forever are the days when Arizona's economy—and that of Phoenix—revolved solely around the "Four C's" —copper, cotton, citrus, and cattle. Instead, the state and, most particularly, the city have found a new "C" to play a key role in their economy—components. Diversification and growth are bywords associated with Phoenix' economy in the 1980s, an economy that depends on industries that include aerospace, electronics and computers, professional services, finance, wholesale distribution, retail sales, and tourism. Employment opportunities continue, despite—no, because of—the continuous boom in population growth.

Phoenix' economy today is based largely on a blend of the high-technology, manufacturing, agriculture, trade, and service industries. More than a quarter of the metropolitan area's largest 180 employers are in manufacturing. In fact, manufacturing of all kinds ranks third in the number of adults employed and the amount of wages and salaries in Phoenix, following trade and services. Manufacturing high-tech products—electronic, aerospace, and computer components—occupies a key, and rapidly growing, role in the economy of Phoenix, where 79 percent of the 85,000 high-technology jobs that exist in Arizona are located. These high-tech firms, in turn, provide a base for attracting related employment in other types of manufacturing and research and development. Today Phoenix ranks third among major electronics centers in the country.

Consider that the Phoenix metropolitan area's first high-tech facility was established in 1949 when Motorola, Inc., began operating here with a six-person facility, and you get a feel for the rapidity with which things have grown. Thirty-five years ago, the state's economy was driven by the "Four C's," and manufacturing was oriented toward the production of basic goods.

"What has emerged over the last 35 years is a vibrant, diverse, high-

Technological industries located in Phoenix include aerospace, electronics, and computers. Photo by Don Stevenson tech manufacturing base with few ties to the traditional strength of the Arizona economy," wrote Robert K. Berg, an economist for Valley National Bank.

Berg credits the federal government's urging for defense-related industries to decentralize with much of the post-World War II growth that occurred in the Phoenix area, although he notes that Motorola was one of the firms that moved to Arizona without the urging of the government.

Other companies that began doing business in the Phoenix metropolitan area in the late 1940s and early 1950s included Garrett Turbine Company of Los Angeles, General Electric, and the Sperry Corporation. Manufacturing output in the late 1940s was estimated at $104 million total in the state. By 1967 it had reached almost $1 billion.

According to the Arizona State University Bureau of Business and Economic Research, high-tech manufacturing industries shipped products valued at $5.4 billion in 1984, accounting for 37 percent of the manufacturing shipments from the Phoenix metropolitan area. (Nationwide, high-tech manufacturing made up only 8 percent of the manufacturing shipments.) And yet the diversification of the economy in metropolitan Phoenix means that the area has been able to successfully avoid the economic instabilities that the Silicon Valley has encountered in California.

Mayor Terry Goddard stressed this point to a newspaper reporter when he reiterated his desire to continue to build on diversity in the economy, though he noted that high technology is important symbolically and in terms of jobs.

"I would not like to see a situation like the Silicon Valley where electronics is 60 percent of San Jose's employment," he said.

All this production means increased employment, not only in

The effect of post-World War II growth, still evident in the look of Phoenix, has been modified by the addition of contemporary architecture. Photo by Susan I. Davison

the industries that do the producing, but also in all the accompanying occupations needed to provide the goods and services for the people attracted by the availability of jobs. In the Phoenix metropolitan area, about 16 percent of the workers are employed in manufacturing, and nearly half of those work in high-technology industries. Other key manufacturing industries located in metropolitan Phoenix include firms involved in the production of machinery, firms in the primary and fabricated metals industry, firms that are in printing and publishing, firms producing miscellaneous plastic products, and firms producing textile goods. Manufacturing makes up 15 percent of the employment structure of Maricopa County, the county in which Phoenix lies and which the city dominates.

Buoyed by the economic attractiveness of its location and business climate, the Phoenix area is expected to continue to lure manufacturing from the Eastern and Midwestern industrial complex.

The growth of high technology, the ease with which high-tech products are shipped, and the proximity of the state to the Mexican border has led international trade in Arizona to tremendous growth in recent years. And with the state's recent decision to open a trade office in Taiwan, Arizona's high-tech industry is expected to continue to expand rapidly in the future.

High Tech in the Sunbelt

When Joseph Campanella listed the pluses that helped his company grow rapidly in the Phoenix area, he put at the top "the spirit of the city."

"A lot of people have moved here. Maybe that makes them a little more adventurous, a little more willing to try new things and do more," he said.

The aerospace executive, who came to Phoenix in 1960 when

Facing page, top: Industry and population increases have led to rapid growth in employment. Photo by Susan I. Davison

Facing page, bottom: One reason why outsiders are attracted to Phoenix is the spirit of the city. Photo by Nyle Leatham

OTWEAR

the industry was still in its infancy, listed next "the cooperative and business-oriented attitude" of government.

"It's not that they give us a lot of favors," he said, "but the bureaucracy doesn't tie you down. You can talk to them, and they talk to you."

Campanella also listed the highly qualified industrial work force, good support industries, competitive labor rates, and attractive climate and life-style that make it easy to recruit and keep professionals. He noted that the executive cost of living here falls far below cities like Los Angeles and New York, but said that he fears that may change in the future. Negatives? Sure, there are some, he said. Number one is the possibility that Phoenix won't retain all the pluses as it grows. Number two is the lack of freeways, he said, adding "but we're building some."

All in all, he said, "Phoenix is a very attractive area for industry."

Enough industry heads agree with him to have created phenomenal growth in the high-tech manufacturing field in the Phoenix area in recent years. Since Motorola established the first high-tech facility in the Valley, expansion has occurred rapidly. Arizona's average annual growth rate in high tech in recent years has been 6 percent, compared to 2.4 percent nationally, according to the Arizona Department of Commerce. A 1985 reference book published in Tucson, *Silicon Desert High Tech Directory*, lists more than 3,000 companies in Arizona involved in high-tech manufacturing, sales, marketing, supply, and services. Seventy-nine percent are located in Phoenix.

From 1970 to 1985, 24,100 new jobs were created in metropolitan Phoenix in computers, electronics, and the aerospace industry. Employment in these areas increased 72.2 percent, to 57,500 persons, with the greatest amount of growth occurring in the electron-

Facing page, top: Computer technology companies like MicroAge flourish in the Phoenix area. Photo by Nyle Leatham

Facing page, bottom: Honeywell employs many in Phoenix. Photo by Nyle Leatham

MicroAge

Honeywell

ics industry and the second highest occurring in the aerospace industry. In Maricopa County employment in the electronics industry rose by 81.5 percent, from 17,800 in 1970 to 32,300 in 1985. In the aerospace industry, 6,400 jobs were added between 1970 and 1985, bringing a 71.1 percent increase. Employment in the computer industry has declined in recent years, but not before 3,100 new jobs were added between 1970 and 1985, an increase of 48.5 percent.

ASU's Bureau of Business and Economic Research, which gathered the above statistics, anticipates continued growth in the foreseeable future. In fact, it forecasts a 40 percent increase in employment in high-technology industries within the county by 1990. That would mean a work force of 80,500 workers employed in high technology, with a direct economic impact exceeding $3.6 billion.

All this represents phenomenal growth by anyone's standards, but even more so when combined with the expectations of some economic observers for overall industrial growth. Manufacturing and wholesale trade is expected to outpace overall employment growth, increasing by 135 percent over the next 25 years.

"Maricopa County has only begun to experience the economic benefits of a flourishing high-technology sector," wrote Lee R. McPheters, of the ASU Bureau. "With foresight and planning, the citizens of Maricopa County will occupy an important place in the reindustrialization that is necessary for a strong America."

Below and facing page: Potatoes are an important export crop in Arizona. Photos by Nyle Leatham

International Trade— The New Frontier

Arizona exports more than $2 billion in manufactured products annually,

a figure that pales in comparison to some Eastern industrial centers, but which represents a growth rate far in excess of that for production in the state. As the Arizona Department of Commerce puts it, because the state's economy depends on new technologies, services, and investment more than "traditional smokestack industries," its future in international trade is synonymous with opportunity.

A look at U.S. Department of Commerce figures reveals that Arizona's exports rose 141 percent in the record-keeping period from 1977 to 1981, compared with a 78 percent increase in the state's manufacturing production in the same period. Over three-fourths of the increase came from growth in electric/electronic equipment and transportation equipment exports, which were the state's leading

Left : Cotton has proven to be one of Arizona's most valuable crops. Photo by Dick George

Facing page: Prudent use of irrigation has allowed the cultivation of the desert. Photo by Dick George

manufactured exports, followed by nonelectric machinery. Primary metals, instruments, food, and chemicals were other major products shipped overseas from the state. In electric-equipment exports, Arizona ranked ninth among the 50 states.

In addition, Arizona's share of U.S. agricultural exports was up to an estimated $404 million, a 42 percent increase from the 1977 level. A long-time Arizona staple, cotton, figured heavily in agricultural exports. Other products included fruits, feed grains, vegetables, and wheat.

In exports of copper ore, even given the distressed state of the copper industry and elsewhere, Arizona ranked first nationally in exports of copper ore and concentrates in 1981, valued at $109 million.

The Arizona Department of Commerce figures that Arizona compa-

nies exported $2.49 billion of agricultural, mineral, and manufactured goods, giving employment to 62,250 Arizonans. That figure has continued to grow, U.S. Department of Commerce officials said.

By 1984 Arizona was exporting $1.9 billion in manufactured goods, $367 million in agricultural products, and $165.3 million in minerals. All those numbers have grown, but more recent precise figures are not available.

photo pageCountries that most frequently turn to Arizona for products are Canada, Great Britain, Australia, Japan, Mexico, and West Germany. However, when it comes to countries that receive the largest dollar volume of Arizona goods, they are, in order, Canada, West Germany, France, England, Mexico, Italy, and Japan.

"We have had tremendous export growth here. It reflects our own growth as a community, but, also, we have the right companies here for export—companies that produce high-cost, low-freight products. We have thousands of things made in this state that go into this category," said Donald W. Fry, director of the Phoenix District Office of the U.S. Department of Commerce.

When Fry moved to Phoenix in 1960 from St. Louis, he was "amazed," he recalled.

"In the middle part of the U.S., the export business was 100 years old, but here there wasn't any tradition of export," he remembered. "There were 60 to 70 viable manufacturers who had exportable products, and only one legitimate local exporter in manufacturing at that time—Goettl Brothers."

Goettl Brothers was shipping evaporative coolers to the Mideast, he said. Motorola, Inc., also was exporting some of the products made at that plant—but all the research and development was carried out in Chicago, so the shipping was being done at the request of Chicago, he said.

Tourists—like these at the Phoenix Zoo—often decide to come back to the city for good. Photo by Susan I. Davison

Phoenix and Arizona increasingly are attracting attention from foreign investors, local financial observers say.

The $4 billion in foreign investments that were made in the state in 1988 ranked Arizona 22nd among the 50 states, according to the Congressional Economic Leadership Institute, and Arizona was on the upward move. Though comparable statistics are not available for the city, most of the foreign investment is centered in the Valley of the Sun.

About 35,700 people in Arizona are employed by companies that have at least some foreign ownership, the institute's study said. Of that number, 43.9 percent work in manufacturing and 37.8 percent work in the trades. Twenty-nine percent work for United Kingdom companies and 28 percent work for Canadian firms.

As a result, the Phoenix Economic Growth Corporation and the Phoenix Sister Cities Commission worked together in 1987 to create the City Office of Trade and Protocol, dedicated to raising the city's visibility in foreign markets, particularly the Pacific Rim. "It's the most active economic area in the world and a logical place to target, given geography, climate, work force, and education and economic base," says Doug Wilson, chief protocol officer and director of the Sister Cities Commission.

During its first year of existence, Wilson's office met with political and business visitors from 35 countries and sponsored the first Phoenix Japanese week—a trade, cultural, and sports event that the city intends to continue annually. A trade seminar conducted on how to do business with Japan drew 500 business representatives. The Japanese consul general in Los Angeles called the event the "largest and most comprehensive event of its type in the Western United States."

"Our office has a unique approach, a dual emphasis on business and culture," Wilson says. "It's not just that we want to do business with other countries, but we want to know *how* to do business with them." The interest in attracting foreign business to the state is spread throughout the community, from the business sector to the education and government sector, he adds.

"Throughout Arizona's business community, the fervor for world marketing is growing," writer Jon Kamman says in an article for *Arizona Trend*. "Although precise statistics are not available at the State Department of Commerce, international trade director James Ferguson estimates that fully 800 Arizona companies are now doing foreign deals, up about 100 from a year ago." Local bankers note much of that interest has translated into real estate investments.

Japanese funding is at least partially responsible for two Valley resorts—the Westcourt in the Buttes and the Scottsdale Princess—and three office and hotel developments—Paradise Village Office Park III, the Gateway, and the Esplanade. One of the earliest Japanese investments was a luxury home development northeast of Phoenix, Pinnacle Peak Village. Another large Japanese investment financed an extensive master-planned community, the Crossings in Mesa.

Much of the current interest in the Phoenix area is a result of the city's and the state's recognition of the importance of foreign trade and investment (Arizona opened an office in Taiwan in 1987). Part of the interest is a result of increased foreign knowledge of opportunities in the United States.

Rick Ryan, a writer for the *Business Journal*, in a column

for that Phoenix publication, noted that Arizona is becoming increasingly attractive to the Japanese. "Our climate, natural beauty, wide-open spaces and multitude of golf courses appeal to the Japanese," he wrote. "Recent surveys indicate that Japanese investment is shifting from primary markets like Los Angeles and New York to secondary markets like Phoenix. Furthermore, Japanese investment in resort properties—something else we have in abundance—

Phoenix' close proximity to the Pacific Rim make it an attractive market to foreign investors. Photo by Tim Marshal

soared 160 percent" in 1987.

Japanese investors say they have become more interested in the Phoenix area as they have gotten to know the city better. The cost of land is much cheaper than it is in their country, and they recognize that the opportunities here are endless.

In the next two decades, Arizona awakened to the importance of the growing international character of the U.S. economy.

In 1961 Arizona exported $29 million in manufactured products, but two years later that amount had grown to $70 million. In the 1970s and the 1980s, growth in the export industry skyrocketed. By 1981 Arizona was exporting $1.6 billion in manufactured products and ranked 27th among the 50 states.

Although U.S. Commerce Department data dates to 1981, a more recent Arizona study indicates that about 23 percent of total manufacturing employment in Arizona is attributable to exports.

Today, the major products exported from the Phoenix metropolitan area are electronic—software, hardware, semiconductors, and communications devices—and measuring and scientific devices—medical imaging devices, for example.

Foreign investments in Arizona are difficult to measure. But observers in that area of business say the number of foreign investors interested in the state—particularly from Canada and Western Europe—is climbing.

In the areas of services and investment, which traditionally are not measured in international trade studies, cross-border transactions are substantial and growing rapidly, according to the State Commerce Department. These include areas such as licensing and franchise agreements, consulting fees, insurance premiums, and foreign student tuition. Receipts could "easily rank with manufacturing's export earnings," the State Commerce Department said.

Tourism in Phoenix is big business, bringing thousands of foreign visitors and millions of dollars to the state. Nearly 12 percent of all West Germans visiting the United States in 1983, for example, came to Arizona. At least 4 percent of all visitors from England, France, Italy, and the Netherlands came to Arizona. Nearly 10 per-

Stars shine above and within the city of Phoenix. Photo by Audrey Gibson cent of all Australians and 4 percent of all Japanese were drawn to the Grand Canyon State. And Phoenix, the state capital, with its resorts, cultural amenities, airport, and central location in the state, is a destination point for the great majority.

The Phoenix area also exports international executive talent. Some 20,000 graduates of the American Graduate School of International Business, located in the neighboring community of Glendale, currently are serving in jobs around the world. The nonprofit school was founded in 1946 by Lieutenant General Barton Kyle Young, commanding general of the U.S. Air Force Training Command in World War II, because of his belief in the need for specialized training to meet the growing demand for international business and government managers.

The land where the school is located is a former pilot-training center that was donated by the War Assets Administration, and the school initially was funded by unsecured loans provided by a consortium of local banks. Today the school operates as a one-year graduate program.

Phoenix businesspeople looking outside U.S. borders for opportunity also emphasize the desirability of expanding efforts to sell in and attract business from the Pacific Basin. Arizona's proximity to the western border of the United States makes its link to the Pacific Basin a natural one, they say.

In October 1987 this rationale led the state to open an Asian branch office in Taiwan, funded jointly by the Arizona legislature and private enterprise. Arizona thus became the first state in the nation to choose Taiwan as its Asian base. There are those who question the wisdom of the state's decision to establish its base in Taiwan, when 30 other states have opened offices in Japan. But State Commerce Department officials said the move was carefully calculated. For one thing, Arizona has exported citrus and cotton to Taiwan for years and therefore has long-established working relationships with government and business leaders there. For another, Taiwan is far less expensive to operate in than Japan. Furthermore, the country is conveniently located to reach out from Korea to New Zealand, Australia, and the Philippines, as well as to Japan.

State officials also cited the fact that Taiwan leaders revere the name of Arizona's most distinguished retiree, former U.S. Senator Barry Goldwater, a factor that has not hurt relations between the state and the country. They noted that Arizona's sister state in Taiwan (which has the same name as the country) agreed to pick up the third year of lease payments on the office, and that Taiwan has a foreign-trade reserve of close to $60 billion. Even before the office opened, Taiwanese officials had indicated that they wished to meet with Phoenix government and business leaders to discuss $5 billion that Taiwanese businesses propose to invest in the U.S. in the future. The electronic firms in the Valley particularly captured their attention.

Two other states—Washington and California—have announced plans to open Taiwanese offices as well.

The U.S. Commerce Department's Fry sees the opening of the office as a crucial move in the future growth of Arizona's export business.

"Arizona must have a presence to be competitive," he said. "We don't have 50 years of tradition. We have tremendous advantages, but a lot of people are just getting acquainted with this state. We're just now coming into another era. The next 10 years are going to see a lot more involvement in all areas. The next 10 to 20 years ought to be really fun here!"

CHAPTER SIX

Mecca for Business Opportunity

When did Phoenix reputation as a vital, energetic business environment begin? Was it in the 1880s when those early merchant families—the Goldwaters and the Goldbergs—arrived to develop businesses that still flourish today? Or was it in the post-World War II era, when population and business began a growth cycle that continues to spiral upward? Or does it go back even further, to the establishment of Phoenix as a town, settled by rugged individualists for whom the traits of resourcefulness, competitiveness, and initiative were inborn?

Whatever the date of its origin, the fact is that the city's ability to en-

Phoenix rate of population growth is second only to that of Los Angeles. Photo by Don Stevenson

courage business opportunity and growth has earned it a national reputation that continues to expand as Phoenix grows.

"Phoenix is second only to the Los Angeles Basin in its rate of population growth," said James A. Chalmers, president of Mountain West, a research company. "We're a major growth center.

"When you have that kind of growth, you have to realize that one-half of the infrastructure in the year 2000 is going to be new. There are lots and lots of opportunities associated with that kind of change."

Terry Trost, chief economist for the Phoenix Metropolitan Chamber of Commerce, said that growth in the late 1980s has slowed a little from the high pitch of 1984 to "more normal kinds of growth."

But put that in perspective, he added quickly.

"There are probably a handful of communities in the country who will have growth similar to ours. While we talk about a slowed rate, there are communities throughout this nation that would kill for the kind of growth we are crying over."

Phoenix emergence as a regional center, economists say, is similar to the fast track that Atlanta followed in the 1970s when it blossomed into a regional center for the South. Economists point to the increasing frequency with which Phoenix has been selected as the location for regional headquarters of businesses ranging from telecommunications to airlines.

In the late 1980s an increasing number of nationally based companies have chosen Phoenix as the site for regional headquarters. Businesses like US West, Thompson Industries, Hexcel Advanced Materials, Ft. Howard Paper, and Rubbermaid have made Phoenix their home. The city's location is ideal for service not only to the rest of the Southwest, but also to Southern California and the international

Businesses from telecommunications to airlines are often choosing to locate regional headquarters in Phoenix. Photo by Don Stevenson

markets of the Pacific Basin and Mexico.

This chapter examines two byproducts of Phoenix growth: Phoenix, the finance, insurance, and real estate center for the state, is emerging as a regional center as well; and small entrepreneurs have found a climate in the city that is particularly conducive to their businesses, encouraging an explosion in small-business activity.

Finance

Reflecting the character of the general economy of the city and the state, financial institutions in Phoenix are healthy and strong.

Phoenix first branch bank was opened in 1877, when an office of the Bank of Arizona from Prescott— the first bank in the Arizona Territory—was established. That small bank later became the National Bank of Arizona.

Above: A Hopi kachina is a well-known part of the logo of the Arizona Bank, the state's third biggest bank, which recently was acquired by Security Pacific. In 1986 Arizona became the first growing market state to allow banks from outside its borders to buy local banks. Photo by Carol Topalian

From those humble beginnings grew the financial community that is centered in downtown Phoenix today.

Recent changes in Arizona banking laws have resulted in a change of ownership for a number of banks in the last few years. In 1986 Arizona became the first growing market to invite other banks centered outside the state to come in and set up shop when a new law allowing U.S. banks from outside Arizona to buy local banks was passed by the Arizona legislature. During 1987, the first full year of operation of Arizona's interstate banking law, five of the state's seven largest banks changed hands, bringing large national financial institutions such as Chase, Citibank, and Security Pacific into the Arizona market.

Today there are approximately 26 banks in metro Phoenix with assets totaling $19.7 billion. Banking (mainly commercial banking) comprises the largest subcategory in the financial industry. The largest bank is Valley National.

The second-largest financial subcategory includes savings and loan associations, credit unions, business credit institutions, and mortgage bankers and brokers. In metro Phoenix nine savings and loan institutions exist, with assets totaling $14.5 billion. The largest savings and loan is Western Savings, followed closely by Merabank. There are 69 credit unions with assets totaling $883.5 million. The largest credit union is Desert Schools, followed by Motorola, Arizona State Employees, and Arizona Telco.

Statistics show that the growth in the industry has been rapid. Statewide, 1986 figures show Arizona banks had $23.8 billion in deposits and $19 billion in loans. That compares with $6.7 billion in deposits and $4.75 billion in loans in 1976.

In addition, a variety of other financial institutions are doing business in Phoenix, including security and commodity brokers, and in-

A landmark in downtown Phoenix, the Valley Bank Center rises 40 stories, acting as a giant mirror for the city's brilliant skies. Photo by Carol Topalian

vestment offices such as mutual funds, trusts, and commodity traders.

Employment in the finance, real estate, and insurance industries also is an important factor in the state's economy.

Statewide, nearly 72,000, or 6 percent of Arizona's 1.2 million workers in 1984, were employed in finance, insurance, and real estate firms, and nearly half of those were employed by financial institutions. Phoenix, the state capital and urban center of the state, is home to most of this activity and employment.

The growth in employment in these industries has been strong and consistent for more than 10 years. Only services and the construction industry have experienced greater increases. The greatest number of new jobs occurred in the finance industry, most within commercial and stock savings banks. There were strong rates of growth in the number of security and commodity dealers and services as well.

In 1985 Arizona banks employed 14,000 workers in 704 establishments, amassing a payroll of $487 million, according

to the Center for Business Research in the College of Business at Arizona State University.

Finance, insurance, and real estate compose 17.7 percent of the Gross State Product. As a group, they rank among the top 10 industries in the state.

Insurance

Like everything else in Arizona, the insurance industry has enjoyed rapid growth. The largest segment, life insurance, has shown phenomenal expansion. While in 1976 the average family in Arizona had $30,500 worth of life insurance, 10 years later that amount had grown to $56,200. In 1976 there was $24.5 billion in life insurance in force in the state, while 10 years later that figure had grown to $71.9 billion.

Employment in the insurance industry in Arizona increased 15 percent between 1980 and 1984, a trend that appears to be continuing. Although the number of agents and brokers earning a wage or salary dipped in 1981, overall employment in the industry increased to 6,300 in 1984.

During 1986 the Department of Insurance issued 6,506 new life-type insurance licenses and 2,745 new property and casualty licenses. A total of 11,911 renewal licenses also were issued. By the end of the year, the number of resident and nonresident licensees in Arizona totaled 36,341.

One-third of all the workers in the insurance industry are independent agents or brokers. Another 23 percent are employed by firms that primarily are engaged in underwriting fire, marine, and casualty insurance.

Health maintenance organizations have become a viable part of the health-insurance market in Phoenix, as they have elsewhere in the nation.

Arizonans have had the unique opportunity to observe at close hand the successful emergence of the Arizona Health Care Cost Containment System, the state's unique approach to the national Medicaid program. Arizona became the first state in the country to provide health care to low-income families using a prepaid HMO insurance plan. A Lou Harris poll showed that since the implementation of the innovative program, the proportion of Arizona's poor children visiting a doctor increased dramatically.

Real Estate

Eighteen percent of Arizona's largest privately owned companies are real estate firms, most of them headquartered in Phoenix.

At a time when the nation is facing rising vacancy rates in commercial real estate, real estate construction continues to grow in

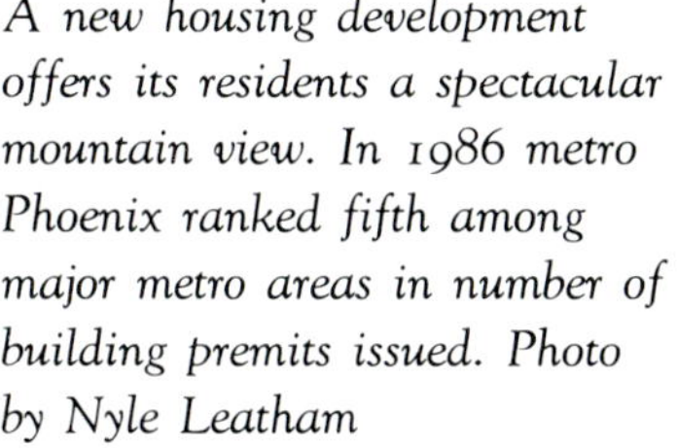

A new housing development offers its residents a spectacular mountain view. In 1986 metro Phoenix ranked fifth among major metro areas in number of building premits issued. Photo by Nyle Leatham

Phoenix. Studies show that nearly one-quarter of Arizona's most successful privately owned companies are construction firms.

And for the past several years, Phoenix has absorbed record amounts of office space, from 2.2 million square feet to 3.7 million square feet a year.

In a six-year period that began in 1980, more than $25 billion in new real estate projects were constructed in the state, placing Arizona among the fastest-growing real estate markets in the country.

The great bulk of the construction took place in the Phoenix metropolitan area, where the greatest boom in population also has occurred. It is no surprise that house construction has been responsible for a large portion of the boom. More people create a need for more housing. The housing sector is responsible for about $10 billion of the $25 billion total quoted above.

But commercial development also has been strong. In the six-year period, $1.5 billion of office construction took place in the Phoenix metro area, with $385 million of that occurring in one year—1985.

"Real estate has been a good industry in Phoenix because of all the other things happening in the economy—jobs, people," said James R. Huntwork, a Phoenix real estate attorney. "All those people moving here have to have places to live and work. That's what feeds real estate."

"The real estate industry is going to be strong in the foreseeable future," the lawyer continued. "There will be cycles. But as long as we preserve the points about our city that make it worthwhile and continue to promote economic development, the real estate industry is going to continue to be successful."

That opinion was echoed by Dennis Knight, a Canadian who—

Housing availabilities in the Phoenix area include convenient, new accommodations for mobile homes. Photo by Nyle Leatham

like many others involved in Arizona's real estate picture—was attracted to the state for its investment potential and has since adopted Arizona as his home. Foreign investments in Arizona's real estate market are growing.

"I think the future is assured," Knight said. "I think we are just beginning."

The construction industry is a key component both for providing space and as a major source of employment. In 1984, the last year for which statistics are available, there were 96,000 construction employees in Arizona—8 percent of the state's total work force. The largest amount by far worked in the Phoenix metro area. That number increased from 52,200 only seven years before.

Margo Kesler had been working for big hotels—first as a catering director, then as a trainer for the sales staff—when she decided to take matters into her own hands.

Mother of one young son, with a second child on the way, she decided to start a business in her home that would provide her with more accessibility to her children and more flexible hours. She knew she wanted to "hop on" the industry she knew best—the service industry—and she had an optimistic philosophy: "If you give better service, there's always room for your business."

"This is just a wonderful climate for new businesses," she says. It was 1982, and balloons were just beginning to be a big decorating item. "The whole balloon thing had

Many Phoenicians are becoming entrepreneurs, opting for self employment to make money. Photo by Ben Marra

just hit the market, was brand new to the Valley, and I hit on that idea," Margo says. "Balloons were popular in bouquets, but I wanted to take it into a decorating for conventions aspect."

Five years later when she sold her business, the competition in the balloon market had become fierce. By then her part-time effort, which had afforded her time to work in her children's classes at school and to be an active participant in their lives, was netting her $35,000 a year. "I was lucky," she recalls. "I was in the hospitality business, planning parties, and fell in with clients, made contact with people who would

need our services."

She also was creative and a hard worker. And she had the enthusiastic support of her husband, Bob, who had bought a small manufacturing company by "mortgaging our home" several years before. He has built up that company, Fyrmatic Industries, a manufacturer of kitchen ventilation systems, and when Margo sold the balloon company, she did so to join Bob in his business.

"Let's face it—it's a lot simpler to go to work for a corporation," says Margo. "But if you have enough confidence in yourself and enough time and energy and you really enjoy what you get into, it's the American dream.

"It's a very big risk, but it's always very exciting, and, of course, you hope that someday there'll be a major payoff."

Although construction growth has not been as rapid in the late 1980s as it was mid-decade, the value of construction awards and of building permits continues to increase annually.

"Buoyed by population increases that consistently rank Arizona as one of the country's fastest-growing states, the construction industry employs approximately one of every 12 Arizonans earning a wage or salary," a publication of the State Department of Economic Security reported.

While the state does not escape the cyclical nature of the industry that occurs nationally, the level of real estate activity in Arizona has remained constant and growing because of the continual demands placed upon the industry by an expanding population.

Entrepreneurship

About one-third of the businesses that are operating in metropolitan Phoenix today did not exist five years ago.

And if that fact isn't startling enough, consider this: New businesses were begun in the Phoenix area during 1986 at a rate of 300 per month.

According to a study by the Phoenix Metropolitan Chamber of Commerce, during a five-year period that began in late 1981, the number of businesses in metro Phoenix grew by 12,027, or 35.5 percent. All sizes of employer groups grew, but the greatest growth was in small business.

"There can be little doubt that robust population growth has done much to fuel the growth of small business," the chamber reported in a summary paper. "These companies are serving the needs of an ever-expanding population."

The chamber study found that more than 40 percent of the new businesses were in the service industry, while 16 percent were in the trade industry, 14 percent were in construction, and nearly 13 percent were in finance, insurance, and real estate. These four sectors of the economy accounted for 83 percent of all new businesses formed during the period.

A similar study, conducted by the Arizona State University College of Business, found that during 1986, eating establishments were the most popular new businesses formed, while auto-repair shops and hairstyling salons followed closely.

During that year, there were 3,646 business start-ups that contributed about 10,000 jobs to the employment scene. That accounted for about a quarter of total job growth in the Valley of the Sun during 1986.

Most of the new businesses were located within the boundaries of the city of Phoenix, and the Valley's typical new business owner was a 40-year-old, married Caucasian male "who already lived in Arizona, had some post-high school education and was employed in the previous year," the study found.

About one-third of the businesses operating in downtown Phoenix did not exist five years ago. Photo by Nyle Leatham

"A lot of people located here believing that they had a better idea," said Terry Trost, the economist for the chamber. "They came out here to get their market niche and branch out as the Valley grew. That wild West spirit makes them feel good."

Interestingly, 7 out of every 10 new businesses formed statewide were started in the metropolitan Phoenix area, and 66 cents of every dollar increase in state personal income occurred in metropolitan Phoenix.

It was statistics like these that led *Inc.* magazine to recognize Arizona in 1986 as having the nation's "most dynamic state economy" and to identify Phoenix in 1987 as the third fastest-growing metro area in the nation, as measured by growth in jobs, entrepreneurship, and percentage of fast-growing companies.

CHAPTER SEVEN

Government: Big Business

Government—local, county, state, and federal—is one of the four largest industries in Arizona, and the largest portion of it is centered in the Phoenix metropolitan area.

Arizona has a reputation of being a state that focuses on less government rather than more, and that fact is reflected in growth statistics for the industry.

Although Arizona's total wage and salary employment increased by 24 percent between 1982 and 1985, government employment rose less than half that amount, according to the Department of Economic Security.

State government is centered in Phoenix. Pictured is the capitol dome rotunda. Photo by Mark E. Gibson

In the future, economists predict, the government share of total employment will continue to shrink.

Part of this will be as a result of continuing federal efforts to reduce budget deficits. Increasing popularity of privatization (the effort to turn over services currently provided by government to private-sector enterprises) will have an impact at all governmental levels.

Employment

Even if one eliminates the employees in the public education system, government workers numbered approximately 120,000 in 1986, or one of every 11 Arizona workers. With education employees included in the count, the number nearly doubles.

Forty-two percent of the noneducation government workers were employees of counties, cities, and towns, while 34 percent were federal employees, and 24 percent were state government workers.

The nation's largest employer, the federal government, has a big impact on employment in the Phoenix metropolitan area, which has two air force bases located in close proximity. Together with postal service employees, civil military employees make up 48 percent of all federal employment in Arizona. Luke Air Force Base, eight miles

west of Phoenix, and Williams Air Force Base, 21 miles southeast of Phoenix, account for the largest share in the Phoenix metro area.

There are 41,500 federal employees in the state, and about 12,000 are in the Phoenix metropolitan area.

Facing page: The Arizona Peace Officer Memorial stands near the Arizona State Capitol. Photo by Matt Bradley

Below: Local government employees, like this City of Phoenix policewoman, accounted for 46,500 of the statewide government employment in 1986. Photo by Matt Bradley

State government is the largest government employer in Phoenix. As the state capital, Phoenix is the center of the business that keeps state government running.

The State of Arizona employs 26,300 workers, 2 percent of total wage and salary employment in the state. Sixty-seven percent of them are in the Phoenix metropolitan area. The largest number of employees are in the Department of Economic Security, which is charged with welfare-oriented and labor-training programs. It is the agency through which federal transfer payments—such as food stamps, aid to families with dependent children, and unemployment insurance benefits—are made.

The next largest state government employer is the Department

Above: This symbol to liberty stands atop the copper-plated dome of the Arizona State Capitol. Phoenix historical lore contends the statue was used in days past by cowboys for target practice. The copper roof was donated by Arizona's mining companies. Photo by Carol Topalian

Facing page: Schoolchildren view Arizona's state seal inside the state capitol. Photo by Mark E. Gibson

of Transportation, responsible for maintaining the state's highway system. Other large agencies, in declining order of impact on employment, are the Department of Health Services, the Department of Public Safety, the Department of Administration, and the Department of Corrections.

Local government accounted for about 46,500 of the statewide government employment in 1986. The greatest portion of local government employees also are located in the Phoenix metropolitan area.

The City of Phoenix is governed through a city manager-council system. The mayor and the city council are elected, and they employ a city manager to carry out the administrative duties of running city government.

In the early 1980s a new district system was approved by the voters, requiring that each of the eight city council members run from designated districts within the city. The mayor continues to run at-large. Supporters of the district system say the new system has made city government more efficient and responsive to the voters.

Public-Private Sector

The City of Phoenix has long been an innovator in utilizing private-sector services to perform city jobs. Cited by the U.S. Chamber of

Commerce for its efforts to involve the private sector, the city utilizes private firms to operate its bus system, provide security and crowd control, collect trash in some areas, tow and store illegally parked cars, and operate the city landfill.

The city has joined hands with the private sector in a number of endeavors, among them the creation of the Phoenix Economic Growth Corporation (PEGC). PEGC was created by the city in 1984 as a nonprofit public-private partnership between the city government and the private sector. Its charter focuses on working to secure economic development that might otherwise not occur if the private and public sectors acted independently.

An example of this kind of joint public-private effort occurred in the development of a downtown city park, Patriots' Square. Preliminary costs for the project were fronted by the private sector, with the city adding public dollars to that early commitment. Private sector funds for a final phase of the project, the addition of a laser beam projection attraction, have been committed.

Fiscal Conservatism

State budget growth is controlled by a heritage of fiscal conservatism as well as by a state constitutional spending limitation formula that went into effect in the late 1970s. State spending is controlled by a formula based on personal income, population growth, and inflation.

Above: The Old Maricopa County Courthouse still houses justice courts for the county. Photo by Matt Bradley

Facing page: This surrealistic bird stands near city hall. Photo by Nyle Leatham

Pages 172-173: Construction on the Arizona State Capitol Building began in 1899 and finished a year later. The neoclassical structure was built entirely of Arizona stone, including malpais rock from Camelback Mountain, granite from South Mountain and tufa from the mountains near Kirkland. Photo by Carol Topalian

Since its beginning as the nation's 48th state in 1912, Arizona has been known for its own unique brand of political conservatism. Arizonans believe in balancing the budget, and the state's constitution reflects that belief in its requirement that the state budget be balanced annually.

The state also is forbidden to incur long-term debt in excess of $350,000, and therefore has no outstanding General Obligation Bonds.

Census Bureau statistics rank Arizona lowest among all 50 states in terms of both debt total and debt per capita.

Taxes

Arizona's tax environment compares favorably with the rest of the nation. Among its pro-business components are the lack of state debt and the absence of an inventory tax, corporate franchise tax, offshore unitary tax, municipal income tax, or tax on income paid to a parent company by a subsidiary when the parent firm owns 50 percent or more of the subsidiary and is headquartered in Arizona.

The state sales-tax rate is 5 percent with an additional 1-2 percent in municipal sales taxes. In Phoenix that amounts to a combined sales tax of 6.7 percent. Sales taxes do not apply to manufacturing equipment, fabrication, or processing of a product, and sales taxes are not levied on personal or professional services or labor costs.

Property-tax assessments are based on eight property classes,

It took a group of Phoenix businesspeople to save Christmas.

When for the first time in 20 years, the city of Phoenix did not adorn itself for the holiday season because its decorations needed to be replaced, the city appealed to the business community for help.

The year was 1987. The Santas and saguaro cacti that had hung from Phoenix lightpoles in past seasons were frayed and worn. City finances were tight, and the council decided it simply could not afford new decorations.

A group headed by KOY Radio General Manager Michael Horne joined with the Phoenix Community Alliance (an organization of downtown and central corridor businesspeople), the Phoenix Chamber of Commerce, and the city to conduct a fund-raising campaign. They called themselves the Scrooge Busters.

It was not the first time

Government has often formed a partnership with the private sector to make Phoenix a better city. Photo by Stephen Burns

the city had worked with private industry in an endeavor to enrich the city, but it probably was the partnership with the quickest results. And the joy it brought to the faces of young and old alike throughout the holiday season of 1988 made the effort all the more worthwhile.

The Scrooge Busters raised $275,000—about $215,000 of which came from the private sector—to purchase an array of holiday decorations inspired by Southwestern themes. The new decorations celebrate the uniqueness of the area— representations of Indian jewelry and cacti abound in pole ornaments and garlands. Turquoise, coral, silver, and copper beads create a highly original seasonal motif.

Mayor Terry Goddard, noting that the city and private enterprise also have joined hands in efforts to purchase a laser-powered attraction for the downtown Patriots' Park and to build museums and a theater, observed that partnerships like the Scrooge Busters deeply enrich the city. "Efforts like this help us have things in this community we could not otherwise possibly afford, and, frankly, they are the things that greatly enhance our life-style here," he said. "Private businesses are helping to stretch community dollars."

Phoenix' tax environment is favorable to business and commerce. Photo by Nyle Leatham

with commercial and industrial property assessed at 25 percent of full cash value—generally about 20 percent below actual market value. Phoenix' average property tax is $10.47 per $100 of assessed valuation. The assessment rate is 10 percent of current value for residential property, 16 percent for vacant land, and 25 percent for commercial property and equipment.

Metro Phoenix does not have a personal income tax. Federal income taxes are deducted before computing state taxable income.

Arizona has the nation's lowest net estate tax and has no gift, inheritance, poll, or intangible personal-property tax.

Tax-exempt industrial development bonds up to $10 million are available for a variety of commercial enterprises and industrial projects through the county or Phoenix' Industrial Development Authority.

"Arizona's tax structure is consistent, predictable, and equitable, and provides a favorable environment for business," said the Phoenix Metrogroup, a consortium of chambers of commerce from various cities in the Phoenix metropolitan area.

The bottom line? The city of Phoenix taxing environment is very competitive with other similar-sized cities, both for individuals and for businesses.

CHAPTER EIGHT

Where the Living Is Easy

P hoenix's richest asset is its life-style. Its climate, its scenery, and its culture continue to draw tourists, corporations, and new residents in record-breaking numbers.

With a generous supply of sunshine, Phoenicians enjoy both participatory and spectator sports year-round. Whether it's the NBA's Phoenix Suns, the Phoenix Firebirds professional baseball team, major league baseball spring training, the ASU Sun Devils football team, or—the newest member to the local sports scene—the NFL professional football team, the Phoenix Cardinals, opportunities for watching abound.

The Phoenix Cardinals are the newest sports attraction in Phoenix. At a home game in Sun Devil Stadium, the Cardinal's Stump Mitchell leaps for a reception over the Washington Redskin's Alvin Walton. Photo by Randy Reid/ The Phoenix Gazette

Symphony performances, opera, the theater, museums, and libraries in a regenerating downtown broaden the choice of entertainment opportunities in the state's capital city.

And Phoenix is a short drive from the 22 national parks (including the Grand Canyon) and 16 state historical and recreation parks that make Arizona a renowned vacation spot. Add to this the cultural influences of nearby Mexico, the chance to explore ghost towns and lost mines, just "hanging out" at nearby guest ranches, and participating in rodeos, pioneer day celebrations, and fiestas, and the opportunities seem endless.

Phoenix also offers a rich supply of human resources, educational opportunities, health-care resources, and housing availabilities.

Recreation and Leisure

With an average 11 days a year below freezing and only 36 days of rain, and with an annual average temperature of 72 degrees, Phoenix

Above and right: The Great Fair of Fountain Hills— a community east of Scottsdale—hosts a hot air balloon race. Photos by Nyle Leatham

Facing page: Dozens of golf courses, both public and private, are popular throughout the year in the Valley of the Sun. This one is the Papago Golf Course. Photo by Nyle Leatham

is a utopian metropolis to those used to having to deal with snow and sludge and gray skies in other parts of the nation.

Phoenix' climate encourages outdoor activities, and residents have the widest range of choices possible. Over 100 professional-caliber golf courses offer year-round opportunities on the links, and more than 1,200 public and private tennis courts help make that sport one of the favorites in the Valley. Water and snow skiing are both only a two-hour drive away.

While the desert is an environment closely associated with the state, water recreation is a very real part of Arizona's—and Phoenix'—life-style. In fact, more boats are owned per capita in Arizona than in any other state. The largest group of the state's 67 natural and man-made lakes is the Salt River Lakes chain, enjoyed by Phoenicians year-round. These include Roosevelt Lake, with over 17,000 surface acres; Apache Lake, with 2,600 surface acres; Canyon Lake, with about 1,000 surface acres; Saguaro Lake, with 1,250 surface acres; and Lake Pleasant, with 3,700 surface acres.

Further away (about 205 miles), Lake Havasu features the reconstructed London Bridge and a surrounding English village, and Lake Powell (about 300 miles from Phoenix) offers scenic

Like the snow? Take a quick trip north. Prefer water sports? Go the same distance—but east.

Part of what has made Phoenix so attractive to new residents and to tourists alike is its central location in the state. Thus visits to most of Arizona's scenic attractions are a mere two-hour drive away from the city.

There are times during the year when an enterprising athlete could travel a little more than two hours to the north of Phoenix and ski in the snow or else a little less than two hours to the east and ski on a lake. What's more, Tucson and all its resorts are only a two-hour drive to the south, with Nogales and Mexico only an hour drive beyond that. In addition, the Grand Canyon is an approximate five-hour drive north of Phoenix.

From the tall pines of the north country to the beautiful desert silhouettes of the south, here are a few of the popular day trips easily taken from the Phoenix area:

—The Grand Canyon, one of the natural wonders of the world, offers spectacular views of canyon walls sculpted by the Colorado River. For the more adventurous,

Not far from Phoenix, scenic trails through the desert offer breathtaking vistas. Photo by Mark E. Gibson

there are nature walks, vigorous hikes, or mule rides into the canyon. Airplane trips to the canyon also are available from Phoenix's Sky Harbor Airport.

—Flagstaff, a few hours north of Phoenix (en route to the Grand Canyon), offers wintertime snow skiing or summertime cool temperatures. Fairfield Continental's Snowbowl is located in the San Francisco Peaks. The city also is a popular destination for those interested in exploring the Hopi or Navajo Indian cultures and reservations. The Museum of Northern Arizona has fine collections of Native American art, and the two reservations are each a few hours' drive from Flagstaff. Both offer memorable experiences and breathtaking scenery. The Hopi Reservation contains some of the most majestic mesa country anywhere, while the Navajo Reservation contains three of the largest known cliff dwellings as well as ruins and pictographs of Indian villages under the sheer, weather-streaked cliffs of Canyon de Chelly. Nearby is the Painted Desert, vast land of desolate beauty, and the Petrified Forest, where giant trees were transformed into stone thousands of years ago by mud and volcanic ash.

—Sedona, a mecca for art lovers, contains the gorgeous red-rock buttes that are unique to the area. It also lies at the base of a spectacular canyon drive, Oak Creek Canyon. A two-hour drive north of Phoenix, the area attracts not only those who love its natural beauty, but also those interested in purchasing authentic Indian and Southwestern arts and crafts. Montezuma's Castle, misnamed for an Aztec king who never saw it, is nearby, a five-story apartment house built by the Sinagua Indians in the year 1250, as is Jerome, a historic mining ghost town that clings to a mountain.

—Prescott, Arizona's first permanent capital in the days when most arrivals came here to prospect gold, is a charming, small community that offers a chance to investigate early state history. Here is the first territorial governor's mansion, the historic 1857 John C. Frémont House, and the restored 100-year-old Bashford House. Popular with Phoenicians seeking a break from the summer heat, Prescott is a two-hour drive north.

—The Apache Trail, so named because it was used by the Apache Indians as a short-cut through the mountains to reach early Salt River Valley settlers, is a twisting, sometimes treacherous mountain road along the back side of the Superstition Mountains, from Apache Junction to Roosevelt Lake and the mining community of Globe-Miami. The trail is a six-hour round trip from Phoenix along sparkling man-made lakes, and it goes past the Tonto Indian Cliff dwellings, which are worth a look.

—The Salt River Canyon, north of Globe about one hour (a total three-hour trip from Phoenix), is a scenic canyon view second only to the Grand Canyon. The highway dips straight to the

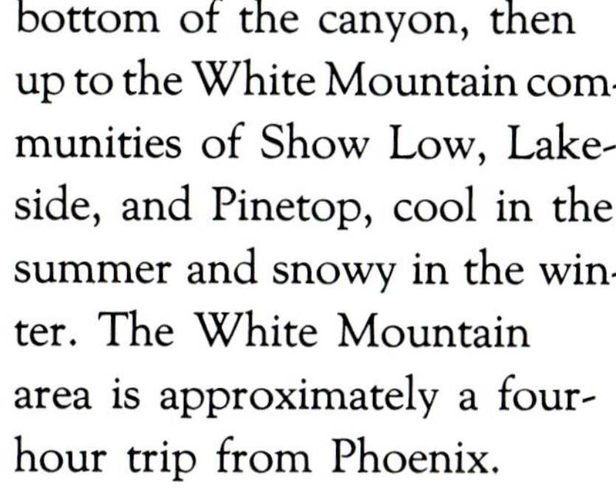
A popular summertime recreation, tubing, draws Phoenicians to the Salt River on a weekend. Photo by Matt Bradley

bottom of the canyon, then up to the White Mountain communities of Show Low, Lakeside, and Pinetop, cool in the summer and snowy in the winter. The White Mountain area is approximately a four-hour trip from Phoenix.

—Tucson, a culturally rich city where Pima Indians, Spanish explorers, and Mexican settlers once lived, is a two-hour drive south of Phoenix. Among attractions in the area are the Arizona-Sonora Desert Museum, old Tucson (a frequently used movie set to simulate the Old West), the 300-year-old San Xavier del Bac Mission, and Kitt Peak, a world-renowned observatory.

—Nogales, the state's best-known border town, is side-by-side with the twin city of Nogales, Sonora, which offers bullfights and a chance to purchase Mexican goods. Those who like to bargain over prices will not be disappointed. Nogales is a little over an hour south of Tucson.

beauty and the opportunity to rent houseboats.

But it isn't necessary to go far to enjoy the beauty of the Arizona desert. Within the city's boundaries, Squaw Peak, Camelback Mountain, North Mountain, and South Mountain all offer trails for exploring. The trek up Squaw Peak, in particular, has gained a reputation with Phoenicians as a pleasant daily routine for keeping in shape while getting a spectacular view of the Valley. The Superstition and McDowell mountains are nearby for city dwellers as well. In all, the Phoenix Parks and Recreation Department has 7 desert mountain parks and more than 150 parks in total. Among the most impressive are:

Papago Park. A geological attraction because of its rock formations, Papago Park houses the Desert Botanical Garden, the only botanical garden dedicated from its beginning to the study of plant life of the deserts and other arid lands.

The park abuts the Phoenix Zoo, 125 acres of rolling hills, shaded paths, and natural environment exhibits that offer the opportunity to view more than 1,000 animals, many of which are endangered species. It is here, for example, that the Arabian

Horseback riding up Squaw Peak is popular with tourists and residents alike. Photo by Charlene Faris

Above: In addition to its animal exhibits, the Phoenix Zoo also has an exquisite floral display. Photo by Mark E. Gibson

Right: Covering 125 acres, the Phoenix Zoo has plenty of room for natural environment exhibits. Photo by Charlene Faris

oryx was saved from extinction. The inspiration for the unicorn legend, the horned oryx has been bred so successfully in captivity here that some have been returned to their natural environment and others have been given to other zoos, such as the San Diego Zoo. The Phoenix Zoo is the largest nonprofit, private, self-supporting zoo in the nation.

Encanto Park. An oasis in the center of the city, this 222-acre park was named with the Spanish word for "enchanted." It features a

Above: From South Mountain Park, one can view the city in the distance. Photo by Mark E. Gibson

lagoon with paddleboats and canoes and a 1948-vintage carousel, restored through citizens' volunteer efforts. When the carousel, a city landmark, was put up for sale by its owner, hundreds of Valley residents rallied to provide the funds to purchase and restore it. A community "save-the-carousel" movement brought together Phoenix' Junior League and local union members of the AFL-CIO in a unique cooperative effort to restore the merry-go-round.

South Mountain Park. This is the world's largest municipally owned desert mountain park. With nearly 16,000 acres, the park encompasses not only unusual rock formations, but also prehistoric Indian petroglyphs, rock carvings, and inscriptions. The panoramic view of the city attracts visitors both during the day and at night. Its trails are popular for horseback riding, hiking, and leisurely strolls.

It was Phoenix's Statue of Liberty project—comparable to New York City's effort on behalf of a tangible symbol in danger of decaying and becoming lost to the future.

Frankly, the Encanto Carousel didn't look like much—20 horses on a worn-out merry-go-round, painted with glossy automotive paint and cracked and weathered in all too many places. It would have been easy to let it go.

But to thousands of Phoenicians, the carousel meant much more. It meant childhood fantasies and life without cares. It meant family outings and birthday parties and dripping ice cream cones. It meant rides that were rewards for good behavior or for getting good grades. It meant memories.

So when the carousel, which had been located in the city's lovely downtown Encanto Park since 1948, was about to be sold off by the private concessionaire who owned it to the highest bidding carnival operator, Phoenicians rallied. A group of mothers formed the Encanto Carousel Fund, Inc. With nothing but a pledge of loans, they approached the media. The result was impressive.

In less than two months,

Canoes and paddleboats ply the lagoon at Encanto Park. Photo by Mark E. Gibson

the group raised more than the $55,000 purchase price of the carousel in donations from hundreds of Phoenix residents. Children sent coins from their piggybanks. Grandmothers sent checks in their grandchildren's names. Businessmen offered donations. And letters of support poured in.

"The enclosed is sent on behalf of my son, Jimmy, who is 15 and autistic," wrote one father. "We can't lose the merry-go-round. Good luck."

"Bless you all for saving the carousel," an 80-year-old woman offered. "You are saving a precious heritage."

"This is probably one of the most worthwhile checks I have sent to anyone in a long time," added a mother who had treasured the carousel as

a child and hoped that her children would also be able to enjoy the ride.

In addition, two key community groups offered to help with the restoration. The Junior League of Phoenix contributed $20,000 and, equally important, a group of volunteers. The AFL0-CIO and 16 local union members offered their labor services at no cost. Many members of both groups explained that they fondly remembered childhood rides on the merry-go-round. Moreover, it was the first time the two diverse organizations had joined hands in a project, and the results were impressive.

The city of Phoenix itself provided warehouse space for the work and allowed for the carousel to be returned to its home in Encanto Park when the restoration was completed. Involved in an effort to clean up and freshen up the park, the city agreed that the carousel that had touched the heartstrings of so many Phoenicians should be a focal point of the new Encanto Park.

The Encanto Carousel was saved—a symbol of the past that would live to be a part of the future for the children of Phoenix.

Deck Park. Site of the city's new Central Library, this 24-acre park is being created over the top of Phoenix' new freeway where it is recessed in the city's central corridor. Deck Park was authorized by the voters in a 1988 election, as was the library, and it is symbolic of the city's commitment to the inner city.

Above and below: The Phoenix Symphony, which enjoys widespread support from the city, is known as a leading national symphony. Photos by Nyle Leatham

A Cultural Bonanza

In the early 1970s, Phoenicians were likely to complain that the city's cultural life had not kept up with its growth. When historians look back on the city's development, they will surely consider the 1980s as the dawning of cultural awareness in the city.

The Phoenix Arts Commission was formed in 1985 and moved quickly to increase funding and support for the arts. With the sup-

port of the city council, the commission initiated a Percent for Art Program that assures funding for public art from every public construction project that takes place. The commission thus created a funding mechanism for the arts where none had existed before, and undertook an ambitious effort to inventory and plan for sites for public art.

While other cities allowed their symphonies to die from lack of support, Phoenix rallied behind the Phoenix Symphony as it moved into major status.

With passage of a record billion-dollar quality of life bond issue in 1988, Phoenix voters made an impressive commitment to its

Right: The Arizona Theatre Company recently produced Candide. *Photo by Tim Fuller*

libraries, parks, art and science museum facilities, theaters, and other cultural institutions. The bond issue contained the largest public arts and cultural proposal ever approved in any city in the nation. In fact, since the bond's passage, representatives of cities from all over the nation have studied the Phoenix example to determine how to gain such widespread popular support for their own cultural needs.

In an election that drew the second highest voter turnout for a bond election in city history, voters approved a massive cultural improvement plan to expand the Phoenix Little Theater and Phoenix Art Museum, provide a new Arizona Museum of Science and Technology, build a new Central Library and three more library branches, add parks and a new indoor aquatic center, and expand other cultural facilities. Thanks to the passage of the bond, a historic downtown landmark—the Orpheum Theater—will be renovated and revived for community events. When completed, it will contain 1,500 seats.

Mayor Terry Goddard said the vote presented "very

strong support for a wide variety of programs" and added enthusiastically, "The overall message is wonderful."

The vote, in effect, determined that Phoenicians wanted a progressive city that would continue moving forward in its development.

Today the city of Phoenix has a vibrant cultural community that includes, in the performing arts, the Phoenix Symphony, the Arizona Theatre Company, the Arizona Opera Company, and the Arizona Ballet Company, along with a long list of local theater companies. The city's growing library system has an outstanding Arizona history collection and a notable "Art of the Book" room. Other cultural entities worthy of note in the Valley are:

The Phoenix Art Museum, featuring a collection of nineteenth- and twentieth-century art, with particular selections from Western American art; a notable Asian gallery that includes collections of Chinese porcelain and cloisonné; and a Spanish colonial room. The museum

Above: This neon contemporary work is in the Heard Museum's art gallery. Photo by Matt Bradley

Below: More than 75,000 artifacts from the Heard Museum's vast collections introduce visitors to the life-style of native Americans and non-western societies throughout the world. These include paintings, graphics, and sculptures. Photo by Matt Bradley

Above: Southwestern history is carefully preserved and presented at the Heard Museum. Photo by Susan I. Davison

Right: A popular attraction for young and old alike, the Arizona Museum of Science and Technology will move into new, expanded quarters in the near future, thanks to the passage of the city's 1988 bond election. The facility is bursting at the seams in its current location in downtown Phoenix. Photo by Carol Topalian

has undertaken an impressive program both to develop its own traveling shows and to bring exhibits from other museums to Phoenix.

The Heard Museum, a collection of more than 75,000 artifacts chronicling 15,000 years of history in the Southwest. The traditions of many prehistoric and living tribes are included, and a wide range of changing exhibits, public programs, children's activi-

ties, and special events focus on the arts of Native Americans.

The Arizona Museum of Science and Technology, a hands-on museum of scientific and technological exhibits intended to spark curiosity about the world. One of the more popular exhibits is "TAM," a female transparent anatomical mannequin.

The Central Arizona Museum, a collection of historic memorabilia from Arizona, particularly focused on preserving the city's past.

The Herberger Theater Center, which features two theaters (one with 820 seats) in downtown Phoenix, designed specifically for dramatic presentations. The smaller theater is convertible for a variety of uses, including theater-in-the-round and as a dinner theater. With the renovation of the 1929-vintage Orpheum Theater and the existing Symphony Hall facility, the downtown theater district will offer a variety of theater options.

Pueblo Grande Monument, one of 22 identified communities the Hohokam Indians constructed in the Phoenix area. This preserved site includes an 85-foot by 41-foot depres-

Above: Just a few blocks from downtown Phoneix, Pueblo Grande Monument is the site of an ancient Hohokam Indian community. Photo by Mark E. Gibson

Facing page: The jewel of Arizona State University is the Frank Lloyd Wright-designed Grady Gammage Auditorium. Photo by Nyle Leatham

Below: World renowned architect Frank Lloyd Wright established Taliesin West, before his death in 1959, and the wintertime home for Wright's disciples has continued to flourish. Located east of Phoenix, Taliesin West is open for tours. Photo by Carol Topalian

Above: A nighttime view of downtown Phoenix, taken from in front of the Phoenix Civic Plaza, shows 100 years of architecture. Photo by Carol Topalian

Facing page: The Rosson House—home to an early Phoenix family—has been restored and is now open to the public. Photo by Susan I. Davison

sion in the earth that once served as a game court and the remains of canals with which these Indian farmers irrigated the arid desert. The exhibit is a few blocks from downtown Phoenix.

Taliesin West, the legacy of architect Frank Lloyd Wright. Located northeast of Phoenix, a 20-minute drive away, Taliesin remains a working colony of disciples of the late architect.

Grady Gammage Auditorium, Frank Lloyd Wright's grand 3,000-seat auditorium located at Arizona State University in Tempe. Gammage, which attracts many entertainers and national touring shows, is an impressive structure that, in addition to being a popular stage for the performing arts, draws the attention of Valley visitors who come just to view the auditorium itself.

Downtown

While the city's commitment to invigorate its downtown area has been a long-term one, the effort really got under way in the 1980s.

194

Among the more significant signs of this are completion of the renovation of Patriots' Square, expansion of the Civic Plaza and redesign of its grounds to include a solar oasis project, construction and renovation of the historic Orpheum Theater, and the addition of the Herberger Theater Center.

Earlier projects that have proven to be popular with Phoenicians include the renovation of the historic Rosson House, the Victorian home of one of the city's early leading families, and construction of Heritage Square, a pleasant center offering both a glimpse of the city's past and a popular gathering spot for downtown outdoor functions.

Rarely has a city so large undergone such an enthusiastic burst of activity all at once, as has been the case of Phoenix in the 1980s. Phoenicians have looked forward for a decade to the end results that will be apparent in the early 1990s. In the meantime, the construction under way in downtown Phoenix stands in stark contrast to the decaying emptiness of many major cities' downtowns.

Patriots' Square. A combined public and private effort to turn an undistinguished block-square downtown park into a unique public space with an amphitheater, refreshment kiosks, and entertainment space that will draw visitors into the city's core, Patriots' Square was designed to be both "people oriented" and to "symbolize the city's move into the future," according to its designer. Architect Ted Alexander, given the task of redesigning the park, saw the job as an

Below: Phoenicians can slip back to the past in Heritage Square. Photo by Mark E. Gibson

Facing page: A canopy of shade structures on the Civic Plaza frame St. Mary's Church. Photo by Matt Bradley

opportunity to create a counterpoint to the "hard mass and rigidity" that necessarily accompanies a downtown.

"I wanted to create something so interesting that anybody coming into the community would want to take a drive for an hour if necessary to see what it's about," he said. "And I have an interest in light. I have done a number of churches, and I'm intrigued by what you can do with light to affect people's moods."

What he did was create a downtown open space featuring fountains, greenery, and an amphitheater. His design capped the creation with its unique calling card—a future-oriented laser beam device that visitors to the square could manipulate. Funding for the laser is coming from the business community.

"The park is a statement of pride and spirit for the entire community, reflecting the vitality and energy of our people," Alexander said. "It's a place for the people of Phoenix."

Civic Plaza. Following closely on a building program that expanded the meeting and convention facilities that were constructed in the 1970s, the city has undertaken efforts to create a unique solar oasis nearby. The oasis proposal, which grew out of a summer demonstration project that was set up on Civic Plaza grounds, will use tomorrow's technology today. Air, water, and plant life will be used to create an environment averaging 20 degrees lower than that around it without wasting precious energy resources.

Superblock. Construction is well under way on an eight-block Superblock project, Rouse Company's $500-million Arizona Center, that will include 2 million square feet of office space, specialty retail stores, restaurants, parks, snack shops, and a 600-room hotel. Developers envision a richly landscaped 3.2-acre garden in the center of four office towers.

Mercado. Just southeast of Superblock, construction on a

$15.8-million two-block Mexican-style Mercado is under way. Featuring two-story buildings, the Mercado will provide 45,000 square feet of offices, 72,000 square feet of retail space featuring Mexican and Spanish products, and a 10,000-square-foot cultural center with meeting facilities.

The $15-million project will be a Mexican-style village of stores, restaurants, and offices, jointly developed by Chicanos por la Causa and the Symington Company.

Square One. Design concepts for an 80,000-square-foot Square One development also have been completed. The shopping center will provide at least 40 specialty retail boutiques.

City officials liken the project to the ambitious undertaking San

The Arizona Heart Institute has existed for 16 years under the guidance of its founder, cardiovascular surgeon Dr. Edward B. Diethrich. For the last 10 years, it has operated out of this structure, which will soon be replaced by a larger facility adjacent to the Humana Hospital-Phoenix campus. Photo by Carol Topalian

Diego successfully completed when it created its Horton Plaza as a downtown redevelopment project. It will be developed by the Trammell
Crow Company.

Renaissance Square. The Trammell Crow Company also recently completed construction on One Renaissance Square, a 26-story,
480,000-square-foot office building. Construction has begun on Two Renaissance Square at a cost of $175 million.

Health Care

Phoenix is a major center of health care and medical science in the Southwest. Among its nationally prominent institutions are the Barrow Neu-
rological Institute and the Arizona Heart Institute. A branch of the
Minnesota-based Mayo Clinic has been founded in nearby Scottsdale
as well.

Many of the city's 13 hospitals, which offer 4,500 beds, have specialties in coronary care, ophthalmology, and arthritis and allergy treatment. Regionally, 33 hospitals with more than 8,000 beds serve the
area.

Health-care institutions comprise a major growth industry for
the area as well. By the mid-1980s more than 80,000 employees in Arizona worked in the health delivery system, with hospitals the major employer. That number has continued to grow, particularly in the Phoenix area. In fact, hospital employment has shown consistent and
rapid expansion over the past two decades, with the Phoenix area the
site of the largest increase.

Education

Phoenix and the surrounding area offer a significant blend of educational resources.

In the adjoining suburb of Tempe, Arizona State University

offers the resources of a major research university only a 20-minute drive from downtown Phoenix.

Comprised of 10 colleges and one school, ASU offers significant resources in basic electronic, semiconductor, aerospace, and telecommunication research, as well as substantial scientific and engineering programs that coordinate with area employers. A second campus of ASU began operations in temporary headquarters in northwestern Phoenix in the fall of 1984, and a 300-acre campus is under construction.

In addition, the Maricopa Community College system has seven colleges in the Phoenix area, with a combined enrollment of more than 70,000 students. The third-largest community college system in the U.S. also includes the Maricopa Skills Center, specializing in job training for many of the area's largest employers. A fully accredited four-year liberal arts private Christian college, Grand Canyon College, is lo-

The University of Phoenix is a private institution that offers undergraduate and graduate degrees in business and administrative fields. Photo by Carol Topalian

cated on a 68-acre campus in west-central Phoenix, and the 10-year-old University of Phoenix offers degrees in business administration and management, nursing, and education.

DeVry Institute of Technology in north Phoenix offers a wide range of technical training and vocational programs, and the American Graduate School of International Management in Glendale, on the west side of Phoenix, attracts students from around the world to its graduate courses in international business. In all, 80 private technical and business schools operate in and around the city.

At the elementary and secondary education level, there are 16 elementary districts and a unified high school district within the city limits of Phoenix. Phoenix also offers a variety of schools to serve the student with special needs.

City government is taking an active role in shaping the quality of education in Phoenix. Mayor Terry Goddard has appointed a Commission on Excellence in Public Education made up of educators, business leaders, parents, and elected officials to examine the educational system in the city and make recommendations for excellence in the classroom.

Housing

The median sales price of a single-family home in metro Phoenix in 1986 was $94,500 new and $79,500 resale, comparing favorably with the national median sales price of $97,900.

As land prices in neighboring California have skyrocketed, the more affordable price of land in the Valley has seemed all the more remarkable. In fact, an Arizona State University study indicated that homes in the Valley were more affordable in 1988 than they had been since 1981.

While housing construction slowed from the record-breaking years of 1983 and 1984, it remains a strong part of the local economy. In 1987, for example, nearly 27,500 building permits for housing were issued—nearly 16,000 of them for single-family homes, about 3,100 for townhouses, and 8,400 for multifamily residences.

Good housing availabilities, plentiful educational opportunities, an array of health-care facilities, and both recreational and cultural entertainment—it all adds up to a rich quality of life that makes Phoenix attractive to the people who choose to call it home.

As nighttime approaches,
Phoenix is blessed yet again
with another beautiful sunset.
Photo by Nyle Leatham

CHAPTER NINE

Threshold of the Twenty-first Century

Probably no one has summed up Phoenix current place as a leading U.S. city better than economist Terry Trost, who said simply, "There are communities throughout this nation that would kill for the kind of growth we are crying over."

Accustomed to phenomenal growth statistics, Phoenicians quake when the numbers slide even slightly. And it is an irony that perhaps only a Westerner can understand, that the people who are hardest on Phoenix are the people who have chosen to live there. Ask a Phoenician about his city and he is likely to tell you it is getting too big, has too much traffic, and has developed too much pollution. He may not remember to mention the phenomenal beauty, the wonderful weather, and the business environment that encourages creativity. He may forget to talk about the advantages of its geographic location, the competitive edge its cost of living has over most major cities, and the tax and governmental regulatory pluses that exist there. It is not surprising, then, that it was *Inc.* magazine, a national publication, not a local one, that rated Arizona and Phoenix among America's hottest business locations. It was not an Arizona food critic, but a New York reviewer—Craig Claiborne of the *New York Times*—who first recognized Phoenix chef Vincent Guerithault as one of the finest French chefs in America. And it is in the national travel magazines that Phoenix's Arizona Biltmore is given its due as one of the finest resorts in the world.

Call it Western modesty. Call it being part of a young city. Whatever, the sense of braggadocio and of total devotion displayed by many native New Yorkers and Chicagoans simply isn't there in your average Phoenician. And perhaps that, too, contributes to what is unique and fresh about the city of Phoenix. Perhaps that partially explains why Phoenicians are willing to try new approaches and to experiment with new undertakings, while the rapid growth the city undergoes constantly brings new players into the power structure.

It is the transferees, the transplants, who most appreciate the virtues of the city. When attorneys James and Patience Huntwork decided to move to Phoenix from Boston in 1977, they did so after a "scientific study" of the country.

"Neither of us had visited here," Jim Huntwork recalled. Their decision to move to Phoenix, he said, was "based on geographical location, futurist studies, and reading newspapers. We decided it was a place where you could get involved and do things, and things were

The Arizona Biltmore is known as a world-class resort. Photo by Don Stevenson

really happening . . . not a town that had reached its peak, but one that was just rolling up its sleeves and getting down to it."

The Huntworks' decision was quickly bolstered by the climate. "We left Boston in a blizzard and arrived in Phoenix in 85 degrees. The palm trees were swaying, the citrus trees were blooming," he remembered. "By the time we got off the plane, we had already made up our minds not to leave."

But will the paradise last? As Phoenix gets larger and larger, can it retain the qualities that make it special while assuming the role of big city and Southwestern business center? Can it retain its pro-

The old makes way for the new in the downtown Superblock project. Photo by Nyle Leatham

business atmosphere, avoid the sprawl and pollution that has marked its neighbor to the west, Los Angeles, and realize the bright future that so many predict lies ahead?

Phoenix Mayor Terry Goddard and the members of the city council believe that it can. "Today we face the compound challenge of developing, protecting, and enhancing our city's environment," Goddard said in his annual State of the City address in 1988. With continued planning and a commitment to pursuing quality of life improvements, he added, Phoenix will "take charge of its future" and "celebrate the incredible resources native to Phoenix and the Southwest."

Regulatory Laws and Taxes

Attorney Jim Huntwork frequently deals with clients from outside the state who ask him how to "work the system" in Phoenix government.

"I tell them it's a fantastic place to work with the authorities because they're honest," he said. "They respond to issues, not to bribes.

"And by and large, their inclination is not to say no. They're much more innovative, compared to a fuddy-duddy, entrenched civil service place."

Bicyclists take a spin in a race around the state capitol. Photo by Nyle Leatham

Duck tamales, lobster chimichangas, and nachos of mild goat cheese? Jalapeno bread, tomatillo salsa, and green bell pepper jelly in a French restaurant?

It's one of the hottest trends to hit the Southwest and, by osmosis, the rest of the country in recent years . . . a palate-pleasing combination of Southwestern ingredients and French cuisine. It's available at four Valley restaurants: Vincent Guerithault on Camelback, La Hacienda and Saguaro in Scottsdale, and 8700 at Pinnacle Peak.

Though the cuisine was spawned by four adventurous chefs in Dallas, Texas, it was Chef Vincent Guerithault who brought it to Phoenix in his small upper-scale restaurant on Camelback Road.

The nouvelle Southwestern cuisine is marked by three characteristics;

(1) The use of native, often spicy hot ingredients;

(2) The cooking technique, which is French;

(3) Its appeal to the eye. Appearance is equally as important and, sometimes, as time-consuming a part of preparation as taste.

Barbara Fenzl, a Phoenix food critic and owner of Les Gourmettes Cooking School, claims this cuisine is no passing fad, but a popular, evolutionary cooking style that's here to stay. "People like spicy food, and they're more adventuresome," she says.

Fenzl also notes that some restaurants like Rox-Sand's (Biltmore Fashion Square) are eclectic, selecting from a variety of cooking styles, using Southwestern nouvelle when desirable, combining Szechuan Chinese with French, and doing whatever else works. It's all part of what she calls "putting together what food should be like."

Chef Guerithault, who came to the United States 12 years ago and to Arizona 9 years ago, was working as a chef in a Valley nouvelle French restaurant when he decided to open his own place.

Trained in Oustau de Baumaniere in Les Baux-De-Provence in southern France, Guerithault worked in Maxim's in Paris before he came to be employed at Le Francais in Illinois, a restaurant *Bon Apetit* magazine has called "America's greatest restaurant." He then arrived in Arizona to serve as chef for a restaurant at Pinnacle Peak that bore his name.

But when Guerithault opened his own restaurant on Camelback Road three years ago, he decided to combine his traditional French training with the Mexican ingredients and recipes he had discovered in his new home. "I wanted to do something very different," he says. "I wanted to do something nobody had done here before."

Guerithault's adoption of the new technique was motivated by two factors: a need to find a style that was different from what other Valley French restaurants were offering and a desire to work with ingredients less expensive than such French staples as caviar and smoked salmon.

"It was a little risky," he admits, but he quickly adds that the cuisine has been popular.

Today, about 40 percent of Guerithault's menu is Southwestern nouvelle, and he believes this cooking method is as intrinsic to Arizona as Cajun food is to New Orleans. "It may be a passing fad in New York or Seattle," he comments, "but we're here in the Southwest. The Mexican influence is so strong. It's like the south of France—the further south, the spicier the food is. People here are more daring; they're not afraid of trying different dishes."

Other governmental advantages listed by business executives who choose to live their lives and run their businesses in Phoenix include: a pro-business climate attributed to Arizona being a right-to-work state; the state's and the city's moderate tax structures; and state and local government constitutional spending limits.

Right to Work. Arizona is a right-to-work state, ranked third lowest in the U.S. in 1986 for unionization among its manufacturing employees. Business executives say the right-to-work principle operates hand in hand with smooth labor relations to keep high productivity. Generally Phoenix has enjoyed a spirit of cooperation, not confrontation, in labor relations. And both business and labor have demonstrated a commitment to the community. A recent effort to preserve a local landmark, a Flying Jenny carousel, for example, brought business and labor together in a joint effort. While business leaders such as Arizona Public Service, American Continental Corporation, Basha's, and KOOL Broadcasting contributed funds towards the carousel's purchase price, the AFL-CIO and 16 local members came forward to donate all the labor for restoration of the merry-go-round.

Taxes. Both the state's and city's tax structures are moderate, with no inventory tax, no corporate franchise tax, and no tax on income paid to a parent company by a subsidiary when the parent firm owns 50 percent or more of the subsidiary and is headquartered in Arizona. Computer software is not taxable, and federal and state income taxes are deductible from gross income in calculating state income tax. The effective corporate income-tax rate is about 5.3 percent, and personal income-tax rates range from 2 to 8 percent.

Spending Limits. State government spending is subject to constitutional limits, and expenditures by local governments are constitutionally limited as well. The state cannot incur long-term debt of more than $350,000; expenditures of state tax revenues cannot exceed 6.5 per-

cent of Arizona's personal income for any fiscal year. Counties, cities, and towns have spending limits tied to population. Spending for school districts also is tied to a limit system.

In 1986 *Inc.* magazine wrote of Arizona, "Economic growth and diversity have been helped along by the 'favorable regulatory climate' that is a favorite of state boosters everywhere—but that, in Arizona's case, seems more than just a cliché." A year later, the magazine ranked Phoenix as the third-fastest growing city in the nation in terms of job generation, rate of new business start-ups, and percentage of fast-growing companies, and the magazine has listed Phoenix among the top five cities when ranked for business climate.

Phoenix government leaders say they will con-

Above: The landscapes of residential areas complement the natural environment. Photo by Susan I. Davison

Below: Careful development of residential areas is crucial to implementing Phoenix' urban village plan. Photo by Nyle Leatham

tinue to remain committed to retaining an atmosphere conducive to encouraging business development in the future.

Planning the Urban Village

The city's urban-village plan, really a series of plans for nine areas identified throughout the city, grew out of a citizen-involved planning process initiated by the Phoenix City Council.

Recognized nationally as an innovative approach to urban planning, it breaks the city into "villages," geographic areas with dense, commercial core areas and outer residential areas.

In effect, the city's general plan seeks to retain the psychological advantages of a smaller community within the boundaries of a large city. Each urban village is designed to contain a variety of housing, job, retail, recreational, and educational facilities, a concept that also is intended to help manage traffic flow and the air pollution problems associated with heavy dependency on automobiles.

Proponents of the plan say it provides for rational development and strong citizen input in the city development and planning process. Critics point out that the concept fails to address how the different urban villages can interrelate and work together. The future success of the plan depends on the city council's continuing commit

ment to tie zoning decisions to the plan's requirements, and members of the council say they are prepared to do just that.

Dealing Creatively with Problems

The urban flight that many Eastern cities are experiencing is not a problem that Phoenix faces; neither is stagnation, lack of opportunity, or any of the other byproducts of declining population. But that is not to say that the city is without its challenges. The problems Phoenix faces today—and will continue to face tomorrow—are problems that come with growth.

No longer a cow town or even the large city with a small-town complex that existed 25 years ago, Phoenix is booming. And with that boom comes a variety of challenges: the air is more polluted than it was a decade ago; the traffic is heavier; and growth puts heavy demands on a finite water supply. Can Phoenix balance the future demands of growth with the continued existence of an outstanding quality of life? It is an issue that is on the front burner of every political gathering, every community forum.

Air Pollution. Arizona's legislature has been forced to face air-quality problems both because of citizen demands and threats from the U.S. Environmental Protection Agency. New legislation requiring the use of alternative clean fuels in automobiles was approved by legislators in 1988.

Facing page: Phoenicians are used to picture-postcard scenes like this one—two Saguaros in the New River area near Phoenix. Photo by Steve Weiss

Below: An azure sky is the backdrop for this distinctive part of the city's skyline. Photo by Mark E. Gibson

At the same time, the Phoenix City Council has begun to implement a number of strategies recommended to it by a regional planning board, including an expanded mass transit system and a detailed public-private partnership to work on carpooling, alternative work schedules, and other improvements. The city also has established a business advisory committee to make recommendations and begin coordination of air-quality initiatives with local businesses.

A 10-year-old vehicle emissions inspection program that is among the toughest in the nation also continues to operate in the state.

Transportation. Part of the initiative supported by the Phoenix City Council under the category of air-pollution control is an intense effort to improve streets and ease congestion.

It should be noted that according to the *Arizona Republic,* the state's largest daily newspaper, the average round-trip daily commuting time for Phoenix workers is 48 minutes, nearly two minutes less than the national average. Even so, traffic is a major concern of Valley residents, and public officials have listened to that concern,

This is nighttime Phoenix, looking south from Pointe Tapatio, a north city Gosnell development. Downtown Phoenix is in the distance (right) and Seventh Street is a blur of light. The red lights on top of South Mountain warn airplanes of the height of radio towers there. Photo by Matt Bradley

anxious to avoid the congestion that plagues some other cities.

In October 1985 Phoenix officials asked voters to approve a one-half-cent sales-tax increase to raise nearly $6 billion over the next 20 years for transportation needs, and 70 percent of the voters agreed. A second vote, seeking an additional half-cent increase to fund a comprehensive program that includes a light-rail, mass transit component, will be taken in February 1989.

That money will fund what transportation administrators in Phoenix call "a balanced transportation system." Efforts already are under way, with funds approved by the public, to add 233 miles of freeways and expressways in the Valley of the Sun. More than 100 additional miles of major streets will be completed in the city in the next couple of years.

But to many, the most exciting aspect of Phoenix's transportation future came in the 1986 creation of the Regional Public Transportation Authority, charged with long-range transportation planning for metropolitan Phoenix. That means everything from carpooling plans to a new mass transit system.

"All of this will keep us from becoming another L.A.," said Severo Esquivel, the city's surface transportation manager.

Water Resources. Arizona took charge of its water future in

Bus ridership has increased 50 percent in the last three years. Photo by Carol Topalian

As the Southwest's leading commerce center, Phoenix is climbing to new heights in economic growth. Photo by Nyle Leatham

1980 by adopting a unique and forceful groundwater management code to protect the future of its groundwater supplies. The state legislature took its commitment to water management a step further in 1986 with the adoption of a comprehensive environmental quality act.

Both measures were landmark legislation, and Phoenix has found their requirements ones with which it can live. There is no question that water conservation will play an increasing role in Arizona's and in Phoenix' future, but it is also true that, as a result, sufficient water supplies will be available to support continued growth in the Phoenix metropolitan area. A large groundwater aquifer and more than one-half million acre-feet of Central Arizona Project water will help meet those needs.

A Young City Facing Its Problems with New Approaches
Phoenix is a young city, alive and aware of the mistakes that older urban cities have made. Born from the ashes of a previous civilization, it is alive with the vibrancy of growth. A combination of cultures, a celebration of the natural beauty that surrounds it—the city speaks loudly of potential and opportunity to the thousands who flock annually to its borders.

Can it live up to the promise? City leaders say the willingness of voters to approve expenditures for freeways and for improved cultural facilities are indications that it can. They point out that more than a decade ago Phoenicians made a ballot-box commitment to maintaining the natural environment that lured so many of them here in the first place when they established the Phoenix Mountain Preserve. And they add that legislative efforts to deal with air pollution and water-resource scarcity are innovative approaches that could not have passed without widespread community support.

Phoenix. A Light in the Desert. A Beacon to the Future.

Phoenix' entrepreneurial spirit is a reflection of the city's growing dynamic business environment. Photo by Nyle Leatham

Networks

Phoenix' energy, communication, and transportation providers keep products, information, and power circulating inside and outside the area.

KAMJ Radio, 231

Arizona Public Service Company, 224-225

KPHO, 228-229

Southwest Gas Corporation, 226-227

Salt River Project, 230

Photo by Nyle Leatham

ARIZONA PUBLIC SERVICE COMPANY

For more than 100 years Arizona Public Service Company and its predecessor organizations have been serving the electrical needs of the state. Today those needs are defined as more than 1.5 million people in more than 200 communities in all or part of 11 of the state's 15 counties. APS serves 45 percent of Arizona's population.

To accomplish this task, Arizona Public Service produces more than 4 million kilowatts of electricity at power plants in Arizona and New Mexico. Some 2.5 million kilowatts of this power is generated by four coal-burning units. Another 1.2 million kilowatts is produced at 3 steam units and 19 gas or oil-fueled units. Three units of the Palo Verde nuclear plant contribute another 1.107 million kilowatts of electricity, and a small hydro generator produces 5,600 kilowatts of energy.

This power load is a far cry from the energy required to light the 12 gas streetlights that originally lit up Phoenix in 1886. That was the year Hutchlon Ohnick (Hachiro Onuki), a young Japanese immigrant, and his financial backers started the Phoenix Illuminating Gas and Electric Company.

As Phoenix grew, so did the need for power. By the late 1890s most of the city was looking to Phoenix Light and Power for its power, and by 1920 the Central Arizona Light and Power Company (CALAPCO) was formed. Although CALAPCO saw steady growth in the acquisition of smaller power companies in areas surrounding Phoenix, the major impetus to growth came in the postwar boom of the 1940s and 1950s.

Beginning in 1946 CALAPCO set one construction record after another as it geared to meet the needs of the many veterans settling in central Arizona. Power companies in northern and southern Arizona saw similar growth and, realizing that Arizona's energy needs could best be served by a single utility, merged with CALAPCO to form Arizona Public Service.

The growth that led to the formation of APS in 1952 still characterizes the company today. In addition to providing electrical energy for the people of Arizona, APS is involved in promoting economic development, participating in campaigns for clean air and

---

Arizona Public Service Company is a leader in solar energy technology. This solar test facility, called the STAR Center (Solar Test And Research), is one of several solar projects built by APS to test the effectiveness of different photovoltaic equipment.

improved transportation, and working with builders to ensure the construction of energy-efficient homes and businesses.

On a more personal level, APS works with customers to help them manage energy costs and introduce them to the firm's many service programs. Services range from community outreach programs and special rate options for residential customers to sophisticated energy audits and installation of advanced thermal storage for commercial and industrial customers.

In terms of its economic impact, APS is the largest property taxpayer in the state and the seventh-largest private employer in Arizona. Nearly 9,000 employees work for APS in both Arizona and New Mexico. Palo Verde alone, which employs more than 2,000 workers, is responsible for millions of dollars being pumped into Arizona's economy each year. APS is deeply involved in nearly every aspect of the economy in each county it serves.

APS is a major cultural benefactor for the Arizona community. The firm annually contributes nearly $1.5 million to social service, cultural, and charitable organizations throughout Arizona. An APS volunteer bureau augments this effort by participating in civic and community efforts such as Arizona Clean and Beautiful and local literacy programs.

On another level Arizona Public Service has been involved in a unique economic development effort: Working with the Phoenix Economic Growth Corporation, the Arizona Department of Commerce, real estate brokers, financial institutions, local committees, and others, APS is actively seeking to assist business and industry already located in the state and to attract new business ventures to Arizona. APS assembles a total proposal that includes banking information, municipal data, transportation costs, tax comparisons, and rate incentives (if qualified) that clients may expect to receive from APS upon relocating to Arizona. Approaching new business as a team effort with other interested Arizona participants puts the strongest proposal before a po-

tential new business.

For qualified customers APS offers clients who relocate to Arizona incentives to take up to five years to graduate to regular energy rates. To be eligible for this incentive program, a company must be a megawatt or better customer and have a minimum load factor of 55 percent or more. Clients must also supply an energy history that supports this fact.

Paul Wiggs, APS' manager of economic development, explains that this incentive program is focused at potential clients who fall into the one- to five-megawatt category. They may be looking for 150,000 to a half-million square feet of space, he says, and are actively being targeted by other economic development efforts. Such efforts are designed to help bring those highly sought after businesses that would otherwise go to some other state.

"The impetus for this program is that we have some areas of the state that have higher unemployment, and new industry would benefit both APS and the community. New customers that operate at 55 percent load factor or greater improve the overall efficiency of our system and lower the average system cost to all of our customers," Wiggs says.

Attracting new business is one of APS' thrusts. However, Wiggs adds that approximately 80 percent of all growth occurring in the state comes from existing customers. "Service after the sale is key to us," he declares. "Service" extends beyond electrical power. It may be defined as helping a client with the permit process, lending professional expertise to assemble electric rate comparisons, and even lobbying for a client's cause.

Finally, community development is key to helping some of Arizona's smaller communities get their economic development efforts running. Wiggs states, "We have assisted and worked with a variety of smaller communities in positioning their city to attract and maintain a diverse business base to keep the community healthy."

Customer service, in the broadest sense, remains the heart of this firm's business. Under the direction of chairman of the board Keith L. Turley and president and chief executive officer O. Mark De Michele, Arizona Public Service Company is dedicated to meet the charge it set for itself nearly 40 years ago: to serve the people of Arizona. Consequently, regardless of the technical improvements to produce and deliver energy or the changing corporate structure of the company itself, that premise—to serve Arizonans—continues to be the driving force behind APS.

APS is project manager for the Palo Verde Nuclear Power Generating Station, located approximately 55 miles west of Phoenix. It is the largest nuclear power plant in the free world and assures Arizonans of reliable energy well into the next century.

APS often uses helicopters to install poles in especially scenic areas. This helps protect the landscape from disruptions caused by vehicles and heavy equipment.

SOUTHWEST GAS CORPORATION

Executives at Southwest Gas Corporation love to talk about natural gas. Ask about gas and the environment, and learn that natural gas is clean and non-polluting. Inquire about cost and discover that gas is more efficient and economical than any other energy form. Question the availability of this fuel and learn that, because most natural gas is domestically produced, Southwest Gas does not worry about supplies being cut off due to international politics. Direct the discussion to safety and hear that natural gas is enjoyed by more than 150 million Americans and has an enviable safety record.

Bring up Phoenix and watch Keith Stewart, vice-president/Papago Division, smile. Since Southwest Gas Corporation bought the long-dormant gas system operated by Arizona Public Service in 1984, the company has made impressive gains both in numbers of new customers served and in public awareness of this fuel source.

Although Southwest Gas appeared on the Phoenix scene as a new face, in reality the move was the operation's third venture into Arizona. The firm had its beginnings as a bottled gas company during the Depression days of 1931 in Barstow, California. It sold liquid petroleum gas to 160 customers. In 1951, when Pacific Gas and Electric Company built its high-pressure natural gas transmission line from the Arizona border to San Francisco, Southwest tapped into the line and converted from propane to natural gas. Expansion into southern Nevada and Arizona followed.

In 1957 Southwest purchased a utility that served the Casa Grande and Clifton-Morenci areas. In 1979 the company expanded again, purchasing the gas system in Tucson. With its most recent move into the Phoenix metropolitan area, Yuma, Globe, and Sierra Vista in 1984, Southwest Gas doubled its customer base.

Today the firm provides natural gas to more than 730,000 customers. The investor-owned corporation, listed on the New York Stock Exchange since 1979, serves more than 2.5 million people in five operating divisions through-out Arizona, Nevada, and California.

"There are a number of advantages to being big," observes Stewart. "Because we operate in three states, we have access to most production facilities in the West. We don't have to rely on a single pipeline as our sole source of supply. We aggressively seek out our own independent contracts." This strategy, plus the favorable Arizona climate, means that Southwest Gas can offer gas to its customers all year around. "We have the supplies necessary for any customer—far out into the future," confirms Stewart. "We offer abundant supplies of natural gas, a fact that industry sees as a real plus."

In addition to a firm supply, Southwest Gas offers stable pricing. As more gas became available during the past few years, prices of the natural resource have actually decreased. "We have to compete with the electric utilities, oil, and propane," Stewart says. "So we do this by providing better service, a dependable resource supply, and energy at a lower cost."

Southwest Gas is promoting cogeneration facilities. Cogeneration basically means that a customer pur-

Southwest's engineers work closely with architects, project developers, and equipment suppliers to design state-of-the-art, energy-efficient, gas-fired heating and cooling systems to meet specific applications.

chases natural gas and uses that energy source to generate its own electricity and heat energy. Not only does cogeneration offer cost savings, it also involves a significant conservation element—energy that is normally wasted or lost with conventional systems is put to work to perform other functions such as providing steam for cooling and other uses. The Princess Hotel in Scottsdale and the Phoenician Resort in Phoenix are among several customers in the Phoenix area that have decided to operate cogeneration facilities.

Currently limited to industrial and commercial users, this is an attractive alternative to both large and small customers. A potential cogeneration customer should have reasonably high energy needs. Potential cogeneration customers include hospitals, hotels/motels, restaurants, resorts, and laundries.

Natural gas is an economical and

Major home builders in the valley are finding the convenience and economy of natural gas appliances are popular with buyers.

efficient source for every gas customer. In homes, for instance, the gas advantage for heating, water heating, cooking, and clothes drying can amount to a savings of up to $200 per year over an all-electric home. Southwest predicts that new uses of natural gas will make this supply of energy go even further, lower costs, and help to reduce air pollution.

For example, aided by two grants from the State of Arizona, Arizona State University and the City of Glendale are preparing to test to determine if they should convert their motor vehicle fleets to compressed natural gas (CNG). Phoenix Mayor Terry Goddard arranged for the car assigned to him by the city to be converted to run on CNG to showcase its fuel cost savings. Because there are no pollutants, engines run more efficiently at a much lower cost with CNG than with gasoline. There is also less wear and tear on engines, which reduces maintenance costs considerably.

Recently Southwest replaced much of the old underground distribution system that served the Phoenix area. The company also conducts regular comprehensive safety education programs for customers, contractors, and fire and safety departments.

"We are fortunate in how our distribution system works within the Phoenix area," says Stewart. "Our major lines circle the city so we have facilities available for new customers vir-

tually everywhere. Our major thrust in the past few years has been to establish trade relationships, for while there has always been commercial activity, now we are penetrating the residential market. Remember," he cautions, "gas was absent from the valley for 10 years. We needed to change the whole approach. Now we are seeing more and more transition to gas."

In Phoenix, transition to gas can be spelled as a broad-based customer market that includes tourism; the electronics, food-processing, and drug industries; as well as hospitals and masonry product manufacturers. "We are extremely proud of what we have

brought to this valley," concludes Stewart. "We are a reliable, fierce competitor and particularly proud of the level of service we provide to our customers. As for the future, we can only promise that we will continue to get better."

Below: Service remains Southwest's key to success. In addition to making house calls to light and adjust appliances when service is initiated, service technicians troubleshoot appliance problems and respond to emergencies day or night.

Bottom: A growing market for Southwest Gas is cogeneration—the on-site generation of electricity and heat as an economical alternative to total dependence on electric utilities.

KPHO

"We're not a typical television station," agrees Dick DeAngelis, vice-president and general manager of KPHO-TV, Channel 5. "We're an extraordinarily powerful and consistent television station with a strong local identity and respected national reputation." The power DeAngelis refers to is not measured simply in kilowatts. Rather, it's measured in viewer loyalty, audience ratings, advertising revenues, and community involvement. No matter what standard is applied, KPHO emerges as one of the nation's top 25 performers. "We habitually rank in the top handful of stations across the country, which is extremely unusual for an independent station," DeAngelis continues. "That recognition comes from our industry peers. We are known as pioneers."

Being a pioneer comes naturally to KPHO-TV. Owned and operated since 1952 by the Meredith Corporation, the station boasts a string of important firsts. KPHO-TV was the first television station in Arizona in 1949. It was the first in the state to telecast local live programs, cover sports events with remote telecasts, and broadcast in full color. In July 1980 the station became the first independent television station in the United States to generate higher sign-on to sign-off ratings than any of its network-affiliated competitors. But ultimately what comes first is the viewer.

"We are a family station," DeAngelis adds. "We gear our programming toward families, both in content and scheduling. That decision keeps coming back to us in any research we do. Our viewers consistently refer to us as the 'family station.'" The general manager explains that an independent station has an important role to play in the community. Program manager Greg Brannan points out that this also provides unique opportunities. "While our policy is not to change schedules casually, we are able to target the audience in our market and program specifically to it. The network affiliates don't enjoy that type of flexibility. For instance, we adjust our lineup in the summer, placing younger viewing shows on in the daytime when kids are out of

school and available."

If there's a secret to KPHO-TV's success, according to Chuck Alvey, station manager, that secret is strong management. "Our department heads are seasoned professionals attuned to the market," he begins. "Our entire staff is very stable and experienced, enabling Dick to fully implement a team approach to problem solving and development of opportunities. While we thoroughly analyze each decision, our collective experience and competitive spirit helps us make choices quickly and decisively." Alvey uses the acquisition of the "Cosby" show as a good example. "Under Dick's leadership, we all spent an enormous number of man-hours researching and analyzing this important show. The effort was both exhausting and exhaustive. When it came time for Dick to make the ultimate decision, we were all a part of it. That kind of decision, we believe, assures our future."

KPHO-TV has a long history of solid selections. Says DeAngelis, "Our long-term goal is to continue doing what we do best, presenting premier off-network sitcoms." Along with "Cosby" other examples include "M*A*S*H," "Barney Miller," "Newhart," "Andy Griffith," "I Love Lucy,"

The KPHO "News 5" team presents "complete, accurate, and early" news with strong local coverage. Shown (from left) are weatherman Stu Tracy, Chris Cochrin, and Roger Downey.

"Three's Company," "Kate and Allie," and "Benson." Yet he is quick to point to the station's programming balance. "Each market is different," DeAngelis says. "Each has its own character, tastes, and life-style. At KPHO-TV we can pinpoint the very unique tastes of the Phoenix market. Its explosive growth brings us people from every part of the United States. That influx and our ability to stay attuned to the viewers contribute heavily to our success as a local television station."

In addition to those highly successful sitcoms the station's schedule is rounded out with first-run syndicated programs, top box office feature films, action hours, children's programs, documentaries, specials, and local news. DeAngelis thinks "News 5" is important to the growth of Phoenix. "I'd like to think that our familiar shows and very localized news helps new families interface with the community," he observes. KPHO-TV offers news twice daily: Monday through Friday at 11:30 a.m. and during prime time at 9:30 p.m., seven nights each week. "We avoid the 'star' system. Our people feature the news," DeAngelis explains. "We have an experienced and efficient news staff that offers strong local news coverage. We are extremely competitive with just two half-hour newscasts, which is why we position our news as 'complete, accurate, and early.'"

As Brannan points out, "Local programming has always been a key to our success, bringing TV 5 a unique local personality. In April 1954 Bill Thompson began hosting a cartoon program as "Wallace." Quite casually, while on the air, he began an interplay with a cameraman in the studio. Ladimir Kwiatkowski soon stepped from behind the camera to in front of the camera and "Wallace and Ladmo" was born. Thirty-five years later the team, including the many characters played by Gerald "Pat" McMahon, is still going strong.

The station's community commitment is equally long running. KPHO-TV lends its full support to community needs. The station produces and schedules a heavy load of local public service announcements and public affairs programs. The biannual "Compas TV Auction" supports the Phoenix Sym-

KPHO-TV, Channel 5, facilities since 1972. Many firsts have been established by the station—the first statewide to telecast local live programs, cover sports events with remote telecasts, and broadcast in full color.

phony, Phoenix Zoo, Heard Museum, Desert Botanical Gardens, and Phoenix Art Museum. And the community responds to KPHO-TV's outreach. Most notably, the annual Muscular Dystrophy Labor Day Telethon raises more than one million dollars each year, one of the largest per-capita outpourings of charitable giving in the country.

"We are active in the valleywide community, both as leaders and participants," says DeAngelis. "People have access to our station." Recognizing the diversity of the communities that make up the Valley of the Sun, KPHO-TV has run a series of half-hour community "Salutes" in a unique Community Service and Sales Department co-venture. People may come from various communities nationwide to live in the various communities in the valley, but KPHO-TV brings them all together, creating a sense of belonging, being home, and being among friends. "We don't want

individuals to get lost in the explosive growth here. The past decade has been an outstanding time for us. The station, thanks to those people, has grown off the charts," DeAngelis says. "We fully intend to be a vital part of that exciting and explosive growth."

The team of "Wallace and Ladmo," with Bill Thompson (left) as Wallace and Ladimir Kwiatkowski (right) as Ladmo, along with the many characters played by Gerald "Pat" McMahon, has entertained KPHO-TV viewers for 35 years.

SALT RIVER PROJECT

Salt River Project shapes the way the people of Phoenix work and live. As one of the country's fastest-growing electric utilities, it provides electric power to more than 500,000 customers and ranks as the third-largest public power utility in the nation. In addition, Salt River Project is Arizona's biggest water supplier, managing a delivery system that provides water from six reservoirs to eight valley cities.

For more than a half-century Salt River Project has led the way to improved standards of living. Its innovations include being one of the first utilities in the West to offer Time-of-the-Day rates to commercial and industrial customers. It was also the first utility in Arizona to offer different seasonal rate structures to all customers. Working with other cities and water users, the Project helps develop water resources such as the Central Arizona Project, programs in groundwater recharge, and water quality assurance.

Drawing from its more than 80 years of service in Phoenix, Salt River Project is in business to provide for future generations. Established in 1903 as the Salt River Valley Water Users Association, it was the first major, multipurpose project formed under the 1902 Federal Reclamation Act. In 1937, to supply electricity to 5,800 rural customers in the area surrounding central Phoenix, the Salt River Project Agricultural Improvement and Power District was created as a political subdivision of Arizona. Together these two organizations form today's Salt River Project.

This utility giant, employing more than 6,000 people, is governed by publicly elected boards that establish policies for the management of the company's business and set electric rates and water delivery fees. In today's competitive energy market decisions are made that offer customers some of the lowest electric rates among Arizona's three major utilities.

Customer incentives for installing high-efficiency heating and cooling equipment help balance the overall demand for electricity—passing the lowest-possible costs on to the consumer. The management team studies the challenges of competition and the impacts of urbanization on the firm's water and electric service areas.

"Salt River Project's rates are set to cover operating costs. Any money remaining at the end of the fiscal year is reinvested in facilities, which reduces the need to borrow money to finance new construction," explains SRP president John Lassen.

The company promotes a business philosophy that Lassen calls "active area development." "Our representatives work closely with major commercial and industrial concerns in other parts of the country that are considering expansions or new offices in Phoenix," says Lassen. "We have and provide the information about applicable rate packages and options that will benefit both the consumer and us."

Salt River Project shares its growth with its community. To better serve the community and to be more involved with its consumers, the firm regularly expands its facilities. In addition to three new regional centers, its nearly completed new Information Systems headquarters is the cornerstone of Papago Park, a 530-acre business and hospitality center. Devoted to meeting the challenges of a growing city, Salt River Project continues to be a foundation for Phoenix' future.

A model of SRP's new corporate headquarters complex in Tempe, which will be developed in stages to the year 2000.

The front entrance to Salt River Project's corporate headquarters in Tempe.

KAMJ RADIO

KAMJ-MAGIC 101-FM has become one of the leading adult contemporary radio stations in Phoenix in just three short years.

KAMJ-MAGIC 101-FM, one of the leading adult contemporary radio stations in Phoenix, is an example of a newly born endeavor that has prospered from Phoenix' growth. In turn, it has shared its success and benefited the community. A three-year-old fledgling station, the "all easy-going favorites" KAMJ is committed to the city's expansion as well as to its listeners.

MAGIC 101-FM's audience, those in the 32- to 49-year-old age group, all came of age during the rock era, which is noted for its largely vocal music. As listeners have matured, so has their musical taste. They now seek a casual atmosphere of relaxing, original vocal music—and MAGIC 101 provides just that. MAGIC's audience represents the second-largest age group in the Phoenix area—a group that includes not just Baby Boomers, but members of the Earning Boom, and consequently, the Super Spenders.

"Our music is only the best and most memorable hits of the past 35 years by familiar artists such as Billy Joel, Kenny Rogers, and Barbra Streisand," says Tony Perlongo, general manager. "Everything about MAGIC 101 matches the mood of the music."

Formerly KONC Radio, EZ Communications, a privately owned company based in Fairfax, Virginia, purchased KAMJ Radio in 1985. Not unfamiliar with the communications industry, the company has broadcasting projects in 11 markets, and EZ Communications believed that the Phoenix market was clearly one of the strongest for establishing a new business. "The radio market has been booming correspondingly with the growth of the Sunbelt—the

advertising has benefited from this growth as well," says Perlongo. "The company saw opportunity to reach a market that was previously served. Our immediate and remarkable success for such a young station is evidence that the principle is accurate."

A staff of 26 makes up the programming, news/public affairs, engineering, production, sales, and administrative departments. But no one department is isolated, everyone works together as a team. The station employs multitalented people and utilizes their capabilities in many different areas, and the newly constructed production facilities have a professional, 32-channel, eight-track studio that delivers the finest-quality production for advertising clients.

The station's 100,000 watts of clear stereo sound cover Arizona 24 hours a day, reaching Tucson and Prescott, and most rural cable systems, which now provide MAGIC 101 to their subscribers. AM radio listeners can enjoy KAMJ's fare over station AM 1230.

The station takes its responsibility of having thousands of listeners very seriously. In addition to using state-of-the-art technology and the most contemporary equipment, it adheres to the highest standards of airing public-service programs that directly affect the community, and delivers frequent news and weather reports that are upbeat and informative. There are no more than four commercial messages per hour, and programs such as "ArizonaViewpoint" examine the top current issues each week. The station's commitments are based on research, ensuring the community's preferences.

Those commitments are complemented by KAMJ's firm philosophy of community involvement. As the station matures, it continues to discover opportunities to participate in events and activities that are culturally significant and that support a variety of causes. "We want to be able to use the power we have to make people aware of what's going on," says Perlongo. "We have an obligation to touch people's hearts."

CHAPTER ELEVEN

High Technology

Phoenix is a mecca for a flourishing high-tech manufacturing and research and development industry.

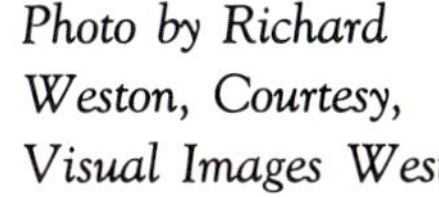
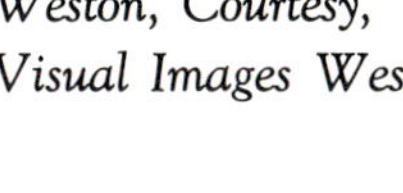

Photo by Richard Weston, Courtesy, Visual Images West

SGS-THOMSON MICROELECTRONICS

The head-turning U.S. headquarters of SGS-THOMSON Microelectronics glistens in the Arizona sunlight. The building represents the southwestern marriage of Italian sophistication and Gallic charm. The company is truly global, with manufacturing and research and development facilities on three continents. The merger in 1987 of SGS and Thomson Semiconductors brought together two European-based companies with large assets in the United States—the Phoenix and Dallas (formerly Mostek) manufacturing factories. Pasquale Pistorio, president and chief executive officer operating from Europe, oversees the corporation, which includes some 17,000 employees and lists revenues of more than one billion dollars.

Pistorio is a former Motorola executive who left a top international position with that company to turn around what was not a profitable semiconductor firm. At the time, in 1980, it seemed like a hopeless task. Japanese producers were battling with U.S. chipmakers, and European semiconductor producers were far behind. However, Pistorio refused to be daunted. Instead he saw a challenge. He determined to make the United States one of his major customers—a bold move by any standard. That Pistorio has achieved this is now history. Within a few years U.S. sales and volume worldwide tripled. His personal commitment to SGS is legendary.

While Pistorio attacked the European front, he put Daniel Queyssac in charge of the U.S. operation. A U.S. citizen born in Paris, former Motorola executive, and now a firm Phoenix booster, Queyssac is known as a quiet and effective leader. Prior to joining SGS as president in November 1980, he had spent the previous two years as director of systems operation for Motorola's International Semiconductor Division, which was in Phoenix. Queyssac determined to move the American operation headquarters from Waltham, Massachusetts. "We needed access to a high level of people specializing in the electronic field," Queyssac explained in an interview published in *Corporate Design & Realty*.

This goal led him to search four market areas in the United States—the Silicon Valley in California; Denver-Colorado Springs, Colorado; Austin, Texas; and Phoenix, Arizona. The head of the U.S. operation has gone on record as selecting Phoenix for various reasons. These include the large pool of manpower, a strong graduate program in semiconductor technology at Arizona State University, excellent climate, and vast tracts of open land that allow room for expansion.

His choice, 20 acres on East Bell Road, proved to be a winner. The headquarters building, designed by GSAS Architects and Architectural Interiors, both of Phoenix, opened in April 1983 to rave reviews for its stunning architectural statement and strong artistic ap-

Colorful, futuristic, and southwestern, the interior of SGS-THOMSON Microelectronics' Phoenix headquarters (below) blends high tech with high energy and complements the exterior (bottom), often compared to a spaceship.

peal. Often compared to a spaceship, the structure incorporates a strong art program that features local artists portraying the American spirit. Colorful, futuristic, and southwestern, the images throughout the interior of the building blend high tech with high energy and complement the exterior design.

But it's what happens inside that makes real news. Under Queyssac's leadership, SGS-THOMSON has staked a major claim in Arizona. Shortly after assuming the presidency, Queyssac presented a market analysis and a major expansion plan, which Pistorio quickly approved. With the ground breaking in 1985 for the addition of a CMOS manufacturing plant adjoining the headquarters structure, the firm added the advantages of home-town manufacturing to its profile. This is a state-of-the-art automated facility, one of the most modern in the world.

The plant boasts a Class One facility that makes it 1,000 times cleaner than a hospital operating room. A complete air exchange takes place every six seconds. Class One is the most advanced form of microcontamination control, which makes it possible to manufacture the intricate six-inch wafer in the Phoenix facility. Local manufacturing means that SGS-THOMSON can provide an even greater depth of service as a broad-line supplier of advanced integrated circuits.

The growth of the firm can be attributed to three fundamental commitments: the timely development of proprietary products and technologies, leadership in innovative packaging design, and overall design excellence. Excellence refers to a position of world leadership in the area of power and high-voltage linear integrated circuits. From automobiles and industrial robotics to disk drives, personal computers, and telecommunications, the products produced by SGS-THOMSON are used in almost every application known to modern electronics.

Today SGS-THOMSON Microelectronics is a major designer and

manufacturer of semiconductor components for almost all electronic systems and subsystems. Now technology and service driven, SGS-THOMSON supplies the world. Queyssac has reason to be proud of his company's ability to establish itself in a very short time during a very difficult economic period. While he was warned that it was unreal-

The plant is 1,000 times cleaner than a hospital operating room. A complete air exchange takes place once every six seconds.

istic to attempt a major expansion into the American market, he proved the Cassandras wrong. Happily, Phoenix has played a big part in that success.

FUJITSU BUSINESS COMMUNICATION SYSTEMS

The computer revolution, advances in integrated circuitry, and telephone deregulation have advanced the business telecommunications industry into the forefront as one of the most dynamic markets of the decade. Over the past several years the Phoenix metropolitan area has been right in the heart of all the action.

In April 1987 Fujitsu America Inc. (U.S. subsidiary of Fujitsu Ltd., Tokyo, Japan) and GTE Communication Systems Corp. (a GTE subsidiary) joined forces to form Fujitsu GTE Business Systems Inc., headquartered in Tempe. The joint venture saw GTE transferring its business systems division into the joint venture, and Fujitsu Ltd., Japan's largest computer company and a world leader in telecommunications and semiconductors, contributing its high-quality manufacturing and technology.

Recently Fujitsu America combined the joint venture into a larger company that includes Fujitsu America's manufacturing and engineering capabilities. The resulting new corporation, Fujitsu Business Communication Systems, has the full capability to manufacture, sell, and service business communication systems with outstanding quality and reliability for U.S. customers.

Fujitsu Business Communication Systems' high-tech training center at South Mountain.

Fujitsu Business Communication Systems' Sales and Nationwide Service Center in Tempe.

Headquartered in Anaheim, California, Fujitsu Business Communication Systems employs about 1,200 people, 500 of whom are located in field service centers nationwide. In addition to manufacturing centers located both in Japan and Anaheim, the firm has sales offices throughout the United States and a nationwide network of distributors. The company also operates technical training facilities in Anaheim, California; Phoenix, Arizona; and Reston, Virginia. The company maintains software/hardware development groups in Anaheim and San Jose, California, and Northlake, Illinois, as well as a technical assistance center in Northlake, Illinois.

Fujitsu Business Communication Systems develops and markets a full complement of advanced voice/data business communications equipment designed to meet the present and future needs of a wide range of customers. These products feature digital voice and data PBXs (private branch exchange or telephone switching systems located on the user's premises) that can serve businesses from as few as 20 employees to *Fortune* 500 companies that employ as many as 10,000 people at a single location.

Every Fujitsu system combines the latest in computer hardware with software that can meet the needs of the most sophisticated user configurations. Specialized applications are designed to fulfill a variety of market requirements, including lodging, health care, retail, and the military. The company also designs and installs private networks for large multilocation organizations.

If the technology of Fujitsu's current products is dazzling, the future is even more impressive. At Fujitsu, the future is being developed today. It is the emerging market of integrated voice and data communications in offices. To a large extent, this future is predicated on the Integrated Services Digi-

tal Network (ISDN), an international standard that brings together voice and data-processing equipment of all forms into integrated information transmission—from voice to data to video. With ISDN, a fully compatible digital communications network can be established worldwide or established at the customer's location as a private multi-location network.

Why ISDN? A glance into nearly any office today will reveal that with the growing number of digital telephones, computer terminals, teleconferencing equipment, and FAX machines, the modern office has a wide variety of non-integrated voice and data equipment. What's more, all this individual equipment means that the user's communications suffer from incompatible interfaces, multiple redundant networks, and network overloads. As a result, transmission is becoming increasingly chaotic and inefficient. With the advent of ISDN and its capacity to transmit a wide range of formats and speeds over traditional narrow-band paired cables, a more compact future is in the offing. With ISDN, separate equipment can be condensed into a single, highly efficient desk-top phone/computer/video terminal.

Fujitsu is a leader in the development of ISDN, and is providing Fujitsu Business Communication Systems with the ISDN technology in the PBX to compete with the leaders for customers in the United States through the 1990s. Fujitsu expects that firms competing in the new ISDN world will be those with a commitment to developing technology and experience in advanced manufacturing of high-quality products. The successful business communications providers will have an established field service network and an installed base of current customers prepared to upgrade their existing systems to ISDN in the future. Even with the evolving world of ISDN technology, this change will not occur instantaneously, and past performance still will count.

The firm's family of products meets all this criteria. Fujitsu's products cover a wide range of business telephone systems. These products have been designed to meet not only the customers' requirements as their businesses grow, but also to respond to the changing needs of the ISDN world of the future.

Fujitsu Business Communication Systems' strength also lies in its existing customers. The company's impressive list of clients includes such distinguished names as the Tennessee Valley Authority, Pacific Gas & Electric, Sears, Westinghouse, Irving Trust, American Express, Texas A&M, Purdue University, the State of New Mexico, and Union Pacific Railroad.

Product development is vital; however, this innovative company is just as solid on service. All of the company's products are supported by the firm's network of 43 service areas located nationwide. In the highly competitive world of advanced business telecommunications systems, Fujitsu believes that the competitive edge will belong to those businesses that not only provide their clients with sophisticated telecommunications and computer technology, but also with top-notch service and support.

At Fujitsu Business Communication Systems, service is as multifaceted as are the manufactured products. Service may entail sophisticated project management, integration of multiple vendors' equipment, and customer employee training. Once the system is installed and running, service can be further explained as the ability to respond to and solve new configuration and application requirements that arise as the customer continues using the system.

Fujitsu Business Communication Systems has such a strong reputation for service that large end-users have contracted with the firm to maintain other telecommunications vendors' equipment. For example, the company has signed service contracts with Digital Transmission Inc., the Irving Trust Co., NYNEX, and BellSouth.

As for the immediate future, Jose Reines, president of Fujitsu Business Communication Systems, Inc., says, "The business communication user of the 1990s will require more advanced and integrated electronic information-transfer equipment than in any other prior period in time. As systems become more sophisticated, customers and customer requirements will become much more complex. Fujitsu's technology and commitment to high-quality products and customer service are essential elements to successfully meeting the business customer requirements for integrated office communications in the 1990s. Our ability to assure unparalleled customer satisfaction provides the competitive edge to Fujitsu Business Communication Systems."

The Fujitsu Starlog™ digital voice/data communications system provides a basic key system or advanced PBX capabilities from 20 to 240 phones.

MECHTRONICS OF ARIZONA, INC.

It's entirely appropriate that the work of space artist Robert McCall dominates the lobby at MechTronics of Arizona, Inc. There the future is an art form. The company offers total integrated manufacturing system service, including precision machining, complex metal fabrication, electronic subassembly, and final system integration, complemented by a competent electronic test organization.

Started in Chicago in 1948 as an electronic assembly plant, MechTronics expanded to the Southwest in 1961. Explains president Michael J. DeMuro, "My father and uncle saw Phoenix as the hub of the Southwest. However, in the early 1960s people in the Southwest didn't want to do business with Chicago. A Phoenix plant was a way to get a foothold here."

That foothold proved a trailblazer as MechTronics boomed with the valley. In 1965 the company moved to a small facility near Sky Harbor International Airport. In October 1986 MechTronics relocated to a 100,000-square-foot plant in the South Mountain Community Redevelopment Area. The site allows for future expansion up to double the present size.

"Most of our work is as a subcontractor to the military and commercial aircraft industry," DeMuro explains. "We specialize in difficult projects with critical tolerances, manufactured and tested to the most rigid military, aerospace, and high-reliability requirements." MechTronics assemblies are used in military communication hardware, and aircraft and helicopter guidance systems. The communication subassemblies are found in satellite networks, Navy shipboard consoles, Army radar track vehicles, and AWACS reconnaissance aircraft.

While MechTronics offers its customers a choice of services, what really sets it apart is the ability to do all three under one roof. "This gives us our competitive edge," DeMuro observes. It's an edge that's honed by a continual pursuit of excellence. That philosophy is featured in the company's brochure: "Excellence is not a fixed position . . . but rather a continuous, unrelenting

pursuit of perfection."

Excellence and perfection have produced results. In 1981 MechTronics was the first Arizona company to receive the Small Business Subcontractor of the Year Award. In 1985 it was named Supplier of the Year by the Motorola Government Electronics Group. Such a fast-track job description requires leading-edge technology. MechTronics employs a CAD/CAM (computer-aided design/computer-aided manufacturing) engineering system that enables it to produce precision products at efficient costs.

Engineering is an important success component, but DeMuro emphasizes the human side of his business profile. The MechTronics' management philosophy states: "The success

The South Mountain Community Redevelopment Area is the site of MechTronics of Arizona, Inc.'s, new building—a showcase for the area.

of MechTronics is the result of the combined efforts of individuals working toward objectives that are realistic, understood, and reflective of MechTronics' basic character and personality." This philosophy was illustrated at the grand opening of the new facility, which featured Bob McCall's futuristic works and Louise McCall's vibrant, gentle flowers. The art said it all: Here is a space-age company that values the human spirit.

Precision is the byword for the craftsmen of MechTronics, a subcontractor to the military and the commercial aircraft industry.

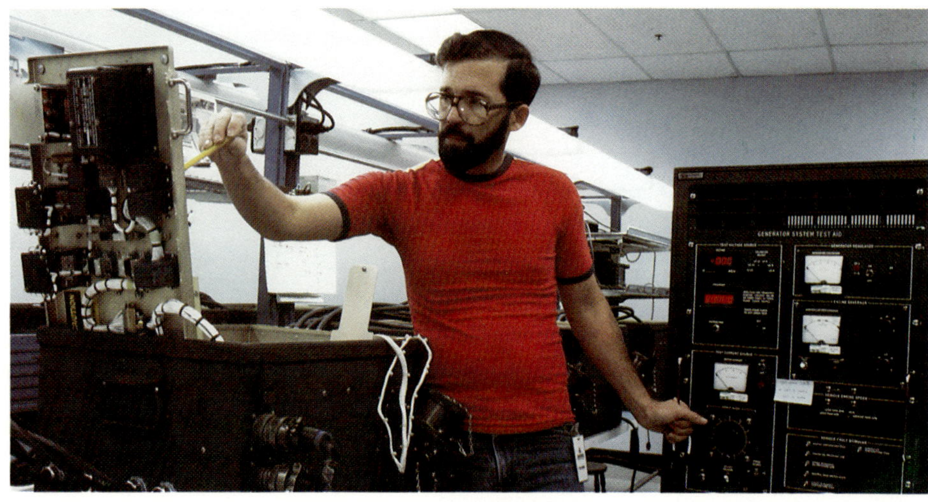

EXODYNE, INC.

To Ralph Rockow, safety engineering and testing is serious business. In 1982 he created a company, Exodyne, Inc., with zero sales. By 1987, having purchased and developed Dynamic Science, Inc., and Exodyne Properties, Inc., Rockow had built Exodyne into a corporation of some 600 employees with offices in 13 states and the District of Columbia, and annual sales exceeding $20 million.

"Dynamic Science has a very distinguished history in both automotive and aviation safety," Rockow explains. "DSI has been part of the Phoenix scene since 1956. Actually, the organization originated at Cornell University Medical College as part of a crash-injury research project in 1942." The project moved to Phoenix in 1956 under the name AvCIR (Aviation Crash Injury Research program), and by the early 1960s the name was changed to AvSER (Aviation Safety Engineering and Research).

In 1968 AvSER was purchased from the Flight Safety Foundation by Dynamic Science, a division of Marshall Industries, and research expanded to include automotive safety testing in addition to aviation safety. By the 1970s the company's scope was ex-

panded to include school bus safety, transbus development, sociotechnical and energy problems, heavy trucks and trains, air bags, pedestrian accident studies, safety standards compliance testing, and crash-severity studies.

Talley Industries purchased the firm in 1976. In late 1982 Rockow, who has been associated with DSI since 1968 as general manager and vice-president under Marshall Industries and president for the Talley Government and Technical Products Group, acquired DSI from Talley. In the next five years he created a diversified contract engineering services company with a broad customer base, including U.S. government military and civilian agencies, and domestic and international private industry. Principal activities focus on research and development, test and evaluation, systems engineering, and related technical, human resources, and support services. The hardware systems of interest include highway passenger vehicles, military vehicles, ballistic weapons, aircraft, and special electronic installations. "The common thread," says Rockow, "is engineering test and evaluation."

The low-key president, who was presented The Ohio State University's Distinguished Alumnus Award in 1979, says he's fortunate that "I have always been confronted with interesting challenges. Following graduate school, I started out working in the

An M-1 Abrahms Tank undergoing a desert dust test. Courtesy, U.S. Army, photography by S. Hanks.

aerospace industry, designing nuclear reactors for space applications and later on the design and development of Intercontinental Ballistic Missiles. At age 29 I was given the responsibility to design and develop a major portion of the descent rocket engine used to land the astronauts safely on the lunar surface during the Apollo program. From there I became involved with automotive safety. The next thing I knew, I was going around the world as a part of a NATO program focusing on automotive air-bag restraint systems and experimental safety vehicles.

"We seek technically oriented people who possess strong interpersonal skills and who demonstrate motivation and dedication. The fun part of managing Exodyne," he concludes, "is that I get to use my own personnel management concepts. We have an eclectic group of executives that are achievement oriented." How does he reward them? "With incentives," he answers. "We pay for performance. And I give my staff freedom to succeed." For Exodyne and Phoenix, Rockow's concepts are paying off.

Rockow was named Entrepreneur of the Year in 1987 by the *Arizona Business Gazette* and the Arizona State University College of Business.

The long-term growth plan for Exodyne, Inc., is to become a mini-conglomerate in technology-oriented businesses and to continue to be a contributor to programs of social value to the city of Phoenix.

Exodyne officers are Anthony M. Solberg, senior vice-president; Ralph A. Rockow, president; and Jerry W. Underwood, vice-president/finance and administration.

IBM CORPORATION

It was 1940—FDR was president, Benny Goodman was the King of Swing, Columbia Pictures was filming *Arizona* in newly constructed Old Tucson, and IBM opened its first Arizona office in Phoenix. The modern Phoenix facility arrived with the latest in punched-card machines, calculators, "Electromatic" typewriters, and an IBM tradition of responsible corporate citizenship. It was the start of a long and mutually beneficial relationship for IBM and Phoenix.

"We're proud to be a part of the Phoenix business community," says Bob Puskar, IBM U.S. Marketing and Services Regional Manager. "We're delighted to have the opportunity to participate in the tremendous growth this area is experiencing, and we look forward to continuing our partnerships with valley businesses."

Indeed, both IBM and Phoenix have grown and changed enormously through the years. For example, in 1940 IBM was a $46-million company with about 12,000 employees, and its main lines of business were time recording equipment and typewriters.

Today IBM has annual revenues of $55 billion and employs some 390,000 people worldwide, offering a broad range of technologically advanced

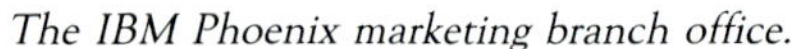

The IBM Phoenix marketing branch office.

information-handling products and computer systems.

IBM's operations in Phoenix over the past five decades have undergone a similar expansion. IBM employed only four salesmen when it opened its doors in 1940 in the 400 block of Central Avenue, enough to handle a sleepy desert town with few businesses and only 65,000 city residents.

By 1968 IBM had about 250 employees working in a new location at 4502 North Central Avenue, and Phoenix had exploded into a major city of nearly 600,000.

Today there are nearly 520 IBM sales, service, and support personnel, most working in a three-story, 127,000-square-foot leased facility at 2850 East Camelback Road. The reason for this growth is simple. Phoenix has emerged as a booming center of high technology, finance, health care, and education, and is now the nation's fastest-growing major city with a population of more than 950,000.

"When I transferred with IBM to Phoenix in 1945, we only had a few schools and some public-sector jobs to handle," says Charles Geoffroy, who is now retired in Phoenix after working 37 years for IBM. "Pretty soon, though, things really started to take off. IBM came up with new technologies and products, and suddenly we had customers in fields that hadn't even existed a few years earlier."

Most Phoenix businesses now use data-processing equipment as a funda-

People—a commitment to excellence.

mental part of their daily operations. As these companies change, so do their requirements. IBM employees in Phoenix, like their counterparts in IBM marketing branch offices everywhere, respond to these needs. They offer solutions, which may range from a few personal computers for an elementary school to an entire system of processors and storage devices to enable a major bank to handle customer transactions more smoothly.

There are IBM products available to meet nearly every data processing requirement, as the corporation has development and manufacturing sites worldwide, including a major facility in nearby Tucson. At the IBM Customer Center in Phoenix, a professional staff provides the latest information on these products. Demonstrations of computer hardware and software are available, and free seminars assist customers in understanding how various products can work together to solve problems.

And the Phoenix IBM branches do their jobs very well. Twice in the past four years local branches have been selected by IBM marketing headquarters as the division's best—a testimonial that they're succeeding in meeting the needs of a growing number of valley customers.

"Our number-one goal as a company is to enhance our partnerships

The IBM Customer Center.

the school, assisting students with their studies, as well as with business career awareness, communication, and interviewing skills.

"The Adopt-A-School program helps enhance educational programs and strengthens the link between industry and education," says Hazel Pope, IBM's Adopt-A-School representative in Phoenix. "The help that IBM employees give can really contribute to a student's success."

IBM employees are also involved in the United Way, Valley Big Brothers/Big Sisters, Literacy Volunteers of Maricopa County, Arizona Drug Abuse Program, Junior Achievement, Scottsdale Arts Center Association, and many other community programs.

More than 40 percent of today's IBM employees in Phoenix have been in the city for 10 years or more. It's clear they like the area, and they believe in working with the community to help make the valley an even better place to live.

"This is where we live and work, and we try to support the Phoenix community whenever possible," says Puskar. "We're a part of this city, and we want to make a meaningful contribution to the quality of life here."

Volunteering through IBM's Adopt-A-School program.

with customers," says Puskar. "We try to understand their problems and offer them not just computer hardware and software, but total business solutions."

Wherever it does business, IBM has traditionally been more to a community than just a business enterprise. In Phoenix, the firm has made significant contributions of money, equipment, and employee time to support education, social programs, and the arts.

That tradition started with Thomas J. Watson, Sr., IBM's first president. Under his leadership the company helped pioneer corporate involvement in the community, just as it led the way in employee benefits, job enrichment, employee education, and other policies and practices.

IBM's leadership in these areas is a natural outgrowth of its commitment to the first and most fundamental of its basic beliefs—respect for the individual. Relations with employees, customers, and the public are guided by that belief, and IBM employees carry it with them into the community. The result is a long list of civic and charitable contributions.

In Phoenix, for example, IBM has played a major role in supporting the Urban League Job Training Center, which provides training and job placement assistance to more than 150 disadvantaged people in Maricopa County each year. The center got its start from an IBM grant in 1982, and the firm has continued its support by donating computer equipment and supplies. In 1987 and 1988 IBM gave $50,000 to support a summer youth work/study program at the Urban League.

IBM also has formed a partnership with South Mountain High School as part of the Adopt-A-School program. Several IBM employees volunteer in the business and math departments at

DIGITAL EQUIPMENT CORPORATION

"We've had a great birth and a great adolescence," says Ed Petrazzolo, plant manager for Digital Equipment Corporation in Phoenix. "All the reasons we chose to locate in Phoenix have been fulfilled."

According to Petrazzolo, 1975 was a vibrant time for growth for Digital. The company needed to expand and looked for a location with talent and access. Phoenix, Albuquerque, and Colorado Springs were all potential sites, but Phoenix was the first plant to open. "We wanted to be in a growing area so that we could grow with it," Petrazzolo says. "We looked for a growing vendor base and a high-tech orientation. Frankly, we were impressed by the other companies that were looking at Phoenix, too. We saw Phoenix as part of the emerging Silicon Desert. With its reliable and skilled work force, Phoenix was in a similar situation to Digital, both vibrant and growing and caring about managing their growth," Petrazzolo continues. "And, finally, there is that lure of the Sunbelt—an undeniable quality of life that Phoenix offers."

Occupying 500,000 square feet of manufacturing space on 92 landscaped acres, Digital's plant is a visible expression of corporate philosophy. Well integrated into the surrounding area, the manufacturing center is vast yet personal, high tech yet low key.

Part of a company with sales of $10 billion per year, Digital Phoenix is a vibrant addition to Digital's 30 plants and more than 110,000 employees. "The utilization of our equipment is second to none," Petrazzolo states. "We are the best producer of networked computer systems in the world."

Offering equipment, services, and knowledge, Digital ties it all together to provide to its customers a total solution. This complete product line makes it possible for the company to build and manage fully distributed computer networks that are easy to expand and maintain, protecting customer investments in software, hardware, and training.

"We like to say that we produce solutions that allow for connecting all parts of an organization from the desk

Digital Equipment Corporation is well integrated into the surrounding area. The manufacturing center is vast yet personal, high tech yet low key.

top to the data center, from the shipping clerk to the president," adds Petrazzolo.

Built in 1975, the Phoenix operation employs 1,000 and consists of three main groups: manufacturing, the headquarters for western distribution, and a regional financial management center.

The Phoenix plant produces VAX systems and printer terminals. VAX systems are minicomputer operating systems, the firm's bread and butter. The location also serves as the distribution center for the western United States and as the control point for products entering and leaving the United States for the Far East and Pacific Basin.

"Our manufacturing operation occupies most of our people and most of our assets," says Petrazzolo who is justifiably proud of his plant's success.

He credits that success to several factors. "We are as competitive a manufacturing location as there is," he begins. "We are committed to manufacturing excellence. Consequently, excellence pervades our thinking; it affects our every decision." That commitment to excellence applies to people as well as product. Petrazzolo notes that in its more than 30-year history, Digital Equipment Corporation has never laid off an employee.

In addition to plant dedication, the plant manager points out that Digital's connection to Arizona State University's School of Engineering is key to his success. "Digital cares a lot about this relationship," he says. "By collaborating on certain projects with ASU, we align professors and students with us. This allows us to aim for more state-of-the-art technology and ultimately get a better manufacturing process and a better product."

Digital's flags have been flying high in Phoenix for 15 years.

To this end, Petrazzolo notes, the plant is dedicated to JIT—or Just In Time, a manufacturing technique that is aimed at eliminating waste. JIT works at the Digital Phoenix plant because the plant is committed to its supply base. Suppliers at this plant are viewed as an extension of Digital's manufacturing capability. Explains Petrazzolo, "We are very happy with our localized supply base. We have a truck that sweeps Phoenix daily to pick up parts and pieces for us and deliver them directly to our manufacturing line."

Finally, the plant enjoys a highly participatory work force. Plant policy does not segregate research and development ideas into any specific functions. At Digital, the work place is a laboratory; consequently, ideas to improve product, manufacturing, or distribution are encouraged from all sectors.

Since establishing the operation in Phoenix, Digital has enjoyed an excellent reputation for sensitivity to community needs. Whether that need is legislation or a communitywide effort for education, Digital Phoenix is in the forefront of such endeavors. In addition to supplying equipment to the Glendale school system and to the Maricopa Community College system, Digital employees are encouraged to be out in the community, giving of their time and talents.

This local policy is in complete concert with corporate philosophy. On the international front, Digital's more than 100,000 employees share a vision of the way that computers can make this a better world. At the same time they recognize the importance of the customer as a key to their own success and the success of the firm. The result is a caring and generous corporate profile. For example, Digital matches, dollar for dollar, employee gifts to schools, nonprofit organizations, and United Way programs. The company also actively supports educational, health care, civic, social, and cultural programs at the national, regional, and local levels.

As the leading manufacturer of computers for advanced research and development, Digital continually searches for new ideas and new technologies. As a research and development company, Digital plays a key role in establishing industry standards that make it easier for different computer systems to work together. The firm invested more than one billion dollars to develop the networking products used with Ethernet.

As more applications are developed for Digital systems, and as more organizations recognize the value of integrating computer resources in enterprise-wide networks, the vision shared by Digital Equipment Corporation and its customers becomes a reality. The network has become the system.

Below: "Excellence pervades our thinking—it affects our every decision."

Bottom: As the leading manufacturer of computers for advanced research and development, Digital continually searches for new ideas and technologies.

ALLIED-SIGNAL AEROSPACE COMPANY

"I was very impressed with the energy and willingness of the work force. If I ever open up a plant again in Phoenix, each of those women will have a job with me." That was founder Cliff Garrett's promise after his plant, which built environmental equipment for high-altitude bombers, shut down at the end of World War II.

Garrett fulfilled that promise in 1952, when the U.S. Air Force required an inland manufacturing plant for the gas turbine auxiliary power units he was producing on the West Coast. The gas turbine product line, along with a pneumatic controls product line, was transferred to Phoenix.

From that product base, five high-technology manufacturing and customer support divisions have grown, employing more than 10,500 people in the valley. Together with a 1,000-employee Tucson division, they comprise today's Allied-Signal Aerospace Company—the third-largest employer in the state. Its five combined divisions occupy more than 3 million square feet of facilities in the valley and maintain a work force that is nearly one-third engineering and laboratory personnel. The company also supports a broad base of local manufacturing and services vendors.

What started as a separate enterprise has doubled in size over the past eight years. Sales have more than doubled, and the Allied-Signal Aerospace Company of today is well diversified, with each division successfully challenging the demanding high-tech world.

Garrett Engine Division is one of the world's leading designers and manufacturers of gas turbine engines for aircraft; among its products, the TFE731 turbofan is the world's leading business jet aircraft engine. "This division is producing and developing more types of aircraft engines than at any other single engine-manufacturing location in the world," says Mal Craig, division president.

Allied-Signal Aerospace Company's success, based on its solid reputation, spans nearly a half-century. Garrett Auxiliary Power Division president F.E. Rick Johnson is proud that "the Auxiliary Power Division has dominated both the technology and production of auxiliary power gas tur-

The Fluid Systems Division of Allied-Signal Aerospace Company's Tempe facility, which produces its power, control, and actuation systems for aircraft, unmanned vehicles, and space applications.

bine engines for nearly 45 years."

The Fluid Systems Division has 50 years of experience manufacturing high-quality products; each second an aircraft engine is started somewhere in the world by one of this division's systems. "Almost as often," says Jim Griffin, division president, "a Fluid Systems Division jet engine thrust reverser is deployed to help an aircraft land."

Garrett Airline Services Division's president, Wilbur Clarkston, explains that this division, with facilities in Alabama and Singapore, is responsible for after-market support of all Garrett-manufactured equipment used by more than 250 airlines worldwide. "We provide support for representatives located in Europe, Africa, the Middle East, and West Germany."

The firm's newest operation headquartered in Arizona is Garrett General Aviation Services Division. "This division provides service and support for all Garrett-built propulsion engines and equipment in general aviation and regional airline use," explains Joe Jackson, president of the division.

Because Phoenix provides a great business environment and a perfect climate for high-tech enterprises, Allied-Signal Aerospace Company has become a major employer in the area and a high-tech competitor worldwide.

Testing is conducted on Garrett Engine Division's T800 engine, being developed for a U.S. Army helicopter. Manufacturing and supporting gas turbine engines is a main endeavor for Garrett divisions in the valley.

AG COMMUNICATION SYSTEMS CORPORATION

"The decision to locate AG Communication Systems' corporate offices and research and development facilities operations in Phoenix wasn't difficult," says Jack M. Kirker, president and chief executive officer of AG Communication Systems. "Quality of life, the proximity of the finest educational institutions in the country, and the availability of a variety of transportation systems were important elements in our selection. Add a high-quality labor force, the climate, and the cooperation we received from state, county, and municipal governments, as well as the chamber of commerce, and there was little choice but to select Phoenix as our home."

AG Communication Systems Corporation is one of Arizona's larger employers with more than 1,300 workers located at its group headquarters in north Phoenix. The firm's campus complex at 2500 West Utopia Road is primarily devoted to research and software development activities for digital telecommunication systems.

Development of the GTD-5 EAX™ family of digital telephone central office switching systems, which were introduced by GTE in 1982, is handled there. Since 1982 more than 10 million lines have been shipped to a variety of telephone companies

AG Communication Systems' main facility, located at 2500 West Utopia Road in north Phoenix.

throughout North America. This firm prides itself on providing local telephone companies with USA-made products that promise top-of-the-line performance and reliability.

As a joint venture of GTE and AT&T, AG Communication Systems develops, manufactures, and markets a wide range of advanced telecommunications systems and equipment for telephone operating companies, business organizations, and government agencies. A state-of-the-art manufacturing facility for digital central office switching systems is located in Northlake, Illinois, and a highly automated manufacturing and assembly of hybrid circuit cards and electronic subsystems assembly is located in Genoa, Illinois. There are more than 4,900 employees at the three facilities in addition to installation and marketing offices located nationwide.

The firm has many firsts to its credit in the digital telephone switching marketplace. Most notably, in conjunction with Mountain Bell and US West, AG Communication Systems provided the first U.S. demonstration of Integrated Service Digital Network (ISDN) primary access (23B+D). ISDN is a dynamic concept that enables voice, data, text, and image to be transmitted at very high speeds over a single, twisted-pair telephone wire. Basic access (2B+D) was also provided. With GTE Telephone Operations-California, more than 1,000 business customers have seen the advantages and future applications of ISDN in the real-world environment.

In Phoenix, AG Communication Systems' accelerated product development translates as an ambitious hiring program for research and software development. In addition, through its president and chief executive officer, Jack M. Kirker, and its many employees, the firm maintains an active community profile. By every measure AG Communication Systems Corporation is committed to quality—both in telecommunications research and design, and in corporate citizenship.

The GTD-5 EAX™ family of digital switching systems provides advanced telecommunications for telephone operating companies and private networks.

MCI

More than 20 years ago MCI began with an idea central to American business—that service, quality, and value can only thrive in a competitive environment. Building upon this concept, MCI has emerged as a remarkable success story in one of the fastest-growing industries of the information age.

In 1974 this company brought the advantages of competition and choice in long-distance telecommunications to Phoenix, which since then has become a major center of operations for MCI and an important link in its network. Located in nearby Wittman, MCI's network junction houses one of the most sophisticated digital switching systems in the world, designed to serve the growing metro Phoenix area. This advanced facility is an integral part of MCI's development of an all-digital network.

MCI's network takes full advantage of both optical fiber and digital microwave. By employing these two technologies, MCI provides a level of flexibility and reliability superior to that of relying upon a single mode of transmission. This enables MCI to use whichever technology is best suited for specific traffic situations or customer needs, with the efficiency demanded by today's home and business long-distance user. Having these options to choose from helps to assure customers that when they elect MCI as their

A view of the Wittman, Arizona, switch facility by photographer Jon Whitaker.

carrier of choice, they can expect the quality and dependability that is the hallmark of MCI. These two values—quality and dependability—describe the core principles of the company's service philosophy.

MCI's service philosophy does not stop with its advanced network. While state-of-the-art technology is vital to the carrier, so are MCI's people, many of whom call Phoenix home. The firm is fully aware that it is people who carry out its commitment to better serve each customer.

Located in the heart of the Phoenix business district, MCI's customer service and telemarketing groups are setting the industry standards in both the delivery of telecommunications services and responsiveness to customers' needs. Employing nearly 300 Phoenix residents, MCI's people bring to the service of its customers the distinct advantage of combining innovation with experienced long-distance service—experience that has been gained by being the industry's most progressive service provider in a highly competitive marketplace.

MCI's people, products, services, and technology give Phoenix access to

the entire world. In partnership with this growing city and its expanding industries, MCI provides telecommunications services as the most responsive company in long distance.

Multiplexing equipment that is housed at the Wittman, Arizona, switch facility. Photo by Jon Whitaker

MCI's local customer service department provides fast, courteous service to Phoenix and surrounding cities. Photo by Jon Whitaker

MICROAGE, INC.

What the factory production line did for the Industrial Age, the microcomputer is doing for the Information Age. More and more people are using microcomputer systems to create, manipulate, and manage information—the lifeblood of business. Although the microcomputer is a relatively new invention, it is already firmly established in the strategies of businesses from giant corporations to small firms.

Many of today's businesses have chosen to work with MicroAge, Inc., when automating their data management functions. Through a network of more than 200 franchised and company-owned locations throughout North America, Europe, and Japan, MicroAge markets microcomputer systems and support to businesses as solutions to information management problems. Each MicroAge location holds authorizations to sell, service, and support products from major manufacturers, including IBM, Compaq, Hewlett Packard, Apple, AT&T, and others.

MicroAge is one of the Phoenix area's principal employers in the high-technology sector and one of the fastest-growing firms ever to start up in Arizona. The firm's international headquarters is located in Fountainhead Corporate Park in Tempe, with a 115,000-square-foot U.S. distribution facility a few minutes' drive to the east.

MicroAge was conceived in 1976. As banking executives, Jeffrey D. McKeever (now MicroAge president and chief executive officer) and Alan P. Hald (now MicroAge chairman of the board) recognized the microcomputer's enormous potential for business data-processing applications. The pair founded the first computer store in Arizona and one of the first few in the United States. Their idea led the way to a new industry—and became MicroAge, Inc., parent company of one of the world's largest and most respected microcomputer reseller organizations —MicroAge Computer Stores, Inc.

The two pioneering entrepreneurs soon realized that microcomputer technologies and market dynamics were evolving rapidly. Once regarded as toys for the home, microcomputers were quickly gaining popularity in offices. Executives, accountants, engineers, and other professionals began demanding microcomputer systems for use as business tools. As businesspeople they wanted value from their hardware and software investment. And nationwide, MicroAge professionals were there to provide that value, with needs analysis, training, and support and maintenance services as integral components of a complete microcomputer system solution.

Other entrepreneurs also recognized the opportunities that the MicroAge focus on value-added solutions offered. They joined the MicroAge network as franchise owners—and led the way to the systems era, configuring products from multiple vendors into integrated office and business systems.

MicroAge was one of the first firms to target and sell to specialized vertical markets—and was one of the first resellers to develop high levels of expertise in selling and supporting multiuser systems and local area networks. These and other value-added marketing and distribution strategies have earned MicroAge a leading industry position. The company completed a successful initial public offering in 1987; its stock is traded on the NASDAQ over-the-counter market under the symbol MICA.

As the industry continues to grow more complex, MicroAge continues to build on its history of success—turning ideas into action and vision into reality. With strong commitments to its value-added strategies, outstanding levels of talent and resources within its network, and a clear vision of the future, MicroAge, Inc., is leading the way to the bright promises of the Information Age.

MicroAge's international headquarters in Tempe.

MicroAge distributes microcomputer products from leading manufacturers to its franchise network from this 115,000-square-foot facility in Tempe.

CHAPTER TWELVE

Manufacturing and Mining

Producing goods for individuals and industry, manufacturing and mining firms provide employment for many Phoenix area residents.

Phelps Dodge Corporation, 250-251

Talley Industries, Inc., 252-253

Superlite, 256

W.L. Gore & Associates, 257

M&D Electrical Parts, 254-255

Ameron Southwest Concrete Pipe Division, 258

Callahan Mining Corporation, 259

Photo by Kevin Cruff, Courtesy, Visual Images West

PHELPS DODGE CORPORATION

When Phelps Dodge moved its corporate headquarters in 1987 from New York City to the impressive Phelps Dodge Tower on Phoenix' North Central Avenue, city boosters cheered. PD has been a major force in Arizona for more than a century. Now the *Fortune* 500 company finally was "coming home." But while that made engaging copy, it wasn't the whole story.

According to G. Robert "Bull" Durham, chairman and chief executive officer of Phelps Dodge Corporation, the principal reason for the move to Arizona was more pragmatic. It wasn't the climate or even the Arizona lifestyle that prompted the change of corporate address. Rather, the driving force behind the relocation was money. "By merging our New York office into our Phoenix office, we're going to realize annual savings of $3.5 million," Durham says.

This focus on costs explains more than just the relocation. It also speaks to how the nation's largest copper producer has been able, in just a few short years, to recover from the effects of a prolonged depression in the price of copper and become one of the rousing success stories of American basic industry. "Our business plan of cost reduction, balance sheet improvement, and significant diversification remains a commitment of Phelps Dodge man-agement," says Durham. "We have made substantial progress on each of these fronts, but we are not relaxing. More can be done, and needs to be done to position this company as one of the leading companies of its size."

Today Phelps Dodge is the largest copper producer in the United States by a wide margin. The firm can produce about half again as much copper as it could in 1981. Even more significant, it is the lowest-cost producer of copper in this country. PD's aggressive cost-cutting strategy has enabled the organization to reduce production costs from well above 80 cents per pound of copper in 1981 to around 55 cents per pound in 1989, and Durham says that programs already under way will drive production costs below 50 cents per pound by the end of 1990.

The corporation's success is firmly grounded in its commitment to finding new and better ways of doing business. With its 15-percent partner in Morenci Mining, Sumitomo Metal Mining Arizona Inc., a subsidiary of Sumitomo of Japan, PD completed a $40-million in-pit crushing and conveying system in its mine at Morenci, Arizona, in 1988.

G. Robert Durham, chairman and chief executive officer, at Phelps Dodge Corporation's Phoenix headquarters.

This installation will enable the firm to completely eliminate rail haulage between the mine and the concentrators.

In 1988, with its one-third partner in Chino Mines Company, Mitsubishi of Japan, PD completed a $55-million solvent extraction/electrowinning (SX/EW) plant at Chino Mines in New Mexico. The plant will produce 90 million pounds of electrowon copper, more than 99.99 percent pure, each year. An SX/EW plant that went into production at the company's mine at Tyrone, New Mexico, in 1984 has been expanded three times since then.

Together the firm's domestic mines and its associated SX/EW plants produce some one billion pounds of copper annually, giving Phelps Dodge the distinction of producing more copper than any other private-enterprise company in the world.

Although copper is the foundation of the corporation, Phelps Dodge also has embarked on an ambitious diversification program. As a first step the firm acquired Columbian Chemicals Company in 1986. With this acquisition Phelps Dodge became a leading U.S. and international producer of carbon blacks—a family of chemical products

Harvesting cathodes, more than 99.99-percent pure copper, at the new Morenci solvent extraction/electrowinning plant.

that includes key ingredients in tires and other rubber-based products. And, in February 1988, the company announced the acquisition of ACCU-RIDE Corporation, North America's leading producer of wheels and rims for medium- and heavy-duty trucks and trailers.

Phelps Dodge also is one of the leading domestic producers of magnet wire. It has interests in copper wire and cable plants in 14 foreign countries, and in mines in South Africa, Chile, and Peru that produce copper, gold, silver, lead, zinc, and fluorspar. The firm conducts an active mineral exploration program in the United States, Mexico, southern Africa, and Chile, looking for a variety of metals—primarily gold and copper.

Viewed from an economic perspective, copper means gold for Arizona. According to a report by the Western Economic Analysis Center in Marana, Arizona, copper companies account for one of every $11 collected by state and local governments in Arizona. The copper industry is a major employer in the state, and copper companies purchase more than a half-billion dollars' worth of goods from other Arizona firms each year.

The relationship between Arizona and Phelps Dodge has been long and fruitful. It began in 1881, when William Church walked into the offices of Phelps, Dodge & Company in New York and requested a $50,000 loan to build a smelter near Morenci. Although the partners in Phelps, Dodge & Company, the predecessor of Phelps Dodge Corporation, had no idea who the man was, they were aware that a number of rich copper finds had been made in the Arizona Territory. Therefore, they asked Dr. James Douglas, a well-known and respected mining engineer and metallurgist, to travel to Arizona to evaluate the Morenci site and several other copper prospects. Upon his return, Douglas filed such a favorable report that not only did Phelps Dodge back Church's operation at Morenci, the company purchased a mine in the Bisbee mining district as well. Thus began a relationship that has flourished

An aerial view of the Morenci open-pit copper mine at Morenci, Arizona.

for more than 100 years.

Today Morenci remains Phelps Dodge's largest mine and largest money-maker. Ore reserves at Morenci and at Phelps Dodge's other two operating mines total one billion tons, and Phelps Dodge has three undeveloped copper ore bodies in Arizona—two near Safford, the other southwest of Prescott—a currently idled mine at Ajo, Arizona, and a promising prospect near Bisbee to rely on in the future.

From his vantage point as chief executive of a flourishing copper giant, Bull Durham is a satisfied man. "I'm not a good-news Charlie kind of guy, but I'd be hard pressed to think of a problem in the near term that would cause us concern," he says. "Frankly, business is a pleasure."

An electric shovel loads 170-ton trucks in the Morenci mine.

TALLEY INDUSTRIES, INC.

Talley Industries, Inc., is an active participant in Phoenix' expanding growth and is a reliable indicator of the city's bright economic future. Since 1960 the company has grown from a small aerospace firm, producing various solid-propellant-actuated devices, to a diversified corporation listed on the New York Stock Exchange.

During its growth Talley Industries, Inc., has been committed to breaking new ground. As an offshoot of its aerospace activities, the firm pioneered the development of automotive air bags in the late 1960s. It was the first company with solid-propellant air bag components in U.S.-manufactured cars, and is a leading producer of complete air bag modules. Talley's future air bag production is expected to grow rapidly, with potential annual revenues exceeding $140 million by 1990.

To handle this dynamic growth, a new, $16-million, high-tech automated air bag assembly plant was constructed in Mesa in 1987—the first facility in the nation devoted specifically to air bag development and production. The plant has the capacity to produce 2.5 million air bag modules annually. By 1990 this facility is expected to employ more than 700 engineers, technicians, and assembly personnel.

After devoting 20-plus years and more than $60 million in research, development, and testing, Talley is prepared to respond to an industry poised for tremendous future growth. At every level Talley Industries is a significant factor in the development of superior products.

This nationwide enterprise was founded by the late Franz G. Talley and a group of experienced engineers and technically oriented investors. Its original business—the design, development, and manufacture of rocket-propelled components and subsystems for military use—continues as one of the firm's major subsidiaries, Talley Defense Systems, Inc.

Dedicated effort and major capital expenditures in the early years resulted in the development of superior products and enabled Talley Industries to grow. By 1967 the corporation desired

William H. Mallender, chairman of the board and chief executive officer, is pictured with air bag components manufactured by Talley's Phoenix area subsidiaries.

to provide a buffer against cycles in aerospace and military expenditures, and acquired a number of diverse businesses, resulting in Talley's emergence as a conglomerate.

A milestone in the building of this multicompany corporation was the June 1973 purchase of the Mobil Five Star-rated Arizona Biltmore Hotel and the contiguous 1,045 acres of undeveloped property located in the heart of Phoenix. Shortly after acquiring the Biltmore, disaster struck. The hotel, closed for the summer, was being updated to meet fire code standards with the installation of a sprinkler system. A spark from a welder's torch ignited insulation materials, and fire threatened the loss of Arizona's distinguished landmark. But with dedication and perseverance, a restored, more luxurious Arizona Biltmore Hotel opened—on schedule—the following September.

Talley then assembled a team of specialists to master plan the property. The hotel was expanded and, after accomplishing the rezoning of the remaining property for commercial, residential, and recreational use, the firm sold the hotel and the surrounding land. This highly successful Arizona Biltmore Estates project was the forerunner of many other real estate projects that have resulted in the recognition of Talley as a premier developer in the Phoenix metropolitan area.

In June 1977 the firm again expanded locally through the acquisition of Universal Propulsion Company, a Phoenix-based manufacturer of rocket catapults, rocket motors, and other solid-propellant and propellant-actuated devices. In 1986 this subsidiary was strengthened when Talley's aircraft escape systems product lines were moved from out of state and integrated into its operations.

The need for more space by Talley Defense Systems and the advantages to be gained from a more centralized Phoenix corporate office led to the relocation of Talley's headquarters. Originally located near Mesa's Falcon Field Airport, the company moved to its own Talley Plaza office complex in Phoenix in 1983.

Today Talley Industries is a diversified designer, manufacturer, and supplier of products and services for government and industry. The broad spectrum of products includes inflator modules for automotive air bag passive-restraint systems, air crew survival equipment and systems, high-reliability electronic components, naval architecture and marine engineering, and stainless-steel products. Talley also invests in and develops real estate, primarily in the Phoenix area. From these diverse industries, the firm provides technology for the nation's—and Phoenix'—future.

Concurrent with its development, Talley has never forgotten that the real key to corporate success involves community participation and spirit. From its inception the company has lent financial support and leadership to charitable and cultural activities, business and civic organizations, and medical and educational institutions.

The firm employs 850 people in its various Phoenix area operations and more than 3,200 people out of state, who comprise the work force of 17 distinct subsidiaries.

"Talley Industries' future growth, in general, will reflect the company's long-established operating strategy," says chairman William H. Mallender. "We enjoy being a conglomerate and think it is a very sensible way to operate, managing a portfolio of well diversified businesses that allows us to realize positive results during difficult times that any one industry might encounter.

"We seek improvement and growth in our operations through internal efficiencies, product line expansion, and acquisitions. Our portfolio of businesses is continually analyzed to ensure that available assets are properly deployed. It is an evolutionary, ongoing process that serves Talley well."

Talley's joint-venture, 11-story office complex in Phoenix is home for the company's corporate staff along with other tenants.

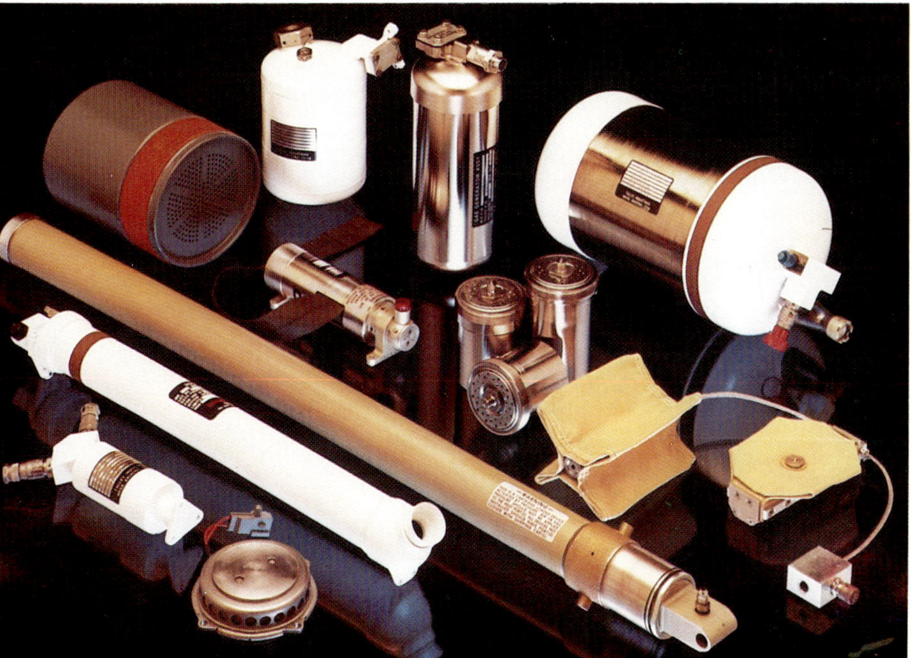

Products of Talley's local subsidiaries include inflators and modules for automotive air bag passive-restraint systems, as well as other solid-propellant-actuated devices.

M&D ELECTRICAL PARTS

At M&D Electrical Parts, nothing is left to chance. Not the company's goals, its position in the industry, and certainly not its products. Reliability and performance are the hallmarks of M&D Electrical, which has built its reputation remanufacturing superior quality starters, alternators, and water pumps. Product excellence has propelled this family-owned firm from a small business in 1973 to its present role as an acknowledged leading supplier in the automotive aftermarket world.

Today, just 16 years after it was founded, M&D employs approximately 200 people in its two plants. Its headquarters facility is contained within a 115,000-square-foot manufacturing center in Phoenix. M&D also has an additional 20,000-square-foot shop located in Gainesville, Georgia. A vast warehouse, also located on the grounds of the Phoenix plant, completes the M&D picture. This facility enables the company to stock a complete backup inventory for its customers.

By all accounts that inventory is staggering. It contains more than 1,000 different kinds of starters, alternators, and water pumps for domestic and foreign cars as well as for a variety of trucks, and agricultural, industrial, and marine applications.

In addition to this regular inventory, M&D also is equipped to manufacture specialty parts upon request. "If we don't have it, we'll make it," affirm M&D spokesmen. All told, the Phoenix-headquartered remanufacturing center turns out approximately a half-million units per year.

While the numbers are impressive, they do not accurately describe this burgeoning company. The secret behind M&D Electrical is its quality. There remanufacturing means more than producing a new part from an old one. Quality is built into every piece of every unit. "Every step of the way we test and retest," observes Ohad Muller, executive vice-president of the firm. "We insist that each subassembly is done correctly before it gets to the final assembly."

Because M&D believes that the surest road to reliability is to prevent failure during use, extreme attention to detail characterizes each step of the remanufacturing process from initial teardown to final test. Whether producing a 100-percent rebuilt part or doing an efficiency rebuild, detail is always paramount.

Such attention to detail has paid off for this rapidly emerging industrial leader. Today M&D Electrical is one of the giants in the automotive aftermarket. Explains Moshe Muller, M&D Electrical founder and president, "This is an extremely competitive business. Over the years, thanks to our fine product, good catalog, and excellent service, we have built up a large list of longtime customers." That client list spans the globe.

The remanufacturing process begins with trained M&D personnel tearing down and inspecting every reusable part of each used starter, alternator, and water pump received in the plant. All parts are scrutinized, evaluated, checked, sorted, and stored for future remanufacture use.

Before any piece can be placed in an M&D starter, alternator, or water pump, it is first remanufactured according to exacting specifications. This means that each nut and bolt is inspected and replated when necessary. Water pump housings are paint dipped for protection. Armatures are rewound in house, and starter drives made on the premises. Solenoids are replaced, field coil assemblies repaired or replaced, and new brushes carefully installed by trained technicians—every step of the way, testing continues on each and every part.

Once the remanufactured unit is assembled, it is tested again in its entirety for reliability and performance. Starters, for instance, are placed in conditions that parallel existing road situations. Alternators and water pumps also must pass such exacting performance standards. Only after each remanufactured part meets the M&D inspection can M&D employees package these units for wholesale distribution.

Entirely a wholesale operation,

M&D has a customer base that includes warehouse distributors and retail outlets throughout the country and the world. Many well-known chains sell M&D parts under their own labels. In addition to its major wholesale thrust, the Phoenix firm maintains a small parts warehouse. There mom-and-pop shop owners can purchase individual parts they need to rebuild starters, alternators, or water pumps for their customers.

In 1989 M&D plans to become involved in the new component assembly

of "pancake" DC motors, used increasingly on vehicles to facilitate automatic seats, wipers, windows, and locks.

Remanufacturing the unit is just the beginning step for this aggressive company. To complete its competitive profile, the firm delivers a level of service that is unsurpassed in the industry. M&D Electrical stands behind every part it remanufactures. Moreover, the firm is committed to timely delivery to its customers. Through its computer-aided distribution system, this remanufacturing center can promise prompt delivery to any customer, either by M&D trucks or through common carrier. This combination of cost effectiveness, quality, and superior service has helped to create the remarkable story that is M&D Electrical.

As is usually the case, there is more to the M&D Electrical story than the mechanics of the operation. The energy behind the firm is the Muller family. Moshe Muller is an innovative and inventive entrepreneur who recognized the opportunities in the remanufacturing market. He established M&D

A remanufacturer of starters, alternators, and water pumps for foreign and domestic cars, M&D Electrical Parts is headquartered in this 115,000-square-foot manufacturing center in Phoenix. A vast warehouse located on the grounds contains more than 1,000 different kinds of the remanufactured parts.

Electrical Parts and, in addition to domestic units, had the foresight to see the potential demand for foreign electricals and was on his way. Out of a combination of intuitiveness and hard work, his business has grown and his ties to Arizona have strengthened.

SUPERLITE

In 1944 Phoenix was a small town, home to servicemen who were stationed at the desert's air bases, and Superlite Builders Supply was a fledgling firm supplying quality concrete blocks for residential and commercial construction. After the war many servicemen returned to Phoenix. They sought sunshine and wide open spaces, and brought with them an increased demand for building materials.

Today, some 45 years later, Phoenix is a big city and Superlite is a major Arizona supplier of concrete block and aluminum windows and doors. More than 300 employees work at production facilities in Tempe and West Phoenix, a raw material mine in Flagstaff, a portland cement/masonry cement-sacking facility, and a sales yard and sales organization in Tucson. Not only is Superlite the largest concrete block producer in the desert southwest, it is one of the largest producers in the world.

Superlite manufactures a wide variety of concrete block products with architectural shapes and sizes in both natural gray and earth-tone colors. Although its image remains in concrete block, the firm is also the largest producer of residential aluminum windows and doors in Arizona. This business resulted from requests from the homebuilding industry for quality aluminum products. Consequently, in 1960 Superlite began producing its own aluminum doors and windows. In addition to manufacturing doors and windows, the firm also supplies skylights, French doors, and garden windows.

Its most innovative product, however, was unveiled in 1984 when Superlite introduced the INTEGRA® concrete block wall system, an engineered wall system for the residential homebuilding industry. In this unique system, every space in the concrete block wall is filled with a special expanding urethane insulation that assists in energy cost savings. This enables the home buyer to obtain a concrete block house with a high energy efficiency. In addition to providing an R-value of 23, which translates into 43 days of energy savings each year when compared to other typical wall systems,

INTEGRA® concrete block walls are 28 times stronger than most residential wall requirements. Yet, because it is a concrete block wall, INTEGRA® remains remarkably affordable. This ma-

A cross section of Superlite products.

sonry system is so unique that it is being patented and is one more reason why the future of Superlite in Arizona is bright.

Superlite is a major supplier of concrete block and aluminum windows and doors to residential builders throughout Arizona.

W.L. GORE & ASSOCIATES

In 1958 the late Wilbert L. "Bill" Gore identified a market opportunity for specialized electronic wires insulated with polytetrafluoroethylene or PTFE, a polymer consumers knew as "Teflon." With the scientific help of his son, Bob, Gore developed the product and established his first wire and cable facility in the basement of his home in Newark, Delaware. The wire and cable business was on its way. By 1967 a second plant opened in Flagstaff.

Within two years, however, Bob Gore, a chemical engineer, began searching for a way to improve the product. He wanted to introduce more air into PTFE, which would produce a greater volume per pound of raw material without affecting the performance of the material. After weeks of frustrating, failed attempts, Gore angrily yanked at the PTFE rod he held in his hands. Amazingly, the rod stretched instead of breaking. The young Gore had accidentally discovered the formula he had been seeking.

Today GORE-TEX is a famous brand name. Best known by consumers for fabrics, it is also used for arteries, veins, and ligaments. W.L. Gore & Associates is the world's leading manufacturer of high-reliability electronic wire and cable products. The company specializes in precisely controlled electrical characteristics, miniaturization, cables with EMI/RFI shielding, and engineered zero-defect assemblies.

At the South Pointe Phoenix plant, the focus is on electronic wire and cable. This facility, which employs 150 associates, produces round conductor ribbon cables in nearly any configuration, high-performance ribbon cables, and zero-defect cable assemblies. "GORE-TEX, which is 70 percent air and 30 percent PTFE, is the best dielectric material used today," explains W.L. Gore associate David McCarter of the Phoenix facility.

The firm, which operates on the lattice system of management, eschews departmental or formal titles. "We are problem solvers," continues McCarter. "The electronic business is a custom business. Our role is to identify a problem and resolve it. Everything we do here is engineered."

That philosophy extends to the plant as well as to its products. McCarter hand-picked the site on Beautiful Lane that fully lives up to its name. The plant, which opened in April 1984, nestles up to the South Mountains and provides a panoramic scene of Phoenix. "Every one of our plants is located in a college town," adds McCarter. "Our headquarters in Newark, Delaware, is home of the University of Delaware. Flagstaff has Northern Arizona University. The Phoenix area has Arizona State University."

As for Phoenix, he points out that he sees it as the hub of the Southwest. "From here we can be at the airport in 12 minutes and, within 1.5 hours, serve Dallas, San Diego, Orange County, San Francisco, and Denver. At times, when you are trying to serve California, Phoenix is closer than being there." He pauses a moment to appreciate the view. "We have access to any resource we need to run a business here," he concludes. "It's the best city in the country as far as I'm concerned."

The W.L. Gore & Associates plant on Beautiful Lane nestles up to the South Mountains and provides a panoramic view of Phoenix.

W.L. Gore & Associates is the world's leading manufacturer of high-reliability electronic wire and cable products. Photo by Richard Weston

AMERON SOUTHWEST CONCRETE PIPE DIVISION

The water history of Arizona is inextricably meshed with the products of the Ameron Southwest Concrete Pipe Division. So is the conveyance of wastewater whether in miles of sewer lines or more local storm drainage systems.

Although Ameron's predecessor companies in California established temporary concrete pipe plants in Arizona intermittently during the first half of this century, Ameron, then American Pipe and Construction Co., did not become a permanent fixture on Arizona soil until it acquired the Hooper Concrete Pipe Co. of Phoenix in 1956. At that time the name was changed to the American Concrete Pipe Co. and so it remained until 1970, when American Pipe became Ameron with its divisions following suit.

Hooper Concrete Pipe had been in Arizona a decade before it merged into the Ameron operation, supplying reinforced concrete pipe for irrigation, drainage systems, sewers, culverts, and water supply lines of gravity or low-head pressure. Ameron continued with these reinforced concrete pipe products and added two new kinds of concrete pressure pipe, concrete cylinder, and prestressed concrete cylinder pipe. They would revolutionize water transmission and distribution statewide.

Ameron's concrete cylinder pipe-manufacturing equipment for the new Southwest Division was moved from a temporary plant site at Alamogordo to Albuquerque, New Mexico, where a permanent facility was established in 1958. Its first order was for five miles of concrete cylinder pipe for the city of Mesa, Arizona. The same year Ameron produced the first order of prestressed concrete cylinder pipe for the city of Phoenix' West Feeder Main. More orders would follow, contributing to the backbone of the city's water system.

Two exceptional projects, however, both begun in 1976, demonstrate Ameron's capability to support Arizona's progressive pattern of growth that always depends upon the availability of water.

When the Central Arizona Project of the USBR became a reality and the Granite Reef Aqueduct began its crawl toward Phoenix, Ameron undertook the manufacture and installation of the largest concrete pressure pipe ever produced. It had an internal diameter of 21 feet, a laying length of 22 feet, and each section weighed about 225 tons. The pipes were used in a series of six inverted siphons, each of which would pass under a river, a dry riverbed, or a dry wash to protect the 333-mile-long canal system from being washed out at critical points. The portable pipe plant to manufacture these enormous concrete pipe sections was designed and built by Ameron's equipment engineers as was the Pipemobile, an extraordinary off-road vehicle that would crawl through each pipe, lift it hydraulically, carry it from the pipe plant into the trench, and install it.

At the far southern end of the Central Arizona Project, the Southwest Division continues to supply prestressed concrete cylinder pipe to carry CAP water into Tucson, the largest city in the United States to have been dependent on groundwater sources.

Also in 1976 the Southwest Division began to supply 36 miles of prestressed concrete cylinder pipe to carry effluent, processed from the sewage of greater Phoenix-area cities, to the Palo Verde Nuclear Generating Station being erected 40 miles west of downtown Phoenix. Underground at the power station were Ameron prestressed concrete cylinder pipe and fittings to serve in the cooling water system that now supplies 1.7 million gallons of water per minute to cool steam from the turbines.

The preceding are just two outstanding examples of how Ameron's concrete pipe products, out of sight and underground in Arizona, have become principal hidden assets to the state's economy.

Below: *Ameron's Pipemobile Mark IV installs a 225-ton concrete pipe section in Granite Reef Aqueduct a few miles northwest of downtown Phoenix.*

Bottom: *Thirty-six miles of Ameron concrete pressure pipe carry effluent from a Phoenix waste-treatment plant to Palo Verde Generating Station.*

CALLAHAN MINING CORPORATION

When Callahan Mining Corporation moved its headquarters to Phoenix in 1980, the company renewed an old relationship. The mining operation had incorporated in Arizona on June 12, 1912—just after the young territory had become the 48th state. No doubt the spirit of Arizona appealed to the Minnesota men who backed a mining venture led by James F. "Jim" Callahan. A native of Galena, Illinois, Callahan had left home at age 18. After working as a woodsman, a farmer, and a cowboy, he landed in Eagle City in the Idaho Territory in 1883. He quickly established himself in the Coeur d'Alene Mining District of Idaho as one of the area's better-known figures.

Callahan's Idaho claims were the beginning of Callahan Mining Corporation, a company that has been listed on the New York Stock Exchange since 1916. Specializing in silver and gold, Callahan Mining today has revenues in excess of $30 million and a reputation for conservatism and fiscal responsibility.

One of the nation's leading silver companies, Callahan Mining employs more than 275 people at various locations throughout the United States.

The Galena mine surface facilities are located in the Coeur d'Alene Mining District and house one of the largest silver mines in the United States. The Galena mine yields more than 3 million ounces of silver each year.

The firm operates with no debt and receives the majority of its pretax income from the Coeur d'Alene Mining District. This area is home to Callahan's largest producing silver mine, the Galena mine, which yields more than 3 million ounces of silver each year. One of the largest silver mines in the United States, the Galena mine is both productive and cost efficient. The company reports that it costs approximately five dollars an ounce, including smelting charges, to produce silver from Galena.

Another major operation for Callahan Mining is Ropes Gold, a Michigan mine. It was discovered in 1880 by Julius Ropes, an Ishpeming, Michigan, druggist, and was worked by him. Later a copper company explored it, but determined in the 1930s that the ore grade was too low for the gold prices that were locked in during that era.

Callahan purchased the Ropes mine in 1975 on the probability that rising gold prices would make the property economically successful. The corporation realized that it could use low-cost bulk undergroud-mining methods to remove the ore. According to Charles D. Snead, chairman and president of Callahan Mining Corporation, "As it turns out, we're able to take what the old-timers left behind and still make profits." After an initial period of capital investment, Ropes Gold became Callahan's principal revenue

Charles D. Snead, Jr., chairman of the board and president.

source in 1986 and now yields more than 40,000 ounces of gold per year.

In addition to its mining operations, the firm also receives income from its investment portfolio and from The Flexaust Company, a division that manufactures lightweight hose and duct for industrial applications.

Snead points out that the move to Arizona was prompted by a variety of factors—not the least of which was the potential for attracting mining and geological talent. Happily, however, the community has also benefited from the relocation. In the tradition of Jim Callahan, Snead and officers of Callahan Mining Corporation quickly assumed active leadership roles in the Phoenix community.

Valley National Bank of Arizona, 262-263

Phoenix Economic Growth Corporation, 264

Arizona Central Credit Union, 265

Sun State Savings, 266-267

Coopers & Lybrand, 268

Blue Cross and Blue Shield of Arizona, 269

Franzoy Corey Engineers & Architects, 270-271

John Carollo Engineers, 272-273

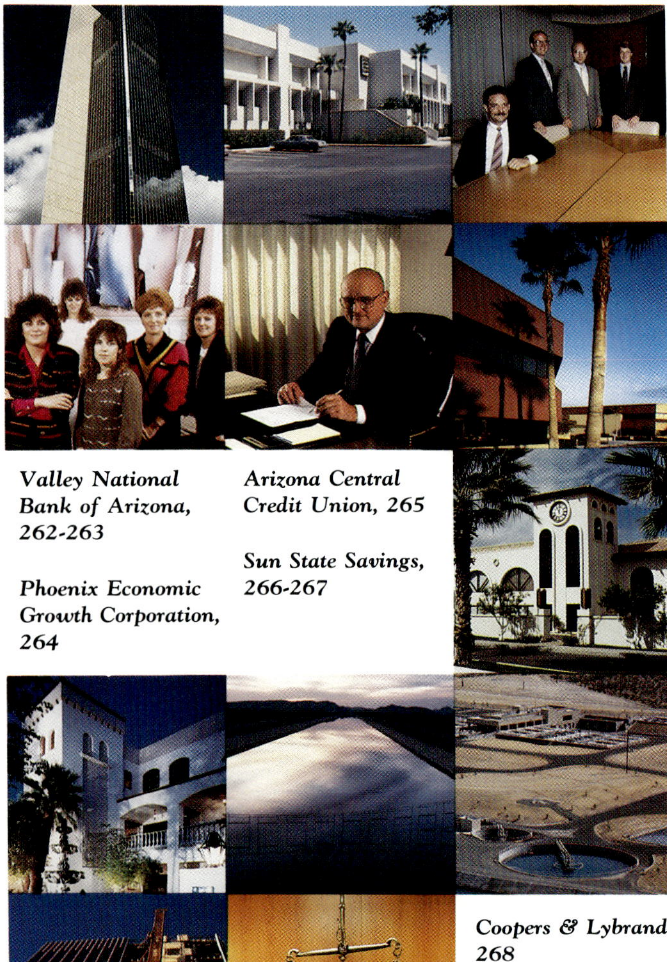

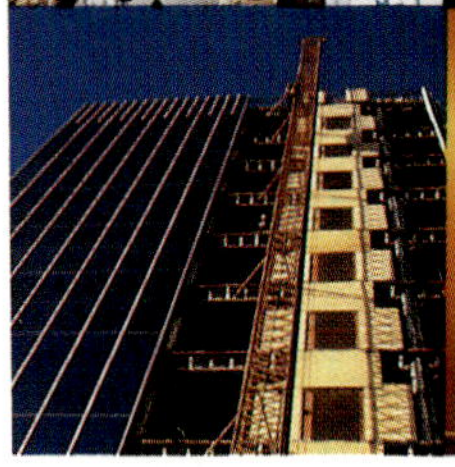
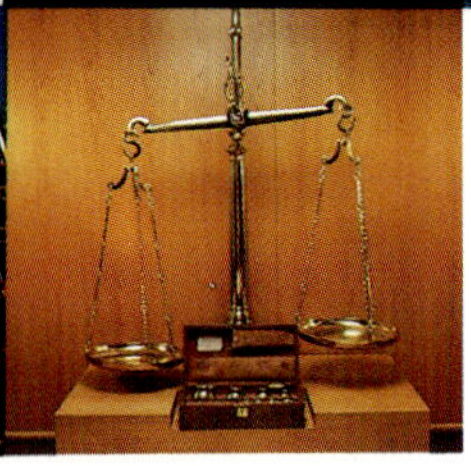

Balmer Architectural Group, Inc., 276

Sunbelt Holdings, Inc., 277

Johnson & Higgins of Arizona, Inc., 274-275

Lewis and Roca, 278-279

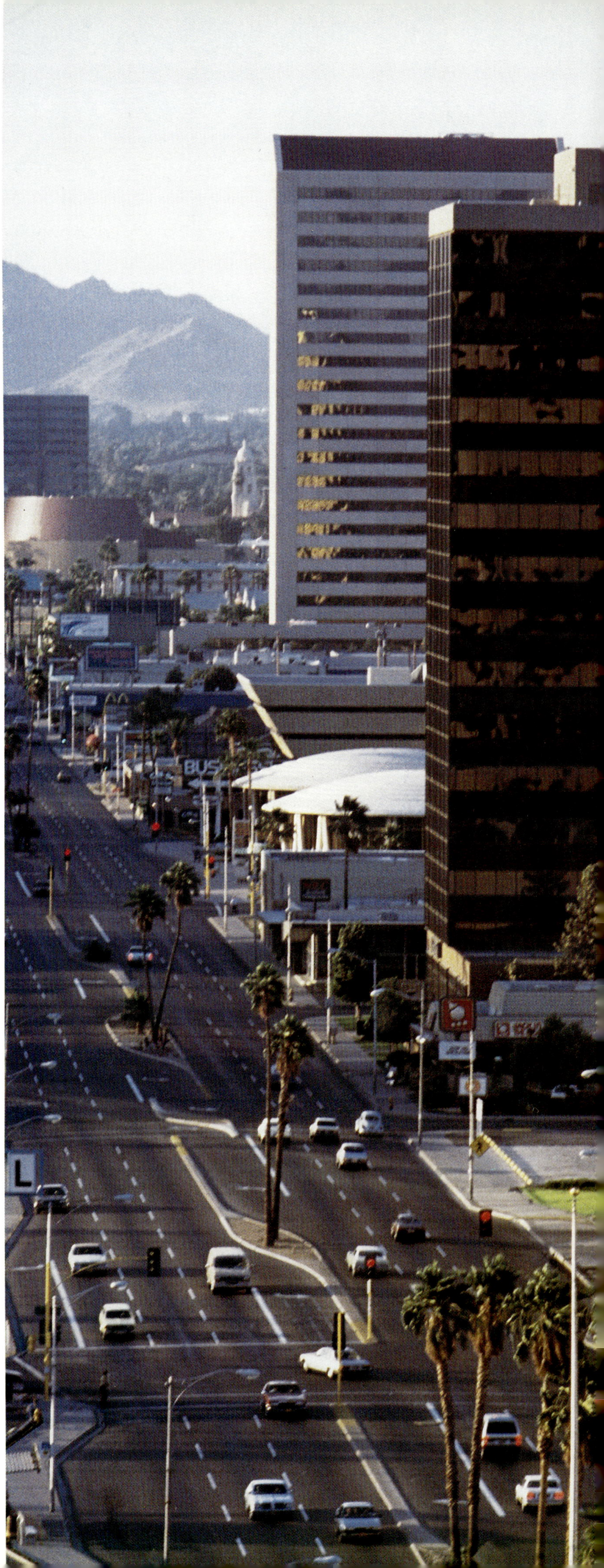

Business and Professions

Greater Phoenix' business and professional community brings a wealth of service, ability, and insight to the area.

CyCare Systems, 280

Chase Bank of Arizona, 281

Fennemore Craig, 282-283

Evans, Kitchel & Jenckes, 284-285

DWL Architects+ Planners, 286

Roberson and Company, 287

Brown & Bain, 288-289

Meyer, Hendricks, Victor, Osborn & Maledon, 294-295

Carroon, & Black/ Olliver Pilcher, 296

Storey & Ross, 292-293

Phyllis Hawkins & Associates, 297

Young, Smith & Peacock, Inc., 290-291

Photo by Paul E. Loven, Courtesy, Visual Images West

VALLEY NATIONAL BANK OF ARIZONA

With roots deep in Arizona soil, Valley National Bank has grown from a small, rural bank located in a general store to the largest bank in the state, with more than $11 billion in assets.

Valley Bank's origin traces back to the Gila Valley Bank and Trust Company, which was established in 1899 to serve the residents and businesses of Solomonville and the surrounding copper-mining communities of southeastern Arizona. As this small pioneer bank grew and prospered along with Arizona's copper industry, its managers decided to invest their personal savings in the rescue of a failing bank in Phoenix. For more than seven years the two banks remained independent institutions but were run by the same president, vice-president, and general manager.

During that time Valley Bank of Phoenix became stable and prosperous, successfully serving the growing agricultural, livestock, and business enterprises of the Salt River Valley. At the same time a declining demand for copper following World War I began affecting the profitability of the Gila Valley Bank. So, in 1922, the two institutions merged and became the Valley Bank and Trust Company.

Growing at a rapid pace along with the Arizona economy, Valley Bank ex-

The I.E. Solomon General Store, Solomonville, Arizona, housed the original Gila Valley Bank, forerunner of Valley National Bank.

panded to 11 branches and $18.8 million in deposits by 1928. But that growth abruptly ended with the onset of the Great Depression. By 1932 deposits had dropped to $6.7 million.

It was a grim time in history. Twelve million unemployed stood in long bread lines. The nation's financial structure was sliding downhill to the lowest point ever reached. It was a time when the bank needed strong, innovative leadership to pull it out of this downward trend—and that's exactly what it got in its newly hired president, Walter Reed Bimson, a poised, vigorous, young banker of 40 who didn't fear the panic.

Instead, Bimson saw this crisis as a great opportunity, a chance to usher the bank into a surge of growth that would make banking history. He delivered a general order that was completely astonishing to the staff: "Make loans! That's the way to recovery. I want this period of automatic loan refusal to end, and end now. The biggest service we can perform today is to put money into people's hands."

During the first 60 days of Bimson's presidency, the bank's old loan portfolio was cleaned out, the new loan-making policy was launched, and new deposit accounts were established. Bimson worked night and day, made flying trips to branches, met hundreds

Walter Reed Bimson: As president, he led Valley National Bank with courageous innovation from the dark days of the Great Depression in the 1930s until his retirement in 1970.

of people, made speeches statewide, and personally restored the public's confidence in the institution. He put his desk just inside the main door, where everybody could see and meet him. Lights burned late, troubles were ironed out, and the bank was readied for action.

It was a masterpiece of timing. Just when America's banking system as a whole was collapsing, Valley Bank gained a head start toward recovery and prosperity. The bank was moving forward while its rivals were still getting over the shock of the Depression.

During this period the institution started acquiring additional branches by taking over state banks that were in trouble. The First National Bank of Prescott was merged with Valley, as was the large Consolidated National Bank of Tucson.

A national charter was obtained in 1935, and the bank changed its name to the Valley National Bank & Trust Co. It was now three times as large as it had been on New Year's Day 1933.

Under Bimson's leadership Valley Bank continued to make history in the years that followed. The bank issued Arizona's first FHA loan in 1935, and was nationally recognized for its aggressive loan program. The employment that resulted from the construction work tied to these loans helped lift Arizona out of the Depression. The bank went on to issue the state's first automobile loan and first mobile home loan, and was the first Arizona bank to offer charge cards.

These innovations continued to bring in more business. In 1936 alone the institution's deposits increased $7.3 million to $32.5 million, and loans outstanding increased $4.1 million to $12.7 million. Another surge took place during World War II; Valley Bank held 53 percent of Arizona's total deposits and 72 cents out of every dollar in outstanding bank credit.

In addition to his keen business sense, Bimson was also a compassionate man. During World War II he made money available to nearly 14,000 of the always-broke GIs for trips home on leave. Throughout the war the bank received letters from parents all over the United States and from boys in the Pacific, thanking the institution for making the trips possible. Some letters came from Gold Star parents, who sought to pay off the balances for their sons who had lost their lives. The bank refused to accept these offers, and in cases where parents actually sent checks, returned them.

Walter Bimson retired in 1970, but before doing so, he established a capable, talented management team to succeed him and carry forward his philosophies and direction. During the next five years the total resources of the bank increased by a remarkable 100 percent—growth that somewhat paralleled that of Arizona. The bank outgrew its headquarters in the Professional Building and moved in 1973 into the newly constructed 40-story Valley Bank Center, still the tallest building in Arizona.

Growth continued steadily throughout the 1970s. By 1980 deposits reached $4.7 billion, and Valley Bank offices totaled 203. In 1981 a holding company, Valley National Corporation, was formed, opening the door for new subsidiaries.

Today Valley Bank has more than 215 branches statewide and better than $11 billion in assets. At midyear 1987 Valley National Corporation acquired Valley Utah Bancorporation, the fourth-largest banking concern in Utah with 36 offices and assets of nearly $900 million.

The future plan for Valley National Corporation is to become a major regional bank holding company in the Southwest. To do so, the corporation will continue to take advantage of expansion opportunities as they arise. But first and foremost, the bank is committed to build on the strong base in Ari-

zona by providing additional products and services to meet the changing needs of its customers, and by contributing to and supporting its home state.

The nation's first drive-in bank was at the Valley National Bank on First Street and Willetta.

The 40-story Valley Bank Center, the bank's headquarters, is still the tallest building in Arizona.

PHOENIX ECONOMIC GROWTH CORPORATION

"As the first partnership between the City of Phoenix and the private community, we are building the infrastructure for sustained economic growth for Phoenix," says Ioanna T. Morfessis, executive director of Phoenix Economic Growth Corporation (PEGC).

Created by Mayor Terry Goddard, the Phoenix City Council, and Phoenix business and community leaders, PEGC was established in 1984 as a private corporation with a public purpose. The idea for the private/public partnership emerged from an ad hoc committee consisting of Mayor Goddard, William H. Mallender, Brian Aby, Lucia Fakonas Howard, Herman Chanen, and Earl de Berge. The committee recommendation was followed by the incorporation of the Phoenix Economic Growth Corporation, and a 38-member board was appointed by the mayor and council.

PEGC's goal is to define, achieve, and maintain the best-possible quality of life for the city of Phoenix. Says Morfessis, "We have a remarkable business story to tell, probably one of the most phenomenal of any city in the country."

Adds Jeff Burt of PEGC, "Phoenix has a strong reputation as a resort destination. It is also our goal to establish Phoenix as the business and financial capital of the southwestern United States."

To accomplish its goal PEGC completed a five-year strategic plan, Phoenix: A Blueprint For Growth, in 1986. This plan is based on the recommendations of The Fantus Company of Chicago, Illinois, which did an in-depth analysis for the corporation and identified needs that must be immediately addressed. These include the improvement of the city's image and role as a corporate business center; strengthening the role of the central business district as a magnet for commercial, cultural, recreational, and corporate facilities; fostering more locally based companies to energize the economy over the long run and increase corporate support for civic, cultural, recreational, and social enterprises; helping the city move away from assembly-oriented manufacturing; and promoting the more efficient and productive use of the city's land and its financial, cultural, and human resources, as well as improving the natural desert, water, and air.

In addition to developing Phoenix: A Blueprint For Growth, volunteers in the private sector have contributed more than 5,000 hours to economic issues, assisted prospective new and expanding companies, responded to countless business groups evaluating Phoenix as a business location, and developed a business information base. By all accounts, PEGC is exceeding the mandate established for it.

Today this aggressive economic development partnership continues to be run as a nonprofit corporation and governed by a board of directors. This board consists of chief executive officers and business representatives from all major areas of the Phoenix economy, and elected and appointed officials from the city government. PEGC provides answers and information regarding a variety of business needs, from market data to financial services, and from site location to setup information and assistance. In addition, the private/public corporation aids in employment matters, business counseling, and advocacy.

"We recognize that the day will come when Phoenix is no longer the fastest-growing city," says Burt, "which is why it was important to do some soul searching early on and identify the direction for the city to follow. The charge of the original ad hoc committee was to point out how to stay competitive in the future. Our in-depth analysis identified our strengths. Now we are capitalizing on them."

The Phoenix Economic Growth Corporation team (left to right): Laurie Scheiber, Judie Scalise, Rhonda Phillips, Jeff Burt, Ioanna Morfessis (executive director), Duriye Luckett, Sandra Bivens, Donna Krouse, Joyce Haver, Cindi Willing, and Ed Standage, not pictured.

ARIZONA CENTRAL CREDIT UNION

The year was 1939, the place was Tucson, and the problem facing those gathered was that while employees of credit unions could save where they worked, they could not borrow. But the solution was clear: start a "credit union's credit union," a new, member-owned financial cooperative whose complete financial resources would be available to them.

The first office of this new organization opened in Tucson—at a dining-room table. By the early 1940s the home office had shifted to Phoenix, and within 10 years the credit union's credit union had grown to 450 members strong.

In 1957 the financial cooperative changed its name from Arizona League Central Credit Union to Arizona Central Credit Union. Growth was evident during this decade as Arizona Central Credit Union assisted existing credit unions that could no longer serve their members by accepting them into their field of membership and offering full credit union benefits. A steady influx of additional members secured Arizona Central Credit Union's role as a leader in the state.

In 1989 Arizona Central celebrated its golden anniversary. Nearly 50 years after its inception, this unique financial cooperative encompasses 45,000 members, employs 75 people, incorporates 5 offices statewide, and boasts an amazing growth record for the past decade, during which time both deposits and assets doubled.

R.J. Zawacki, president and chief executive officer since 1971, explains, "We definitely planned on this. We set goals and objectives, and we achieve them. Much of our success is attributed to our excellent management team. This team is very solid. We've worked and learned together for a long time." In addition, he notes, Arizona Central offers excellent services such as nationwide ATM access and checking accounts with no monthly charges. "And we were the first credit union west of the Mississippi in the VISA debit-card program. Basically, we offer service, smiles, and convenience."

Zawacki caps this winning combination with historic perspective. "Credit unions are unique," he says. "I don't know of any other financial institution in this country that operates on and promotes a membership concept. Our institution is member owned, democratically controlled, permits members to vote on the financial policy and operation, and returns profits to its members. Arizona Central is a family institution," he adds. "Once a member always a member. No matter how big we grow, since Arizona Central is owned by its members, we never lose that personal interest."

Zawacki predicts a golden future. "We are the third-largest state-chartered credit union in Arizona," he says. "The majority of our members come from Select Employee Groups (SEG). Since our growth is tied to the growth of Arizona and Phoenix, it's our policy to open branches in fast-growing areas. As for our overall goal, we are gearing up to become our members' primary financial institution. We plan to be able to handle every financial need."

Arizona Central Credit Union's home office in Phoenix.

SUN STATE SAVINGS

When Edward Janos organized Sun State Savings in 1978, he was certain that he had a winning idea. Just one decade later everyone else would agree with him. Today this high-performance, real estate-based financial services company is in the top 10 percent of the nation's savings and loans; its assets have grown from $2 million to more than one billion dollars. Despite its youth it is one of the leading lenders in Phoenix.

A unique deposit and lending philosophy and enterprising employees have put Sun State Savings on the fast financial track. Almost from the day that Sun State first opened its doors, in March 1980, it has been referred to as the fastest-growing financial institution in the state. Within three years that description was modified to the fastest-growing major financial institution in Arizona. As of 1987 assets, loans, and income showed compound annual growth rates of 26 percent, 26 percent, and 33 percent, respectively. Return on assets has averaged more than 1.7 percent during a five-year period ending in 1987.

"A lot of people don't know what to make of us," says K. Michael Million, corporate communications director. "It's almost unheard of to take the assets of a savings and loan from $2 million to more than one billion dollars in eight years—or for that matter to see stockholders' equity go from $2 million to $45 million in the same period." Crediting the company's rapid expansion to a combination of good management and being in the right place at the right time, he adds that Sun State has built its assets and profits by betting on Phoenix, taking calculated risks with developers, and playing off a deregulated environment that permits thrifts to enter into real estate joint ventures and direct property ownership.

From the start Janos knew who he wanted Sun State to serve and where he wanted his new thrift to be. He targeted his savings and loan to appeal to larger depositors—people with serious dollars to invest who seek executive service and high interest rates. By concentrating on savings, not transactions or number of accounts, lower costs compensate for higher interest rates. This deliberate focus has paid off. "Today our average balance is more than $20,000," Million points out. "We only compete with banks on the high-end scale."

Janos also decided to buck the trend and open with a single financial office. He chose an upscale location in the affluent Camelback Corridor. "Janos was certain that people would be willing to travel—even a long way—for the services we offer at this office," Million explains. Again the financial executive was correct in his instincts. The Sun State Savings office opened with three employees in 1979. Today it counts more than 200 professionals among its staff.

Until September 1987 that office constituted the whole of Sun State Savings. Then the thrift opened a regional facility in Sun City. This office met with such immediate success that in May 1988 Sun State opened a regional facility in Sedona, deciding to target additional regional offices in metropolitan Phoenix.

Janos tailored his loan portfolio as carefully as he did his deposit profile. Determining that he would not attempt to be all things to everyone, the savings and loan was positioned to be a force in residential lending. Its commitment to residential lending translates three ways. Sun State earns fees and interest through all three phases of the single-family housing cycle: It lends to established builders for land acquisition; it makes interim loans to finance construction; and finally, it makes permanent loans to the home owner. Over the past 10 years Sun State has established substantial relationships with many of the larger, national building organizations.

Above all, its real estate lending concept encompasses total community development. Sun State Savings finances communities, not just projects.

In addition to emphasizing and targeting real estate lending, Sun State Savings also has been committed to a program of direct real estate investments since 1984 with the acquisition of 14 parcels of undeveloped land in the metro Phoenix area. Over the past five years these joint ventures have contributed more than $13 million to Sun State's pretax earnings.

"Some of these areas have been virtually ignored by the traditional savings and loans," says Gregory E. Janos, president and son of the founder. "We take a careful look at all our investment opportunities, but are not averse to pursuing a nontraditional route if it meets our qualifications. We pride ourselves on knowledge and service."

While its carefully delineated deposit and loan philosophy helped spearhead this thrift into prominence, its entrepreneurial employee base has provided the energy to realize the vision. Sun State actively searches out employees who are candid, resourceful, knowledgeable, and willing to go the extra mile. Explains Million, "Many Sun State people have run their own businesses, or have held top executive positions in other companies."

Although a variety of factors contribute to the growth of this remarkable savings and loan, chairman Janos is quick to credit Phoenix for Sun State's sustained increases. "The thrift's earnings are a direct result of the Phoenix area's thriving economy, particularly the real estate market," says Janos. "And our projections indicate the growth of this area will continue unabated."

Sun State Savings executives happily anticipate a new era for their young company. Observes Greg Janos, "You might say we've come of age—especially in the way we think about the company. Even recently we wouldn't have dreamed of competing head-to-head with some of the state's largest banks and savings and loans. Today we are doing just that."

Edward J. Janos, chief executive officer and chairman of the board of Sun State Savings. The real estate-based financial services company is one of the leading lenders in Phoenix.

COOPERS & LYBRAND

From its offices on the 25th floor of the Valley Bank Center, Coopers & Lybrand has an excellent view of the Phoenix scene. One of the world's largest accounting and consulting firms, Coopers & Lybrand opened its Phoenix office in 1960. Today this office includes more than 100 employees, all of whom, notes Michael J. Marrie, managing partner, take the Coopers & Lybrand commitment to heart. "C&L's commitment is taken very seriously," Marrie emphasizes. "It's not just words. We accept this as our mission statement."

The statement reads in part: "Our first commitment is to consistently maintain the high level of quality service our clients expect . . . We are committed to developing individual initiative and to helping our people fulfill their potential. Finally, we are committed to fostering a sense of teamwork among our people and with our communities."

These cornerstones—quality, individual initiatives, and teamwork—have characterized the firm since its founding in Philadelphia in 1898. Today Coopers & Lybrand is the third-largest accounting firm in the United States, with offices in nearly 100 cities and more than 500 offices in nearly 100 foreign countries. Providing a broad range of financial services to large and small clients, the worldwide team numbers 36,000 partners and staff.

In Phoenix, the C&L office consists of three disciplines: general practice, tax, and management consulting. "We stress being business advisers first and accountants second," says Marrie. "We try to make our clients self-sufficient." All three areas are growing rapidly, thanks in part to being located in such a high-growth center. "It's gratifying to live in a new city and be part of its growth and development," Marrie observes. "Professionally, the growth of the Phoenix area provides us with a lot of opportunities. It enables our staff to fully utilize their expertise, to provide more services, and to expand the partner group. Ultimately, we hope to add a fourth discipline—actuarial, benefits, and compensation consulting."

Marrie points out that the Phoenix business community is well serviced by the Emerging Business Services (EBS) approach of Coopers & Lybrand. This functional service provides expertise in accounting, tax, and business advisory services geared to growing businesses and high-potential start-up companies—a recognized need in a high-growth city. Tax planning, financial

Quality, individual initiative, and teamwork are promised to Coopers & Lybrand clients worldwide and fulfilled locally with the guidance of (from left) James E. Leonhard, partner; James J. Walsh, director of personnel; Charles R. Smith, manager; Stephen A. Clark, partner; Lori C. Mann, manager; and Bruce V. Bush, manager.

statement services, personal financial planning for key management, executive compensation and employee benefit plans, as well as mergers and acquisitions are just some of the services EBS provides.

Even during off-hours employees maintain their commitment. The firm has a long tradition of community action, Marrie notes. "We are involved in the Pace Setter program for the United Way campaign, and our entire office is actively involved in the community, from the Phoenix Art Museum to the Arizona Theatre Company to the American Diabetes Association. When we recruit new talent from Arizona State University, the University of Arizona, or Brigham Young University (three heavily recruited area schools), we look for those who have been very involved in campus activities. Then, as new staff, we expect them to keep up that level of involvement in our community. It's good for their personal development and it's good for Phoenix."

BLUE CROSS AND BLUE SHIELD OF ARIZONA

When the forerunner of Blue Cross and Blue Shield began operating in Arizona 50 years ago, Phoenix was still a wide-open town. The state was reeling under the effects of the Depression. Growth had slowed to 15 percent per year—the slowest increment in any decade in the century. Copper and cattle prices tumbled, and farm prices fell drastically. Private construction was at a near standstill. It was hardly an auspicious time for a new business.

Yet on February 23, 1939, the Blue Cross and Blue Shield Plan of Arizona began operating as the Associated Hospital Service of Arizona to bring the concept of prepaid medical care to residents of the state. In the ensuing 50 years the Plan grew with the state to become synonymous with health care insurance in Arizona.

As the largest health care insurance business in the state, Blue Cross and Blue Shield of Arizona is a not-for-profit corporation that provides health coverage to hundreds of thousands of individual and group subscribers. The company has also served as the fiscal intermediary for the Medicare program since its inception, processing Medicare Part A claims on behalf of Arizona's Medicare beneficiaries. Explains Robert B. Bulla, president and chief executive officer of Blue Cross and Blue Shield of Arizona, the Phoenix-based Plan is one of 77 Blue Plans around the country. Nationwide these organizations provide health coverage to more than 75 million Americans.

Blue Cross and Blue Shield of Arizona's current headquarters is located east of Interstate 17 near the Northern exit.

Today the Arizona Plan employs more than 500 people in the company's north Phoenix headquarters and additional staff in the Tempe, Flagstaff, and Tucson offices. Each regional office features its own electronic claims processing, which localizes customer service and spreads out volume that was previously handled only by the Phoenix headquarters. Together the offices process an average of 35,000 claims per week, paying upward of $170 million annually.

The Arizona Plan has branched out since the mid-1980s to incorporate a number of new services and products to meet a variety of needs for individuals of all ages as well as employer groups. HMO Arizona, the Plan's health maintenance organization, and Home Care Plus, a home-based long-term care plan, are just two of the many new products.

The Plan is dedicated to keeping close track of all the developments in medical technology. It also strives to maintain the proper balance between fees for medical providers and quality service to subscribers.

"Our attitude is to try to be the calm in the middle of the storm," Bulla points out. "We know that health care is a tremendously volatile marketplace. But we've been able to create new products and services, and be a positive stabilizing force for this changing industry, rather than just reacting to what's happening around us." Emphasizing that "everything we do is pointed toward the ultimate benefit of our subscribers," the executive notes that in the past few years the Plan added wellness and counseling programs, an HMO tied into a national network, and a number of other value-added services.

Although the success of the Blues can be measured in revenues generated and rising employment statistics, Bulla prefers to find satisfaction in the human arena. "We are in a business where what we do benefits individuals and families a great deal, physically and psychologically. That happens on a daily basis and that's rewarding to all of us at Blue Cross and Blue Shield of Arizona."

Striving for customer service excellence is a Blue Cross and Blue Shield of Arizona priority.

FRANZOY COREY ENGINEERS & ARCHITECTS

An engineering/architectural firm, Franzoy Corey is headquartered in Phoenix and provides start-to-finish services to its clients.

One of the largest engineering firms in Arizona with its corporate headquarters in-state is a sleeper. But Franzoy Corey Engineers & Architects likes it that way. With growth statistics that indicate a 35-percent increase in revenues for five straight years, the independent, privately owned engineering/architectural firm is assured that its name is well known in the circle in which it travels.

Those circles are wide and varied. Specialties include water resources, transportation, architecture, construction services, land development, water/wastewater, airports, agricultural engineering, and planning. "We are different in the Valley of the Sun," observes Fred C. Corey, president of Franzoy Corey. "It's unusual to find very many firms that offer both engineering and architecture under one roof."

He continues, "In 1978 we started out with seven people in Phoenix as a water resources firm offering both engineering and irrigation management services." The company originated in Arizona in 1971 with Eugene Franzoy, currently chairman of the board, as a branch office manager of a Nebraska-based engineering and architectural firm. "Today we are a multidisciplined entity with 110 employees, 7 directors, and 15 shareholders, specializing in providing the infrastructure for an expanding population. This includes

rural as well as urban growth," adds Franzoy.

With the opening of a civil engineering office in Phoenix in 1982, the acquisition of Lakin Architects, Inc., and the formation of FC Civil Engineering Company in 1983, the stage was set for a major consolidation. In 1985 the companies became reorganized as Franzoy Corey Engineers & Architects. While the firm had built its reputation on water resource expertise, having been involved in many water resource and irrigation development projects (both Indian and non-Indian) in its first in-state 10 years, the newly expanded company was poised to more totally serve the needs of a growing state and metropolitan area.

The staff of Franzoy Corey offers strength in several distinct disciplines. Each discipline is under the direction of a seasoned professional. N.W. "Bill" Plummer, director of water resources development and construction services, also oversees water resources business development. Robert Zicafoose is in charge of the airport and land development discipline. Mark Courtney heads up civil engineering, including roads and streets, water/wastewater, and public works. Earl

Tankersley is the head of the Support Services Group, which includes surveys and computer-aided drafting and design. James M. Lakin is in charge of the architectural disciplines, and Gary Parker manages the water resources disciplines, including hydrology and hydraulics.

Franzoy Corey has more than 1,200 man-years of experience in planning, investigation, design, construction, and implementation of development projects in the southwestern and midwestern United States. Principals of the firm have more than 200 man-years of experience. The engineering management staff, project managers, and division managers bring more than 300 man-years of experience.

The company provides clients with start-to-finish services—from conceptual studies through construction, and operation and maintenance of water resource developments. In addition to its engineering, planning, design, and construction disciplines, Franzoy Corey also assists clients with federal-, state-, and municipal-funded programs, and expert witness testimony at the state and federal levels. The Computer Support Group provides services for feasibility studies, site selections, design and construction, support software, and facilities management. In-house scheduling, budgeting, and project control are provided by the firm, which utilizes a critical path method (CPM) tracking system that ensures cost efficiency and timely schedules.

All divisions subscribe to the overall philosophy expressed in the company's mission statement: "Franzoy Corey's purpose is to provide the highest quality of diversified professional services and leadership in the engineering and architectural profession while maintaining profitable controlled growth, client satisfaction, a reputation for honesty and integrity, and a productive work environment. The company believes in fostering an environment of honest, clear, and open communication through a cooperative spirit of teamwork and training for self-improvement, which enhances employee positive self-image and a sense of security.''

Adds Corey, "Our management style is to care for our clients and our people. We lean toward participatory management and encourage cross-training within the company. In addition to technical seminars, we also make available personal seminars on nontechnical subjects. For instance, we put our entire firm through personal self-talk evaluations. We pride ourselves on trying to stay on top, and, as a result, we have received awards for our management style."

Staying on top has meant a subtle shift in emphasis from its water image to its present focus as a multidisciplined firm. The civil division is involved in the planning, design, and construction services for various municipal, county, and state roads and freeways, and water and wastewater facilities. The firm also has extensive experience in airport design for military, general aviation, and reliever airports.

Its architectural division encompasses both commercial and residential architecture with a special expertise in designing libraries, and operations and maintenance facilities for the Southwest. Typical services available include site and master land planning, innovative building design, architectural programming and system analysis, remodeling and rehabilitation, interior design, and park and recreational facilities development.

Wastewater collection and treatment projects utilize Franzoy Corey expertise in hydrology, hydraulics, and

The Franzoy Corey board of directors.

sanitary engineering. Services include major wastewater-collection systems, on-site wastewater-treatment facilities, resource recovery, sludge management, wastewater studies, pollution control, landfills, storm-drain systems, and flood-control systems.

In every project, professional services are provided through the careful selection of a project team from the various disciplines with a project manager, selected by the firm's principals, who exemplifies the technical and manage-

ment skills warranted for a project and client. This commitment to personal, excellent, professional service has secured Franzoy Corey Engineers & Architects a leading position in the engineering and architectural fields.

Below: Franzoy Corey engineers' expertise helps to bring water to Phoenix.

Bottom: The firm's civil division is involved in planning, design, and construction services for various municipal, county, and state roads and freeways.

JOHN CAROLLO ENGINEERS

John Carollo Engineers (JCE) has been providing consulting engineering services to cities, towns, municipalities, and industry since its beginning. John Carollo, a civil/sanitary engineer, joined Sam Headman and Ben Ferguson, electrical and mechanical engineers, to form Headman, Ferguson and Carollo in 1933. While JCE's major concerns were water and wastewater management, the partners were called upon to meet special needs during World War II and were actively engaged in the design and construction of defense facilities. In addition, John Carollo served as a major in the U.S. Army Sanitary Corps from 1943 to 1945, and earned the Legion of Merit Medal for outstanding contributions toward research in sanitation.

Peacetime brought growth for the Southwest, especially the city of Phoenix. The firm played a major role in this growth process by designing innovative civil engineering projects to solve water, wastewater, and other societal needs, while still protecting and enhancing the environment of the Southwest.

Several years after Headman's death in 1954, Ferguson left the firm to pursue other interests, and the company became known as John Carollo Engineers in 1957. John Carollo continued the high standards of engineering excellence that the firm had established during the previous decades. Until his untimely death in September 1971, Carollo gave personal attention to each project the firm undertook, passing along his engineering expertise and his knowledge of the Southwest to each new generation of engineers.

JCE's excellent reputation is carried on today by its current partners, assisted by associates and a technical staff of more than 100 in the Phoenix office. The firm has nearly 300 employees in all of its offices, which include Phoenix and Tucson, Arizona; and Fountain Valley, Walnut Creek, San Bernardino, and San Diego, California. *Engineering News Record* (ENR) ranks JCE as one of the top 500 design firms in the country.

Over the past half-century state-of-the-art technology in water and wastewater treatment has changed dramatically. At the forefront of this technology, JCE played a significant role in the Department of Health's decision to revise regulations regarding maximum permissible filtration rates for potable water. JCE later successfully installed the state's first high-rate dual-media filters, effectively doubling the potential filtration capacity of water treatment plants. More recently JCE has been a leader in the development and dissemination of information on the Arizona Environmental Quality Act.

Since its inception JCE has worked with the city of Phoenix to create water and wastewater treatment facilities to meet the growing area's demands, and has designed the initial phases of all of the city's water treatment plants: Verde, Squaw Peak, Deer Valley, Val Vista, and Union Hills.

Most recently JCE completed the Union Hills Water Treatment Plant, the first direct-filtration plant to be accepted for use in the State of Arizona. JCE is currently designing an 80-million-gallon-per-day expansion.

JCE has worked with the city of Phoenix, providing metropolitan wastewater treatment and disposal since 1958, when it designed the first 5-million-gallon-per-day trickling filter plant at a site in southwestern Phoenix at 91st Avenue and the Salt River. The concept was developed for a regional wastewater treatment plant serving the eight communities of the Southern Regional Operating Group.

In 1964 JCE designed a 45-million-gallon-per-day activated sludge plant at the 91st Avenue site, followed by a

The initial phase of all Phoenix water treatment plants, including this Union Hills facility in north Phoenix, has been designed by JCE.

15-million-gallon-per-day addition in 1968, another 30-million-gallon-per-day addition in 1975, a 30-million-gallon-per-day addition in 1979, and a 30-million-gallon-per-day addition in 1984, bringing the plant's capacity to 150 million gallons per day. JCE master planned the facility for 240 million gallons per day, and if growth in the valley continues at its present rate, major expansions of the facility can be expected every five years until the plant reaches its master-planned capacity.

The design of the 91st Avenue facility incorporates a number of energy-saving features, including high-efficiency motors, high-pressure sodium lighting systems that reduce energy consumption, a computer control system that minimizes energy use in major plant processes, and the use of waste digester gas to fire plant boilers.

Another special feature of the facility is the reuse of nearly 100 percent of its by-products. By use of a digester gas scrubbing system, digester gas is processed to pipeline quality and sold to a natural gas company for resale. Some effluent from the plant is piped to the Palo Verde Nuclear Power Plant and utilized as cooling water; some effluent irrigates nearby crop land; and some replenishes a nearby marshland wildlife habitat.

Influent and effluent lines grew with the plant. The Salt River Outfall was completed in 1962. The 99th Avenue interceptor sewer, carrying flow from the north, was finished in the late 1970s, and the Southern Avenue Interceptor (SAI), carrying flow from south of the Salt River, was completed in 1985.

Playing a major role in the SAI project, JCE performed routing studies and conceptual design for the proposed 20-mile, large-diameter sewer in 1981, and was ultimately responsible for the detailed design of one of the segments and the construction management for the entire project.

Continuing to play a role in the growth of the Phoenix Metropolitan Area by providing transportation engineering services, JCE recently completed the East Papago and Hohokam Expressways Corridor Location Study and Preliminary Design for the Arizona Department of Transportation (ADOT).

John Carollo Engineers is proud of its contributions to the growth and prosperity of the Phoenix metropolitan area and plans to continue its commitment to the valley by providing innovative solutions to the valley's engineering challenges.

Above: John Carollo Engineers provided the location study and preliminary design for the Hohokam and East Papago Expressway extensions in eastern Phoenix and northern Tempe.

Right: The 91st Avenue Wastewater Treatment Plant, designed by JCE, serves eight cities encompassed in the Southern Regional Operating Group (SROG).

JOHNSON & HIGGINS OF ARIZONA, INC.

In the middle of the nineteenth century, Henry Ward Johnson and Andrew Foster Higgins met with sea captains and shipowners to evaluate the risks that a ship's cargo would face on the open seas. Risks, in the mid-1800s, were defined as pirates, storms, and spoilage. More than 100 years later Johnson & Higgins representatives still evaluate risk as employees of the world's largest, privately owned network of consultants and insurance brokers. Today J&H provides clients worldwide with sophisticated risk management consulting, insurance brokerage, and employee benefit consulting services.

To the casual observer, the Arizona desert may seem a world away from the open seas, but to Johnson & Higgins, Phoenix was a logical expansion step. "Historically , J&H has opened branch offices in growing economic areas," explains Thomas F. Hartley, Jr., of Johnson & Higgins of Arizona, Inc.

"By the early 1970s the J&H office in Los Angeles was handling several Arizona-based clients. Therefore, the Phoenix branch was opened in 1974 to provide more localized services to those clients and provide growth opportunities for J&H in the rapidly expanding Arizona market. Since then we have brokered the property and liability insurance coverage for the Palo Verde Nuclear Generating Station, assisted Samaritan Health Services in establishing an offshore captive insurance company for professional liability coverage, placed special coverages for the Central Arizona Project, assisted the Arizona Biltmore in settling the insurance claim following its major fire, and provided a full range of our services to more than 200 other clients. As current valley businesses and public entities continue rapid growth and more corporations move their headquarters to this area, the opportunities for the J&H-Phoenix branch to serve their risk management and employee benefit needs will expand."

Since opening with five employees, the Phoenix branch has grown to more than 60 personnel and was the fastest growing of J&H's U.S. offices in 1987. J&H of Arizona is part of a network of 155 J&H offices that circle the globe. Forty-nine J&H offices exist in major cities in the United States, and 10 offices stretch coast to coast in Canada. Forty foreign offices and an additional 56 affiliates and exclusive correspondents in principal business and financial centers in 48 countries complete the Johnson & Higgins network.

Above all, the company prides itself on its client-oriented approach. It maintains a long legacy of excellence in

J&H personnel meeting with the Ramada risk management team (left to right): Loren Newland, Ramada; Ned Armstrong, Ramada; Tom Hartley, Johnson & Higgins; John Will, Ramada; Wayne Smith, Johnson & Higgins; and Ric Glover, Johnson & Higgins.

Ramada's Tropicana Hotel in Las Vegas, Nevada.

insurance brokerage and consulting. Because it remains a privately owned firm, Johnson & Higgins professionals are responsible to no one but J&H clients. Although the firm began business doing "average adjusting"—the sharing of losses from ships' cargoes—it quickly established an attitude of embracing change. Early on, Johnson & Higgins charted a course to meet clients' needs. That course has led it into some interesting waters and ports.

Most recently J&H has responded to the increasingly technological world of computerized analysis, modern communications, and global concerns by creating specialized departments. These include property, casualty, employee benefits, international, marine and aviation, and risk management services. Each client enjoys the benefit and support of a professional team approach while employing an account manager system that personalizes service. Because J&H clients have needs in many fields, the firm places the full resources of each of its departments and all of its offices at the disposal of every client.

A canal section of the Central Arizona Project.

J&H personnel visiting a pump station with the risk management team from Central Arizona Project. From left (standing): Tom Clark, C.A.P.; Bob Sedillo, Johnson & Higgins; Bernie Hynes, Johnson & Higgins; Mert Bean, Johnson & Higgins; and (seated) Pete Anthony, C.A.P.

Throughout its history the business philosophy of J&H has remained consistent: dedication to acting as an extension of its clients' own staffs. By offering an expert, steady, professional hand, J&H helps minimize risks and costs in an uncertain world. To that end, the firm has developed unparalleled resources to identify, analyze, and solve the unique problems of each client. Adds Hartley, "Because we represent the client, we offer an objective, independent opinion. We do not sell any company's products and we don't insure the risk ourselves. We are brokers in that we place insurance with companies that do accept the risk, but we are consultants in that we work for the client and assist with evaluating and implementing noninsurance solutions."

Working for the client takes many forms at J&H. In the multilinguistic world of international employee benefits, this can involve auditing of the existing programs of clients' foreign operations. Over the years J&H has perfected a questionnaire to assemble details on the design and funding of benefit programs in each country. As part of this program, it makes recommendations for specific local benefit plans, including cost calculations country by country, which are supported by surveys of competitive practices in the labor market. The J&H Risk Management Services Department helps solve risk management problems by means other than standard insurance. As part of its service, the department maintains liaison with the management of more than 125 captive insurance companies in Bermuda, the Cayman Islands, and the United States. The modern Marine and Aviation departments address the insurance needs of businesses transporting goods of every description, as well as passengers. Transportation takes many shapes: ship, tanker, and barge; plane, jumbo jet, and space shuttle; truck, train, and pipeline.

In its long history of service, J&H has become a dependable professional resource for its clients. Whether researching the complex and changing world of risk management, analyzing property insurance, planning for casualty insurance, or exploring the domestic and international realm of employee benefits, Johnson & Higgins of Arizona, Inc., is the voice of experience.

J&H personnel discussing the Palo Verde Nuclear Generating Station insurance program with members of the APS Risk Management Department (left to right): Fred Lindy, APS; Joel Bertuzzi, Johnson & Higgins; Norman Cocanour, APS; Graham Walker, Johnson & Higgins; and Jim Brackney, APS.

Palo Verde Nuclear Generating Station—operated by Arizona Public Service (APS).

BALMER ARCHITECTURAL GROUP, INC.

"Phoenix has an entrepreneurial spirit," says Wesley R. Balmer, president of Balmer Architectural Group, Inc., "and it is being expressed through development. Phoenicians relate to our growth and development as a symbol of the 'newness' many moved here to find."

This attitude has contributed to the dramatic impact Balmer Architectural Group has had on the valley. Land planning, corporate offices, retail, hotel, and industrial design are specialties of the company. "We are a hands-on firm, maintaining contact with our clients from preliminaries to post-completion," Balmer notes. "Our clients appreciate our intense interest in their projects, which is one reason we enjoy a solid repeat clientele base."

Satisfied clients include GTE, Ramada, and Quality Inns International. "One of our first projects was a 90,000-square-foot facility for Ingram Paper. Six years later we designed an addition to that building that more than doubled its size," Balmer explains. Valley growth and vitality, coupled with creative service, have led the Balmer Architectural Group to design such diverse projects as Mercado at Scottsdale Ranch, Paragon Corporate Center, and Suntech Business Park.

In response to the demand for quality space planning and attention to detail in high-end office complexes, the Balmer Interiors Group was established in 1986. Today interior designers and space planners share the same goals as the architectural division—to ensure quality and excellence, both inside and out.

"One of the things we enjoy most is working as a team member with a developer in transforming a large tract of urban land to marketable product," Balmer observes. An example is Suntech Village in Chandler, an award-winning, 80-acre, mixed-use project that includes patio homes, a medical complex, retail, and multifamily housing. "It's very exciting to work a concept all the way through, helping both the developer and the community create new ideas. Ultimately, we enjoy being part of something as positive as

building, and we respect that what we design will be here for a long, long time."

Flexibility and sensitivity have made Balmer Architectural Group, Inc., a leader in its field, and recognition has included five consecutive design awards from Tempe during the mid-1980s, and awards for design and master planning from the cities of Chandler and Phoenix.

Paragon Corporate Center, Phoenix. Photo by Mark Boisclair

Below: Quality Inns regional headquarters, Phoenix. Photo by Mark Boisclair

Bottom: Mercado del Lago, Scottsdale. Photo by Mark Boisclair

SUNBELT HOLDINGS, INC.

The story of Sunbelt Holdings, S.A., is one of vision and action. Formed in 1981 by Tor Andenaes as a sister company to The Andenaes Group of Oslo, Norway, Sunbelt has its roots in successful investment and development of property. Its U.S. subsidiary, Sunbelt Holdings, Inc., is headquartered in Phoenix.

An investment firm with assets principally in real estate, Sunbelt focuses its activities in the Southwest. The strategy of the company is clear cut: identify underutilized properties and, through the application of carefully considered and meticulously implemented strategies, elevate the value of the holdings.

Says Arthur Cunningham, vice-president/marketing, "Phoenix' diverse economic base and proactive attitude has contributed to and supported Sunbelt's success. The city's development of a climate to cultivate growth, and to attract new business and the relocation of businesses to the valley strengthens our projections for the future."

At present, Phoenix Gateway Center, a Sunbelt development that is one of the largest mixed-use projects in Phoenix, amply illustrates Sunbelt's approach to investments. Transportation is a key ingredient to all the company's holdings. The Phoenix Gateway Center, which is designed to contain more than 3.2 million square feet of premier office, hotel, and retail facilities, is located at the focal point of the valley's transportation system—just minutes from Sky Harbor International Airport. This same concept—keying real estate to transportation—is seen in additional holdings Sunbelt has in the East Valley and in Texas.

From its founding in 1981 in the Grand Duchy of Luxembourg to its Phoenix Sunbelt connection, Sunbelt Holdings, Inc., has moved confidently forward. Its story reflects the evolution of Phoenix, for it is an account of dramatic growth and dynamic success.

The amphitheater area between One and Two Gateway at the Phoenix Gateway Center was completed in 1985, and is utilized year round by tenants and various community organizations. Photo by Sue Bennett

Truly a landmark building, Three Gateway, the first 11-story mid-rise at the Phoenix Gateway Center, opened in August 1988. Photo by Jack Kustron

Sunbelt continues to plan for growth with investments such as southeast valley land acquisitions in Chandler, Arizona. Photo by Sue Bennett

LEWIS AND ROCA

Few major law firms have such unconventional beginnings as Lewis and Roca. In the late 1940s Phoenix was still a very new town. Orme Lewis, however, was old Arizona—his family having been in the state since the 1870s. A graduate of George Washington University College of Law, Lewis opened his law office in 1947 in Phoenix. Soon Paul Roca joined him. By 1949, when Harold Scoville, a former county attorney and superior court judge, joined them, the group formalized their arrangement.

On January 1, 1949, the three entered into what they called a "Declaration of Nonpartnership." As John P. Frank notes in *Lewis and Roca: A Firm History,* this document enabled the founding partners to pool their possessions, especially their collection of books. As the engagement proved successful, the partners "married" the following year, creating the foundation for one of Arizona's most prestigious law firms.

On June 1, 1950, Lewis, Roca and Scoville announced itself as a partnership. Nearly 40 years later that partnership flourishes as a premier, progressive, full-service law firm. More than 130 lawyers cover every specialty in business and litigation practice.

At Lewis and Roca, business and transactional work is organized into four main practice areas: real estate, corporate, tax, and finance. Within these practice areas, specialties include health care, environmental law, and bankruptcy. This structure is historically compatible with Lewis and Roca's interdisciplinary approach, and is based on the recognition that most modern business transactions demand a mix of specialties. This philosophy is essential when handling extremely sensitive and complex transactions such as the acquisition of the Phoenix Suns basketball team in 1987.

The real estate practice of the firm concentrates on transactional work, such as the acquisition and disposition of improved and unimproved real property, commercial and industrial leasing, and real property secured lending both for lenders and borrowers. This area in-

Orme Lewis. © 1983, Yousuf Karsh

cludes ongoing representation of developer clients, assisting them in planning residential and commercial projects, and drafting and negotiating development-related agreements with other developers, contractors, and governmental agencies. Lawyers prepare deed restrictions, reciprocal easement agreements, and residential property owners' associations.

In its tax practice, Lewis and Roca lawyers do corporate tax, exempt organizations, partnership tax, employee benefits, state and local taxation, and tax controversy work. They serve a variety of clients, from small emerging businesses to large, established, multistate corporate groups.

The specialty of corporate law includes transactional, securities, public finance, and general corporate work on behalf of private and public corporations in Arizona and elsewhere. The bulk of corporate work exists in the areas of securities, including private and public offerings; corporate transactions, including mergers, acquisitions, and reorganizations; and public finance, including bond counsel and issuers' counsel representation.

In the field of finance, Lewis and Roca lawyers represent major banks and finance companies in all areas of banking and commercial finance. The firm advises clients on state and federal compliance regulations, and the negotiation preparation of secured and unsecured loan documentation. Environmental and natural resources focuses on a variety of problems involving corporate counseling and litigation in areas that include protecting water rights, dealing with the recovery of damages for contamination, and defending corporations against governmental enforcement actions regarding compliance with the environmental laws. Corporate counseling is increasingly important in this field of law.

Lewis and Roca's litigation practice supports and complements all aspects of its wide-ranging business and transactional work, while at the same time providing other forms of full-service litigation. As with the transactional work, Lewis and Roca's litigators often follow an interdisciplinary approach, recognizing that many types of litigation involve a wide array of subject matters.

The corporate and commercial litigation encompasses traditional commercial contractual disputes, such as those arising under various articles of the Uniform Commercial Code or in real estate disputes. However, much of it involves highly specialized types of commercial matters, including franchise litigation, corporate disputes, securities matters, natural resource questions, and health care. It also involves business litigation between corporate and commercial parties such as antitrust, intellectual property, and trade practices disputes. The firm has been among the leaders in the Southwest in developing expertise in defending and prosecuting complex business wrongs, including securities, RICO, and shareholder derivative claims. These matters arise not only in courts but before state and federal regulatory agencies.

Lewis and Roca has a large, fully developed labor and employment practice. In those areas the firm represents both private- and public-sector entities.

The firm also provides a full construction law litigation practice. The problems involved cover all aspects of disputes that arise during the represen-

The four-foot-tall brass-and-marble scale has graced the main reception lobby since the early 1970s. The scale was purchased by Paul Roca while on a business trip to San Diego. Orme Lewis discovered the complete set of weights in an antique shop in Chicago while on a business trip. Photo by Gary DiBartolomeo

tation of major private and public construction. Lewis and Roca represents construction clients at both the state and federal administrative level, as well as in courts of general jurisdiction.

Traditionally Lewis and Roca has also engaged in a fulltime criminal practice. This long-established criminal expertise has become more and more important as various enforcement agencies vigorously prosecute a wide array of commercial and corporate matters. These problems encompass tax disputes, investigations by various regulatory agencies, as well as more traditional criminal work.

The litigation practice is not limited to these corporate and commercial areas, however. It is a leader in workers' compensation and products liability. Likewise, Lewis and Roca is involved in many complex and difficult personal injury and professional malpractice matters and attendant insurance problems that arise in those kinds of cases.

Lewis and Roca has a history of commitment to being on the leading legal edge. It was the first major firm to break the employment barrier and recruit women in 1969. As early as 1970 it hired paralegals. Before this was mandated, Lewis and Roca believed that lawyers should contribute to the improvement of the law and the legal system. It has been the most active single office in the state since 1955 in keeping the civil and appellate procedural rules of the Supreme Court current with the best thinking of the state and the country. Public service at Lewis and Roca often means hands-on labor. Lawyers serve on civic as well as professional boards. Above all, the firm values diversity. To this end, it maintains its original spirit. Who would have imagined that from a Declaration of Nonpartnership such a passionate legal history would emerge?

Lewis and Roca's circular brass stairway was designed by Taliesen Associated Architects. Courtesy, Frank Lloyd Wright Foundation

CYCARE SYSTEMS

CyCare Systems is under the guidance of James D. Dyer (left), president, and Jim Houtz, chairman, chief executive officer, and founder.

While the nation worries over the escalating cost of health care, a company headquartered in Phoenix has a solution. According to James D. Dyer, president of CyCare Systems, manipulating information (what is called clerical medicine) represents a significant portion of the nation's health care tab. But Dyer does more than diagnose the problem, he also proposes a cure—CyCare Systems.

Founded by Jim Houtz in 1967 in Dubuque, Iowa, as Computer Consulting Service, CyCare is one of the nation's leading providers of physician group practice information management systems. Employing more than 1,400 people in 20 offices across the country, CyCare serves more than 5,500 clients nationwide, ringing up sales of nearly $100 million annually.

Early on Houtz pinpointed that the processing of information for the health care industry would be CyCare's niche. He quickly established a policy of acquiring small regional firms that would aid him in both serving and seeking his chosen client base. By the time the company went public in 1981, CyCare was writing software and reselling hardware. The first vendor to offer patient scheduling and a full range of processing options, CyCare soon developed a broad marketing base.

By 1984 the firm was growing at a rate of 37 percent per year. But onetime system sales were representing roughly 60 percent of total revenue. Houtz decided to shift direction. Recognizing new opportunities in the health care industry, Houtz began to reposition CyCare. The operation expanded into the health maintenance organizations (HMO) market, while at the same time acquiring companies that would strengthen its position in the practice management market and enable CyCare to enter the hospital inpatient care market as well.

Its decision to get into the full hospital information system product line was a critical strategic move—but one that will pay off handsomely. It also reaffirms CyCare's philosophy, which is to serve that set of institutions that wishes to lay out a plan to bring its information systems together and into operation as an integrated unit that offers a total institutional solution rather than as several scattered pieces.

The market leader since 1981 in information management systems to group practices, CyCare has consolidated its management, marketing, and accounting teams in Phoenix. CyCare maintains its Dubuque facility as a corporate information center. This center, which processes more than 12 percent of all U.S. physicians' bills, makes CyCare the largest post office in the state of Iowa.

The CyCare story is enhanced by its statistics. In recent years the firm has sustained a 30-percent growth rate while emphasizing profitability. But numbers are only a part of the picture. People make CyCare special—specifically people with entrepreneurial spirit. As Houtz explains, "Rather than having a company that is led by an entrepreneur, we have a company that is a collection of entrepreneurs, each trying to build new products and marketing programs in their own spheres of influence."

People, product, and service give CyCare Systems its competitive edge.

CyCare Systems, one of the leading providers of physician group practice information management systems, is headquartered at 44th Street and East Camelback Road.

CHASE BANK OF ARIZONA

Chase Bank of Arizona, with one billion dollars in assets and 500 employees, is the fifth-largest bank in Arizona. A wholly owned subsidiary of Chase Manhattan Corporation, Chase Bank of Arizona was created October 2, 1986, when Chase Manhattan Corporation acquired Continental Bancorp of Arizona, the holding company for Continental Bank.

The advent of Arizona's interstate banking legislation made it possible for Chase Manhattan Corporation, with approximately $100 billion in assets, to expand its national banking efforts and bring the resources of a global bank to the Arizona marketplace.

Chase Bank of Arizona combines the personal attention and service of a small bank with the global resources of its parent corporation, while building on the strengths of its predecessor. Continental Bank, successful for 40 years, was well known for its mortgage financing and commercial real estate expertise. Chase Bank of Arizona has utilized this foundation to become one of the state's top mortgage lenders.

Chase Bank of Arizona offers a wide array of banking products and services such as checking and savings accounts, as well as unique investment, mortgage, and business banking products.

Within its first year of operation Chase Bank of Arizona became a financial product innovator with such investment products as the Market Index Investment Account, which gives customers an opportunity to make investments tied to the stock market without risking their principal; Vista Mutual Funds, which offer a choice of eight no-load (no commission charged) mutual funds; and the Self-Directed Certificate of Deposit, which gives customers a choice of a fixed or variable interest rate. Chase also has a private bank that provides first-class solutions to meet the financial needs of customers who require highly specialized financial services.

The bank also has an extensive corporate lending and finance division as well as a unique capital markets division, staffed with officers experienced in employee stock option plans, private placements, and mergers and acquisitions.

To better serve its customers, Chase Bank of Arizona has expanded its service with the Chase Convenience Banking Center, giving customers 24-hour telephone access to account information. The telephone-based unit is staffed with professionals who offer product and service information during the business day and extended evening hours. In addition, individuals can have access to their checking and savings accounts by using a Chase 24-Hour Bank Card, MasterCard, or Chase Visa Bank Card. Chase Bank of Arizona is part of the PLUS system, an automated-teller-machine network that gives customers access to their accounts throughout the United States, in Canada, and in selected foreign locations.

Chase Bank of Arizona, built on strong local, national, and international banking resources; a tradition of excellent service; and a commitment to meeting the needs of its customers, plays a leading role in the financial services market in Arizona.

Below: Chase Bank of Arizona combines the personal attention and service of a local bank with the global resources of its parent company, Chase Manhattan Corporation.

Bottom: The Chase Bank of Arizona Financial Center administrative offices. The bank, a subsidiary of Chase Manhattan Corporation, is the fifth largest in Arizona.

FENNEMORE CRAIG

The law firm of Fennemore Craig reflects both the past and the present in Arizona, both its history and its modern-day growth. To mark the celebration of 100 years of continuous existence, the firm shortened its name from Fennemore, Craig, von Ammon, Udall and Powers and moved into new offices in downtown Phoenix. These changes were not the result of any dissatisfaction by members of the firm, but rather emphasized the firm's commitment to grow and change to meet new demands for legal services while maintaining its traditional standards of practice. The relocation of the firm's offices to the Renaissance Square project also evidenced the firm's participation in the development of downtown Phoenix.

The law firm that has ultimately become Fennemore Craig was formed in early 1885 by Louis H. Chalmers and Richard E. Sloan. Its offices came to be located at 100 West Washington Street in Phoenix, now the site of the First Interstate Bank of Arizona building, in which the firm maintained offices for several years before the recent move. By 1912, the year Arizona was granted statehood, the firm had built a practice involving major clients in industries instrumental in the state's early development—mining, railroads, banking, and transportation.

The firm's name—Fennemore Craig—derives from Harry Fennemore, who arrived in Arizona in 1912 as an attorney for the newly formed Mountain States Telephone and Telegraph Company, and Jubal Early Craig, who joined the firm in 1927 and continued as a partner and partner emeritus until his death in 1974, shortly before his 100th birthday.

Fennemore Craig's location provides direct access to the state and federal courts; city, county, and state government offices; and the financial, business, and development sectors of the city. The firm also has an office located in the heart of Scottsdale, Arizona, to serve the thriving real estate and commercial enterprises in that city and in the east half of the valley. Over the past 10 years, the firm has grown dramatically from 30 lawyers to approximately 120. The firm is organized as a professional corporation, consisting of director-shareholders and associate lawyers. It employs a sizable staff of legal assistants, many of whom have previous experience in such areas as nursing, zoning, or probate.

Fennemore Craig has a long-standing tradition of devoting substantial effort to public and professional service. During the past three decades members of the firm have served as president and members of the Board of Governors and House of Delegates of the American Bar Association; president and members of the Board of Governors of the State Bar of Arizona; and president and members of the Board of Directors of the Maricopa County Bar Association. Lawyers in the firm serve on committees, sections, and Young Lawyers groups for the ABA, the state bar, and the county bar.

With respect to community service, Fennemore Craig encourages its lawyers to contribute and to participate in numerous ways. Numerous types of pro bono representation are pursued, ranging from time informally donated to community organizations to formal programs operated by the State Bar of Arizona and the courts. Firm lawyers serve as board members or on advisory committees for state and local governments, school districts, nonprofit foun-

On the left of this 1902 photo is 100 West Washington and on the right is the future site of One Renaissance Square, the present home of Fennemore Craig.

A panoramic view of the city of Phoenix provides a spectacular backdrop for the offices of Fennemore Craig at One Renaissance Square. Pictured is the main reception area.

dations, arts and cultural organizations, neighborhood or home owners associations, and service groups.

Fennemore Craig has been fortunate over the years to serve a distinguished and diverse clientele. The firm is proud to have been associated for several decades with major clients who have played key roles in Arizona's development, including railroad, telecommunications, mining, and lumber and wood-products companies. The firm also serves as counsel to automotive and related companies, manufacturing enterprises, real estate development organizations, and contractors. Insurance clients include life and health, property, casualty, malpractice, and title insurers. Other business clients are involved in areas of substantial growth, such as health care, banking and financial services, high technology and computers, and investment partnerships. The firm's individual clients are equally diverse, ranging from small-business owners facing regulatory problems to investors with substantial assets or retirees who require thorough estate and tax planning.

Fennemore Craig provides a full civil and business practice for its clients. Litigation matters range from complex litigation to small business claims, and from agency proceedings or lower court matters to extensive trial and appellate advocacy. Business matters may vary from relatively simple contract or lease drafting and interpretation to delicate and complicated financial or commercial transactions. The firm provides advice and representation of the same caliber as other large national and metropolitan firms, and at the same time offers expertise in state and local matters.

In the commercial and real estate areas, Fennemore Craig's representation and services include commercial and consumer banking; loan and conveyance closings and document preparation; lease negotiation and analysis; partnerships and syndications; natural resources, water, and environmental matters; public lands; creditors' rights and trustee's sales; secured transactions; and construction contracts and performance.

In tax and corporate law, the firm offers a wide range of representation and advice, such as incorporation; securities and bonds; franchises; pension and profit sharing; employment and labor matters; mergers, acquisitions, liquidations, and reorganizations; limited partnerships, S corporations, and nonprofit and exempt organizations; tax and business planning, tax litigation; and estate planning and probate.

Examples of the firm's litigation practice areas are personal injury and products liability; medical and legal malpractice, design liability, and bad faith; toxic and hazardous substance cases; aviation law, business torts, and property and casualty claims; antitrust and trade regulation; labor litigation, including NLRA, OSHA, workers' compensation, and wrongful discharge; utilities; environmental and natural resources; real estate, probate, and tax litigation; administrative and legislative practice; and zoning matters.

Fennemore Craig has grown along with the city of Phoenix and the practice of law in Arizona, yet it also strives to maintain a sense of tradition, a perception of Phoenix and its life-style tempered by history. Despite its growth, Fennemore Craig still values professionalism in the practice of law and the wisdom and experience of its senior lawyers. Now in its second century of legal practice, the firm looks forward to its continued association with the city of Phoenix with pleasure and enthusiasm.

EVANS, KITCHEL & JENCKES

Step off the elevator into the offices of Evans, Kitchel & Jenckes, and you sense the presence of Arizona history. Located on the top three floors of the 20-story Phelps Dodge Tower, Evans, Kitchel & Jenckes' suites are warm with wood paneling and accented with interior decor in the federal style. The style and the mood are ideal for this firm, which traces its roots to the days when Arizona was a territory and Bisbee the center of commercial activity.

Although Evans, Kitchel & Jenckes is the contemporary signature of this Phoenix firm, its history originated with two Bisbee lawyers, Everett Ellinwood and John Mason Ross. On June 29, 1910, Ellinwood and Ross, graduates of the University of Michigan and Stanford University, announced their association for the practice of law in the *Bisbee Daily Review.*

Today the firm's practice in business planning, civil litigation, and real estate is complemented by its special expertise in government relations, labor, finance, banking, taxation, estate planning, bankruptcy, public utilities, environmental, natural resources, water, and health care law. At least one of the firm's 75 lawyers is familiar with most areas of law affecting businesses.

More than 3,000 companies—from closely held family partnerships to multinational and *Fortune* 500 corporations—are clients of Evans, Kitchel & Jenckes. The firm's Phoenix and Scottsdale offices provide clients with ready access to its eight decades of legal and business experience.

From his vantage point of a 35-year association with the firm, senior partner James M. Bush notes, "We have done more in the environmental area than anyone else in Arizona. Our association with clients such as Phelps Dodge goes back years and years." Observing that the firm's natural resources practice is the state's oldest, Bush commented that Evans, Kitchel & Jenckes

Clients are greeted by the warmth of the federal-style decor in Evans, Kitchel & Jenckes' reception area, which is in keeping with a law firm that traces its roots to the days when Arizona was a territory.

has long had a prominent voice in shaping and applying mining and water laws on both the state and federal level. In recent years, he added, the firm has taken an active role in drafting the Water Quality Act for Arizona, one of the toughest clean water laws in the nation. Clients of the firm have interests in mining, surface and groundwater rights, mineral leasing, and public and Indian land purchases, sales, trades, and use rights.

Evans, Kitchel & Jenckes has been active in the field of government affairs on other fronts as well. One of the firm's founding partners was a delegate to Arizona's Constitutional Convention. Another served on the historic Colorado River Commission. Bush directs the firm's government relations practice and has served on a number of legislative commissions and task forces to deal with problems of taxation, education, and health care as well as water and environmental matters. Evans, Kitchel & Jenckes recently became the first law firm in Arizona to retain on staff a nonlawyer public affairs executive, who has a background of international, national, and state government relations experience and service as an executive for a major multinational corporation.

In addition to its expertise in environmental and water law, the firm also maintains an active practice in commercial law, litigation, corporate finance, and banking. Businesses nationwide present Evans, Kitchel & Jenckes with a mix of finance, securities, and banking issues that require the creation of manageable and profitable solutions. The firm's corporate lawyers advise clients on a variety of financing devices available to expand or further capitalize their enterprises, including public securities offerings, private placements, tax-exempt financing, credit agreements, acquisition financing, project financing, leveraged leasing, and interest exchange of currency swap agreements. The firm also handles prototype venture-capital transactions and the structuring of tax-exempt notes to finance pollution-control projects. In addition, it has participated in Eurodollar loan agreements with several money center banks.

The firm provides its clients with advice in partnership and shareholder disputes in corporate control matters. Evans, Kitchel & Jenckes has successfully managed shareholder control disputes in both large publicly held corporations and small closely held businesses. The firm also counsels boards of directors and corporate management on legal issues, including director and officer liability and personal indemnification.

Evans, Kitchel & Jenckes has an extensive and well-established trial practice. More than one-third of the firm's lawyers devote their time and energy to litigation. The firm's experience includes trials and appeals at every level of state and federal courts.

The firm's commercial litigators handle cases involving construction, securities, and real estate. It has a well-developed litigation practice in corporate and partnership law, mining and natural resources law, environmental matters, labor and employment law, public utilities, and taxation matters.

Insurance companies are regular clients of the firm in the expanding area of bad faith litigation, defense of accident, health and life insurance claims, and in cases involving coverage disputes. The firm's personal injury practice includes the defense of product liability and medical malpractice cases, as well as the representation of self-insured employers in workers' compensation litigation.

Evans, Kitchel & Jenckes is concerned about the expense and cost effectiveness of modern litigation. The firm works with clients to minimize the cost of legal proceedings and, where possible, seeks alternatives to litigation as a means of resolving disputes. The firm is accustomed to preparing action plans and litigation budgets when requested by clients.

Evans, Kitchel & Jenckes' real estate lawyers advise domestic and international clients involved in the purchase, sale, and development of property in Phoenix, throughout Arizona, and across the Southwest. The firm's clients include owners of ranch and agricultural properties, shopping centers, high-rise office buildings, garden offices, industrial facilities, and entire town sites, as well as developers of resorts, convention centers, condominiums, apartment complexes, and planned residential communities.

Evans, Kitchel & Jenckes advises

Senior partners James M. Bush (left) and Edward C. LeBeau have spent their entire legal careers with Evans, Kitchel & Jenckes and practice in the areas of government relations and real estate law, respectively.

clients on federal, state, and local taxation issues. The firm's tax lawyers are well versed in planning clients' business transactions to minimize the impact of such taxes. Its tax lawyers also assist clients preparing for tax audits and litigating tax issues.

Employers in many different industries consult Evans, Kitchel & Jenckes on a comprehensive range of employment and labor law issues. In addition, the firm's public utility clients include producers and distributors of electricity, water, and natural gas, as well as wastewater service companies, telephone and other telecommunications concerns, and commercial and industrial users of public utility services. The firm provides representation in rate cases, financing approvals, certificate proceedings, and general administrative matters before the Arizona Corporation Commission and other regulatory agencies, as well as in utility litigation matters. The firm's transportation clients include railroads, trucking companies, aviation interests, and automobile manufacturers.

Evans, Kitchel & Jenckes' bankruptcy practice is structured to provide the information and advice necessary for informed decisions in this difficult area. Clients in this field include lenders, lessors, trustees, and other creditors.

Nearly 80 years after Ellinwood and Ross founded the firm, Evans, Kitchel & Jenckes continues its rich tradition of service to clients and dedicated leadership to the community.

DWL ARCHITECTS + PLANNERS, INC.

While riding the train from his hometown in Barrington, Illinois, Richard E. Drover, founder and current board chairman of DWL Architects + Planners, Inc., never envisioned the sophisticated, energetic design firm that has evolved during four decades. "Who would have predicted that the valley would grow from an unsuspecting 100,000 to 2 million people?" says Lawrence E. Metcalf, DWL's executive vice-president. "This fortuitous combination of economic growth and of two talented individuals laid the groundwork for DWL."

The DWL legacy began in 1949, when Drover joined Frederick P. Weaver to found Weaver & Drover Architects. In 1969 the company reorganized as Drover, Welch & Lindlan Architects, and made its current transition to DWL in 1984. What began as a partnership involved in residential design launched one of the most respected architectural planning firms in the Southwest.

The group's success is illustrated in many familiar buildings throughout Arizona. From industrial environments and community developments to office buildings, both commercial and municipal, DWL's creations make up some of the region's most beautiful marriages of site and structure. In addition, the firm's 15 years of experience in the health care market have made it one of

Sun Devil Stadium's South Entrance Expansion—Arizona State University, Tempe.

the top health care designers in the country.

Now recognized throughout the West, DWL has expanded its services on a regional basis. From the Aleutian chain in Alaska to the Colorado Mountains and the Gulf Coast of Texas, there is evidence of its notable achievements.

The Phoenix-based firm is composed of architects, planners, and interior designers with diverse but complementary backgrounds. "Our team approach to project management allows the assignment of personnel with exactly the right qualifications for each client's specific needs," says James F. Lindlan, president of DWL. With four active principals, management provides strength in all activities, including planning, design, production, and construction.

DWL's research-oriented approach has paved the way to completing a significant number of firsts in the Phoenix metropolitan area. The company designed the first drive-in bank,

the first radiation oncology unit, and the first inpatient and outpatient dialysis units.

In conjunction with its exceptional innovations, DWL is also associated with projects that are significant in size and have unusual characteristics: Arizona State University Activity Center, one of the largest assembly areas in the state; the ASU campus pedestrian mall system; the largest parking garage in the city of Phoenix; Sky Harbor International Airport Terminal Three; and projects such as Terminal Four at Sky Harbor, which will be completed in 1990.

Difficult and unusual projects are welcome challenges at DWL, where "Architecture is a problem-solving process to environmental issues," says Carleton W. Van Deman, principal responsible for design. Through this and other philosophical values, and its organizational framework, the company has maintained a reputation for success. "Our recognition of the value of art in architecture and of the extreme importance of aesthetic considerations give substance and guidance to our approach to design," says Lindlan.

DWL Architects + Planners, Inc., bestows its architectural expertise on one of the nation's fastest-growing metropolises. Echoing the optimistic sentiments of the firm's staff, operations vice-president Michael L. Haake says, "We are proud to be a part of and have an impact on Phoenix' future growth."

DWL Architects + Planners, Inc., designed the Phoenix Sky Harbor International Airport Terminal Four, which will be completed in 1990.

ROBERSON AND COMPANY

One of the oldest recruiting and placement firms in Arizona, Roberson and Company was founded in 1967 by Jack V. Roberson, a certified public accountant. After operating his own personnel firm and C.P.A. practices, he formed his new recruiting company to address what he saw as a growing demand for a professional personnel consulting firm specializing in accounting and executive positions. As the company grew, it widened its focus into the administrative, manufacturing, health care, sales, and technical fields.

The staff is composed of former business executives, all of whom have a high degree of expertise in the field that they service. As a result, Roberson and Company's clientele is among the most prestigious in Arizona.

To position itself in this dynamic marketplace, Roberson and Company has adopted a successful service strategy. Response time to customer requests is continually scrutinized; project implementation is emphasized; and ongoing training assures that the staff maintains the expertise needed to provide all clients with first-class service. In addition, the firm sends out a monthly newsletter, the *Roberson Review.* Thousands of Arizona business people receive this publication, which helps to keep the entire business community abreast of human resource activities. This newsletter also includes profiles of some of the firm's qualified

The recent move to 1300 East Missouri is part of a commitment by Roberson and Company to grow with the valley.

applicants.

The company places a priority on understanding the applicant's needs, skills, and chemistry. It also spends as much time as necessary with the client firm to ascertain what type of individual is best suited to each business or professional environment. This method has proven so effective that the organization offers a one-year warranty on every placement.

Since its inception in the mid-

The professional staff of Roberson and Company provides a high degree of expertise to its clients. Pictured (from left) are Ursula Cunneen, Don Shively, Stephen D. Silvas, Richard Van Waes, and Jean Anne Silvas.

1960s, Roberson and Company has established an impressive history of successful recruitment, evaluation, and placement of thousands of skilled personnel. Ethics is a major force behind the firm's growth.

In June 1987 Stephen D. Silvas became president of Roberson and Company. Silvas brings to the firm an extensive background in administration, as well as the human resource and technical disciplines. With him the management team plans to continue expanding the organization to better serve the growing Phoenix community. Roberson and Company's move in 1988 to larger offices at 1300 East Missouri is evidence of this commitment to support the needs of clients and grow with the valley.

Dedicated to integrity and professional competence, Roberson and Company today prides itself on its ability to provide state-of-the-art service to the Phoenix area. But serving its clients is only part of the success equation. Roberson and Company actively supports various professional, business, economic development, and community organizations. By generously giving back to the population it serves, the firm positively impacts the entire community.

BROWN & BAIN

Brown & Bain combines an international reputation for its expertise in the protection of intellectual property, particularly in the semiconductor and computer hardware and software industries, with a commitment to its Arizona and regional clients in commercial banking, real estate, securities, tax and transactional work, as well as litigation. The firm's dedication to providing work of uncompromising quality has led to representation of many leading and emerging companies in Arizona, California, and throughout the Southwest. Founded in 1960, the firm has a total of 95 lawyers in its two offices in Phoenix and Palo Alto, California.

Among the Arizona companies that the firm currently represents are Citibank (Arizona), the Metropolitan Bank, Burns International, Universal Development Corporation, Babbitt Brothers Trading Company, Holsum Bakery, Chandler Regional Hospital, and Edgcore Technology. In addition, Brown & Bain represents national clients such as Apple Computer, IBM, Intel, Unisys, United Technologies, and many other *Fortune* 500 companies. The firm also enjoys a growing media law practice, including representation of the *Arizona Republic,* the *New Times,* the *Mesa Tribune,* and the *Scottsdale Progress.*

The phenomenal economic growth in Arizona, particularly in the Phoenix metropolitan area and in California's Silicon Valley, has been a major at-traction for investors worldwide and thus, a catalyst for the development of the firm's corporate practice. Brown & Bain's corporate department is organized informally into specialty practices, including mergers and acquisitions, corporate and public finance, banking, bankruptcy and commercial transactions, tax, real estate, and health care.

Arizona and California are among the first states to permit interstate banking, and the firm recently represented Great Western Bank & Trust, a major regional bank, in its merger with Citicorp. Brown & Bain also has represented several national firms purchasing companies in the Southwest, including a subsidiary of Ashland Oil in its $150-million purchase of Tanner Southwest, Inc. Other recent merger and acquisition work has involved Arizona's most successful chain of retail and grocery stores, a microelectronics manufacturing firm, several financial institutions, an equipment leasing company, a mining and chemical company, a hospital, transportation companies, a nonprofit country club, and a chain of recreational centers.

Brown & Bain has represented a number of issuers in both the public offering and private placement of securities. For example, the firm recently

---

Jack Brown, name partner and senior member of the firm.

completed the initial public offering of International Leisure Enterprises, a major resort development company. In addition, the firm is among those nationally recognized and qualified to serve as bond counsel in connection with the issuance of tax-exempt obligations.

Brown & Bain regularly counsels high-technology start-up companies regarding various business matters and may assist such entrepreneurial ventures in obtaining needed capital from venture capitalists and other private and public sectors. The firm also drafts and helps negotiate technology development and license agreements for Arizona companies such as Alpha-Graphics, Edgcore Technology, Talley Industries, The Western Design Center, and others, as well as national companies such as Apple Computer.

For nearly two decades the firm has represented Citibank (Arizona) and its predecessor in its lending, enforcement, and workout transactions. The firm also serves as general counsel to the Metropolitan Bank. Other commercial and banking clients include Borg Warner Acceptance Corporation, Continental Illinois, First National Bank of Chicago, Manufacturers Hanover, and Morgan Guaranty. The firm's work for such clients includes counseling concerning commercial paper, lien priorities and security interests, bank regulatory, and other commercial matters. The firm also prosecutes and defends commercial disputes that may arise in these areas and represents entities, primarily creditors, involved in bankruptcy proceedings.

In growing metropolitan areas such as Phoenix and Palo Alto, the development of real estate is an essential and highly visible activity. Brown & Bain has represented several of Arizona's most active developers of commercial, residential, and resort properties. Among the recent real estate matters handled by the firm are the representation of parties engaged in the sale of a 4,000-acre parcel to developers of a proposed planned community in a complex transaction involving consideration in excess of $80 million; the

proposed development of a 50,000-acre planned community involving esoteric financing, water, and real considerations; the acquisition and syndication of a historic Colorado lodge and adjacent properties with a view to the development of a time-share program; and other projects, including real estate syndications, the purchase of apartment units valued at approximately $30 million, and the development of office complexes throughout Arizona.

Many of the firm's corporate clients benefit from an integrated approach to transactions that combines the efforts of lawyers from different practice areas. For example, Brown & Bain's real estate and banking groups recently coordinated, without resorting to burdensome Chapter 11 proceedings, the special reorganization of one of the largest home builders in Arizona and Colorado. The firm has been responsible for restructuring $80 million in secured indebtedness owed to approximately 15 different lending institutions, for selling or raising equity capital in numerous parcels of developed and undeveloped land, and in satisfying $4 million in mechanic's lien claims and trade payables held by nearly 200 different creditors.

Brown & Bain's national reputation for excellence in litigation rests largely on the firm's record of mastering complex facts and diverse disciplines and technologies. The work of Brown & Bain lawyers recently has ranged from probing almost metaphysical questions about the nature of computer microcode (on behalf of Intel) to constructing econometric models in a complex plaintiff's antitrust damages case to studying cultural anthropology and prehistoric archaeology (in connection with its continuing representation of the Navajo Tribe) to conducting a detailed analysis of Arizona's system of indigent health care.

The firm regularly prosecutes and defends trade secret suits and advises high-technology companies with respect to the protection of their proprietary information. The firm has served as counsel in such matters to IBM, Apple Computer, General Instrument,

Randy Bain, name partner and senior member of the firm.

Intel, Zilog, Unisys, ROLM, and many others. Most recently Brown & Bain has litigated cases for such corporations in Massachusetts, Pennsylvania, New Jersey, Texas, Florida, Delaware, Maine, Ohio, and Oregon, as well as California and Arizona. Some of the cases handled by the firm in this area include prosecution of actions on behalf of Apple Computer establishing the copyrightability of operating system software and audiovisual displays and to halt the sale of personal computers containing unlawfully copied versions of the Apple operating system, and the prosecution of actions on behalf of General Instrument, Home Box Office, and Showtime/The Movie Channel to protect the satellite distribution of television programming.

Brown & Bain has been active in prosecuting and defending antitrust cases. For example, the firm represented Fairchild Camera and Instrument Corporation and was lead counsel for all plaintiffs in the multidistrict cases against Data General Corporation that successfully challenged the unlawful tie-in of computers to computer software. After reinstatement by the court of appeals for the Ninth Circuit of a jury verdict in Fairchild's favor, Data General, to avoid a damages trial, paid $52.5 million to Fairchild.

In recent years the firm has devoted increasing resources to securities litigation and to the defense of corporate officers and directors in shareholder derivative and class action suits.

At present the firm is assisting in the prosecution of a securities fraud action on behalf of Chemical Bank as trustee for purchasers of bonds in the face amount of $2.25 billion issued by the Washington Public Power Supply System to finance two defunct nuclear power plants.

The firm has earned a national reputation for its work in defense of the media's First Amendment rights and in prosecution of suits to ensure freedom of information and access to government. In 1984 Sigma Delta Chi, the society of professional journalists, presented Brown & Bain with its National First Amendment Award "in recognition of [the firm's] strong and continuing efforts to preserve and strengthen freedom of the press and the First Amendment."

Most recently, the firm participated as co-counsel in prosecuting the impeachment charges against former Governor Evan Mecham for "high crimes, misdemeanors, and malfeasance in office." Brown & Bain presented the charges to the Arizona Senate in a trial that lasted six weeks and resulted in the first impeachment conviction of a governor in 59 years. The landmark senate trial was carried on live television throughout Arizona and was given substantial attention by the national and international media as well.

YOUNG, SMITH & PEACOCK, INC.

Positioned in one of the most dynamic areas of the country, Young, Smith & Peacock, Inc., has, over the past 25 years, grown with Phoenix and the state of Arizona. Today it is poised to prosper with the emerging Southwest.

Founded in 1965 primarily to focus on equity trading and municipal distribution, this company is the only Arizona-based member of the New York Stock Exchange and the largest investment banking firm based in Arizona. With professionals in public and corporate finance, a full complement of investment executives, and a support structure of dedicated employees in operations, accounting, and other in-house positions, Young, Smith & Peacock has become the premier investment banking firm in the Southwest.

The acquisition of Young, Smith & Peacock in 1988 by American Continental Corporation added strength and vitality to what had been a local firm. The acquisition enabled the Phoenix company to not only increase its capital, but also its presence in other southwestern cities. The firm opened a branch in Tucson, Arizona, adding to its existing Laguna Beach, California, office. Mesa, Scottsdale, Sun City, and Albuquerque branches have since been opened. As the Southwest continues to emerge in national importance, Young, Smith & Peacock will expand to serve a growing clientele.

CORPORATE FINANCE

Young, Smith & Peacock has dramatically increased the size and scope of its corporate finance department. This increase has been in response to the growing capital needs of the Southwest.

The firm's mergers and acquisitions, leveraged buyouts, and public and private offering activities are not confined to a single industry or size of business. Most important is a management team that is involved and adaptable to a changing environment and, second, is past experience that demonstrates the viability of the business. Some past financings have included placing initial private equity for America West Airlines, the initial public of-

The corporate trading room at Young, Smith & Peacock's Phoenix headquarters.

fering for Inertia Dynamics Corp., and a private placement of debt for Fidelity National Financial, Inc.

The corporate finance department is committed to offering innovative and flexible solutions to meet specific corporate finance objectives. The senior management team takes an active leadership role in the structuring and marketing of private financings, providing clients with substantive, high-quality service. Young, Smith & Peacock is proud of its ability to produce value-added results for its clients.

PUBLIC FINANCE

Fulfilling one of the firm's goals since its founding in 1965, Young, Smith & Peacock had provided more than $4 billion in capital funding for Arizona municipalities by the end of the calendar year 1987. Specifically, the firm serves Arizona communities in two distinct ways. It has a tradition of establishing long-term relationships with emerging Arizona communities, while at the same time maintaining a focus on developing investment banking relationships with established municipalities. Municipal clients look to Young, Smith & Peacock for its independence, local expertise, and strong municipal underwriting capabilities.

CORPORATE TRADING

Such trading has been a cornerstone of Young, Smith & Peacock since its inception, and today the firm is a market-maker in more than 100 over-the-counter corporate securities. These securities represent a broad range of issues, including those of corporate finance clients, regional and national issues, and those of special interest to the firm's investment executives and their clientele. The trading department serves institutions, money managers, individual clients, and Young, Smith & Peacock investment executives.

MUNICIPAL BONDS

Young, Smith & Peacock makes a market in virtually every tax-exempt bond issued in the State of Arizona. Active in both the initial underwriting and the secondary trading of bonds sold for the public improvement of Arizona, this department incorporates the municipal sales force, the municipal trading and underwriting desk, and the unit trust trading desk. Because of its Arizona specialty, Young, Smith & Peacock is able to present many investment opportunities to its clients that are not available elsewhere. Although the firm prides itself on anticipating changes in the marketplace, safety and high yield are the hallmarks of this department. No bond sold in the history of the firm has defaulted.

INVESTMENT SERVICES

Above all, Young, Smith & Peacock is a client-oriented firm with investment professionals representing a variety of capabilities. Investment executives have the resources of the entire firm at their disposal. Familiar with Southwest offerings, these professionals are equally at home with the entire spectrum of financial products: real-estate-secured receivables, high-yield corporate bonds, rated and unrated municipal bonds, and real estate participations.

As financial markets continue to change, this Arizona-based company will continue to expand the scope and size of its client services. The firm of the future, Young, Smith & Peacock assures investors who seek capital preservation and appreciation access to the best ideas and transactions available in this emerging, dynamic region.

Investment executives counsel two of Young, Smith & Peacock's clients.

STOREY & ROSS

Since the formation of Storey & Ross in 1981, the group of six lawyers who started the firm have propelled an idea for a highly focused real estate and commercial law firm into one of the state's largest firms. "We are known to our clients as 'people who get things done,'" says Richard Ross, one of the founders. "Our success is attributable to a unique blend of skills, opportunity, and attitude."

The founding partners decided to put together a law firm to represent the real estate and business community. "At that time this was a relatively new concept," recalls Ross. The firm represents sophisticated clients who recognize the quality of product delivered with a different approach to client service than other Phoenix firms.

As lawyers for the business community, Storey & Ross attorneys focus on assisting their clients in analyzing, planning, structuring, and completing transactions. While the role as legal counselor requires honest, objective assessment of the client's position, the emphasis is on imaginatively and creatively getting the job done. The firm takes the time to learn the issues of their clients' industry. Experience under fire makes the firm's lawyers practical and result oriented.

Storey & Ross takes the time to identify its clients' legal needs by learning how they think and feel about their business and what their goals are. They find out where they have been, where they are now, where they are going, and why. This process allows the firm to better assist their clients in achieving their objectives.

The firm's aggressive growth has extended its practice beyond Phoenix to a national and international level. "We represent our clients in more than 20 states," Ross continues, "and we have enjoyed working on a number of important transactions for our European and Asian clients." Storey & Ross has cultivated a state, national, and international network of legal, professional, financial, and other business relationships. This network allows the firm to provide or obtain services on behalf of its clients in many locations other than Phoenix.

Richard Ross credits this network to another of the firm's practices: "Storey & Ross calls on the best outside help necessary to provide quality representation. We are interested in assembling a complete team for our clients—a team that consists of the client, Storey & Ross, and all other business and legal consultants who may be needed." The firm is equally comfortable operating as team leader or team member and in either capacity, believes that coordination, cooperation, and communication among all team members is essential to achieving the client's objective. Storey & Ross is organized into three departments: commercial, real estate/finance, and litigation.

The commercial department handles a broad spectrum of services for business clients from many industries, including corporate organization and reorganization, public offerings and private placement of corporate and real estate securities, partnership/joint venture and real estate equity finance, related tax planning and analysis, financial institution and insurance regulatory practice, insurance risk management analysis, and estate planning. Examples of commercial clients represented by Storey & Ross include Inertia Dynamics Corp., Crafco, Mutual of New York (MONY), and Johnson Wax Development Corporation.

The real estate/finance department participates in a broad variety of real estate planning and transactions, including acquisition and disposition, development, design and construction, condominiums, PADS and PUDS, leasing, real estate regulatory and brokerage practice, related natural resource and environmental practice, and related tax planning. The firm's reputation in the field of real estate law has secured an impressive client list for Storey & Ross in all segments of the industry, including major national, regional, and local home builders such as Pulte Homes, LJ Hooker Homes, and Richmond American.

The real estate/finance department, which actively represents the firm's clients nationwide, also concentrates on negotiations ranging from fairly simple to very sophisticated and complex loan transactions of every kind. These activities include participating loans, real estate and nonreal-estate-secured loans, unsecured loans, multilender participations, leveraged buy-out financing, industrial development, and other tax-exempt financing. In addition, the real estate/finance department provides counsel to borrowers for proposed transactions. Because of its breadth of experience in representing financial institutions and developers, the firm has been very active as counsel to clients in "work out" situations. Among the many major financial institutions represented by the firm are Citibank, First Interstate Bank, and Great American First Savings Bank, FSB.

The litigation department provides a broad scope of services that include dispute resolution, arbitration, litigation arising out of commercial and real estate settings, special investigative counsel, employment and labor matters, insurance, white-collar crime, administrative agency proceedings, bankruptcy, creditors' rights, and appeals. Litigation clients include American Title Insurance Corp., Coldwell Banker, Pixley Richards, and the Arizona House of Representatives.

How does such a young firm attract so many substantial clients? According to Norman C. Storey, the answer is "attitude and talent." The firm has made a commitment to hiring top legal talent who all share a common attitude of pursuing excellence in the practice of law and providing responsive service to its clients. Accordingly, Storey & Ross has attracted a Wall Street lawyer with extensive experience in securities, mergers and acquisitions, as well as a former member of the Justice Department and former judge who is now a well-known trial lawyer. In addition, the former Director of Insurance for the State of Arizona joined the firm to head its insurance practice.

Although originally the firm grew by incorporating knowledgeable and seasoned attorneys into its practice, Storey & Ross has balanced its focus in

recent years to also attract talented young lawyers. Storey notes that the firm now recruits at more than 20 different law school campuses nationwide.

Storey & Ross is a believer in giving back to the community and encourages its attorneys to be active community citizens. Lawyers give time to the Phoenix Symphony, the Phoenix City Club, Cystic Fibrosis, Valley Partnership, the Madison School Foundation, the

Overlooking downtown Phoenix from atop Squaw Peak are (left to right) Richard Ross, Norman Storey, and Lawrence Petrowski.

Phoenix Art Museum Men's Arts Council, the Center for Innovation, Lincoln Hospital, Phoenix Memorial Hospital, and many other civic organizations. "Our firm is an example of the true phenomena of Phoenix," marvels

Ross. "Only in Phoenix could a group of six lawyers, then ranging in age from 28 to the mid-30s, come together with this idea and turn that concept into a major law firm of more than 30 lawyers in such a short period of time." Ross agrees with Storey that "the key has been, and always will be, one of attitude—a desire and commitment within each firm employee to strive for and achieve excellence."

MEYER, HENDRICKS, VICTOR, OSBORN & MALEDON

Meyer, Hendricks, Victor, Osborn & Maledon is a firm that takes pride in the caliber of its attorneys. Mid-size by Phoenix standards, Meyer, Hendricks has charted its growth deliberately since its formation in 1971. Today more than 50 lawyers complete its roster. Of this number, 11 have served as law clerks to justices of the United States Supreme Court. "We recruit nationally, aggressively, and selectively," notes Ed Hendricks, chairman of the firm's hiring committee. "Given the firm's high recruiting standards, clients can call upon any attorney in the firm with confidence."

Approximately half of Meyer, Hendricks' attorneys practice in the area of commercial litigation. The firm's litigation covers a broad spectrum of substantive areas, including antitrust, general contract, real estate, securities, and trade secret law. Meyer, Hendricks litigates in state and federal courts and before administrative agencies. In addition to commercial matters, the firm's trial attorneys handle constitutional, criminal, medical, health care, personal injury, and products liability cases. The firm's commercial litigation group takes pride in a tradition of staffing large cases with fewer lawyers than do most other firms. Not only is efficient staffing more cost effective for the cli-

Bill Maledon (left) and Ed Hendricks (right) head up the firm's litigation practice.

In 1990 the firm will be headquartered on the top three floors of one of the Phoenix Plaza towers located on the Central Corridor in downtown Phoenix.

ent, but the firm believes that it is a better way for young lawyers to develop quickly by assuming greater responsibility early in their careers.

The other half of the firm is comprised of business lawyers experienced in antitrust counseling, business acquisitions and financings, intellectual property law, environmental and water law, land use regulation, health care, real estate, securities, and tax. Meyer, Hendricks has recently added a number of senior lawyers to strengthen certain specialty areas, including state and local government relations, bankruptcy and debtor reorganizations, and environmental law. All of these practice areas have grown significantly in recent years.

Although Meyer, Hendricks has substantial experience in virtually every type of commercial litigation and corporate transaction, the firm does not seek routine legal work. Its real strength is in handling complex matters for sophisticated clients. Examples include representing the City of Phoenix in negotiations for the development of a privately owned and operated multisport stadium complex, representing a franchiser of computer-assisted health assessments in its formation and initial public offering, representing a 4,000-acre planned community development, representing institutional investors in the sale and leaseback of a nuclear power facility, and representing the sellers in an acquisition by a municipality of a water ranch consisting of 140,000 acres of agricultural lands and their water rights.

The firm also has served as co-lead counsel for 44 defendants in the multidistrict cement antitrust litigation, represented 34 heirs of Harvey Firestone, Sr., in trust litigation against the largest bank in Ohio, defended licenses and hospital privileges for physicians nationwide, pursued and defended major first-party bad faith insurance claims, and served, on behalf of a *Fortune* 500 company, as head of a steering committee for a superfund cleanup site involving more than 100 parties and as lead negotiator with the Environmental Protection Agency.

In addition to its full complement of major transactional and litigation work, the firm maintains a strong commitment to pro bono activities. Meyer, Hendricks believes that attorneys and law firms should contribute their expertise to the community and to individuals who otherwise might be denied access to the legal system. The firm has devoted annually as much as a half-million dollars of attorneys' time, in addition to advancing more than $100,000 in costs, for pro bono activities. Its recent cases include obtaining a new trial for a prisoner on Arizona's death row, briefing and arguing a case before the United States Supreme Court on behalf of the Association of State and Local Governments, and litigating a consumer class action in state and federal courts against various financial institutions.

The firm's commitment to creating an attractive professional environment for its lawyers has reaped benefits. Paul Meyer, one of the firm's founders, notes that in the past three years the firm has attracted five senior lawyers from other large Phoenix firms. Meyer believes that "Meyer, Hendricks has an incredible opportunity to be master of its own destiny, which includes the ambitious goal of remaining among the handful of Phoenix firms that clients turn to when they need assistance with a particularly challenging business transaction or complex lawsuit."

(From left to right) Paul Meyer, David Victor, and Jones Osborn lead the firm's business lawyers.

CORROON & BLACK/OLLIVER PILCHER

President Mike Metzger (left) and chairman Wick Pilcher share an optimistic view of their company's continuing role of prominence in the Valley of the Sun.

Corroon & Black/Olliver Pilcher traces its roots in Arizona back to 1903, when Phoenix was nothing more than a tumbleweed town. In 1950, when Bill Pilcher and Don Olliver took over the firm founded by Olliver's great uncle, the agency's total annual commission income was a mere $600. However, both the city and the firm blossomed dramatically during the next quarter-century.

Today Phoenix is one of the country's major metropolitan areas, and Olliver Pilcher is an integral part of Corroon & Black, a prominent New York-based *Fortune* 500 company that has become the fifth-largest insurance brokerage firm in the world. Before the merger in January 1986, Olliver Pilcher was the largest independent insurance agency in the Rocky Mountain area, surpassing 75 million in annual premiums.

Corroon & Black/Olliver Pilcher remains an autonomous entity in the valley with a staff of more than 150 employees. As chairman William Pilcher II and president Michael C. Metzger like to point out, the firm is virtually unchanged, with 95 percent of the staff the same as before. The oldest and largest insurance agency in Arizona takes pride in its business volume—the sixth-most-productive subsidiary out of 63 Corroon & Black divisions in the United States.

This thriving Phoenix operation writes more group benefits insurance and more personal lines than any other Corroon & Black division. The parent company supports the agency in new ways. "They have an excellent reputation across the country, especially in the construction business," says Pilcher. Metzger notes that "Corroon & Black is the nation's largest broker in bonding, so its expertise complements our local talents."

The firm's new corporate headquarters on North 16th Street provides an inviting work place for more than 150 members of the Corroon & Black/Olliver Pilcher insurance brokerage firm.

Whether personal or commercial lines, an inherent part of the company's philosophy has always been the importance of specialization. Through the years the firm has served Arizona's unique insurance needs with coverage for everything from airplanes to Arabian horses and including yachts, aviation, vacation homes, fine arts, professional athletes, and animal mortality. The company also handles everyday personal lines such as home, auto, and life, as well as a full range of commercial business insurance.

The services that made the business successful in the past continue to be its strengths. Corroon & Black/Olliver Pilcher works with 40 percent of the valley's schools and a number of locally based corporations, and traditionally serves the Phoenix Suns basketball organization. Sponsorship of local sports has always been an integral part of the company's marketing philosophy. It sponsors events such as the annual Thanksgiving Turkey Trot in Mesa and a 10K race that attracts roughly 1,000 runners each year for a charitable cause. The firm also directly supports numerous charitable and civic organizations in Phoenix.

From its early days serving the Old West Territory of Arizona to its present position as an insurance industry leader, Corroon & Black/Olliver Pilcher has been a proud participant, for more than 80 years, in the spectacular growth of the Valley of the Sun.

PHYLLIS HAWKINS & ASSOCIATES

The first recruiting firm in the state to specialize in legal and medical executive recruiting, Phyllis Hawkins & Associates has built a stellar reputation in an extraordinarily short time. From only an idea in 1985, Phyllis Hawkins has created a firm that is known not only throughout Phoenix and Arizona, but nationwide.

Today Phyllis Hawkins & Associates is housed in an uptown, Central Avenue building and is staffed by a carefully recruited and trained professional team. The company can point to a record of successfully filling positions in construction, accounting, and real estate, in addition to its legal and medical executive placements.

As Phyllis Hawkins tells it, the initial concept to specialize in law and medical executive recruiting was not a difficult one to sell. "This is an extremely competitive business," she acknowledges, "but I quickly realized, as I gained experience in executive placement, that this was an area that would be responsive to a specialized approach."

In the beginning, Hawkins says, she did a lot of educating. "This was a fairly new idea for the legal offices in the Phoenix area," she admits. "We had to explain that we operate as a broker." Today her firm recruits nationwide and has an impressive roster of satisfied clients. On occasion the organization has helped lawyers find placement outside law into other careers, she adds.

Recently the firm developed another area of specialty in the legal field—mergers and acquisitions. "I see this as a trend in law," Hawkins predicts. "Our knowledge of the legal community is useful in identifying a good merger candidate," says Hawkins. Then, once a candidate is identified, the company leads the client through the steps necessary to accomplish a successful merger. Throughout the transaction the firm acts to keep communication open and talks on track so that progress is not stalled by the press of daily business.

To find the right people and the right placement takes expertise and

Phyllis Hawkins has created a recruiting firm known not only in Phoenix but nationwide.

time. Hawkins has both. She is an active member of the Phoenix community, and her professional training includes a master's degree in education, and extensive postgraduate hours in counseling and educational psychology. "I serve on the Excellence in Education committee for the mayor and have given countless volunteer hours to various civic endeavors."

As for time, Phyllis Hawkins & Associates works efficiently to meet client needs. Above all, the firm values client time, and, consequently, has a policy of extensive client interviewing that is not only geared to gather information about the position, but also to assess what type of person the client is seeking. Questions are in depth and wide ranging, and cover the philosophy, goals, and personalities of the princi-

pals involved.

Each candidate undergoes an equally thorough interview. "I look for a fit," concludes Hawkins, "one that matches both personality and skills. I never present more than three candidates to a client and sometimes, only one. I explain to my clients that this is not a resumé mill. A client is paying for my expertise, my recommendations."

Concludes Hawkins, "A client wants an employee who will remain with them. We have the same goal. To this end we will do our utmost to provide candidates who not only match the job description, but who also will share a client's enthusiasm for the business."

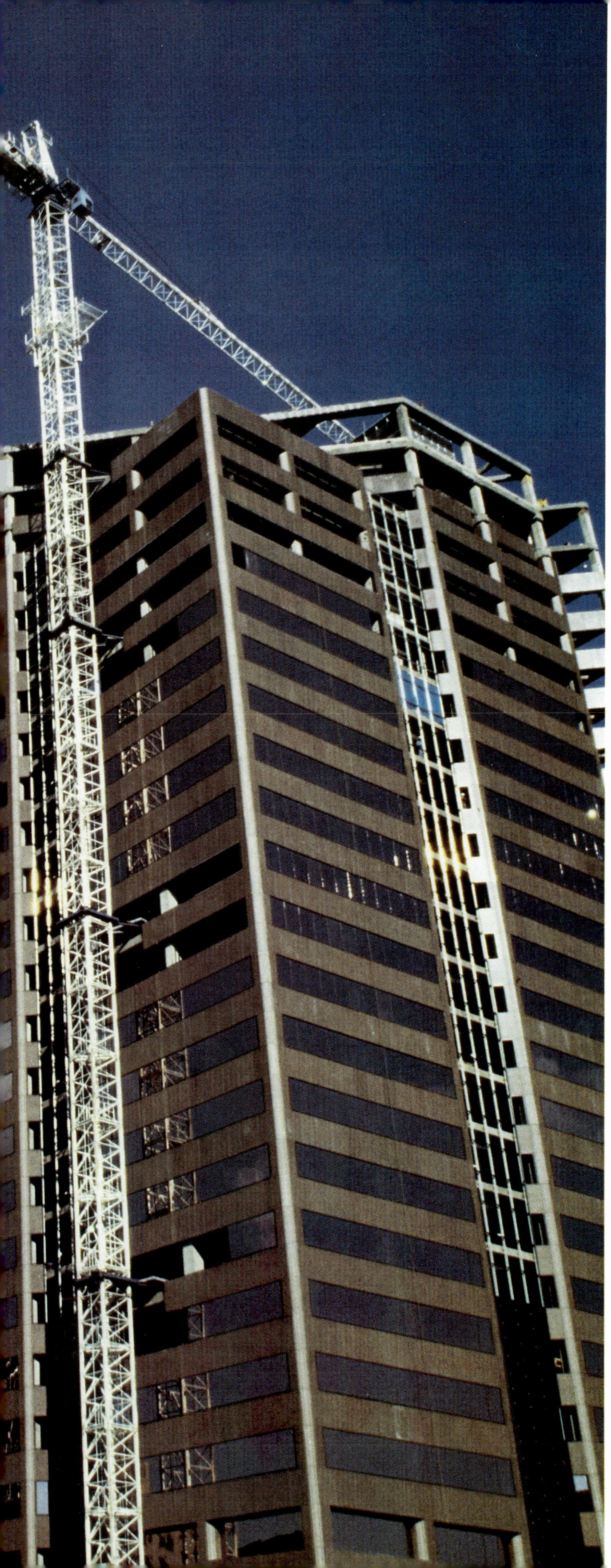

CHAPTER FOURTEEN

Building Greater Phoenix

From concept to completion, Phoenix' building industry shapes tomorrow's skyline.

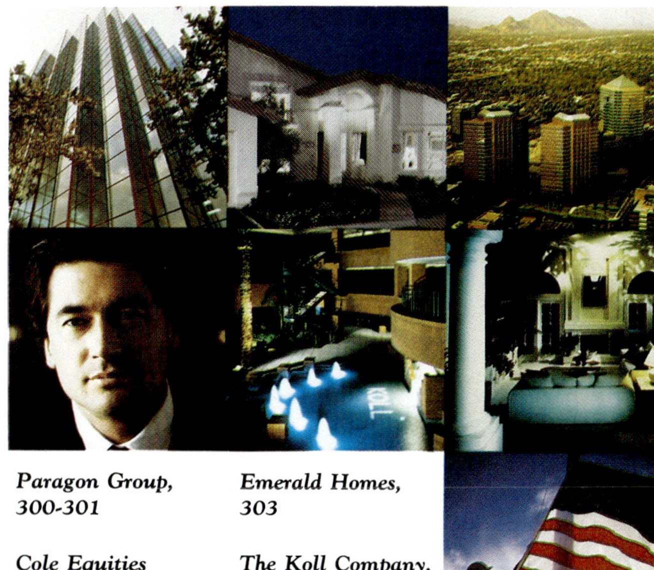

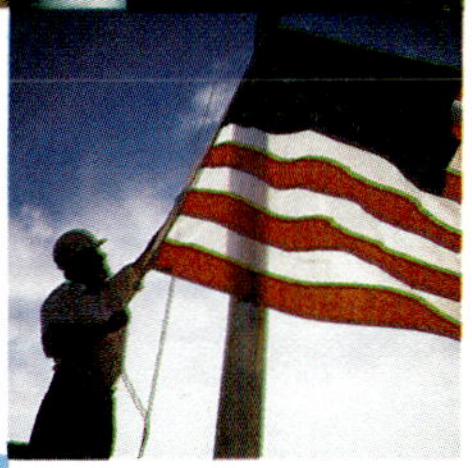

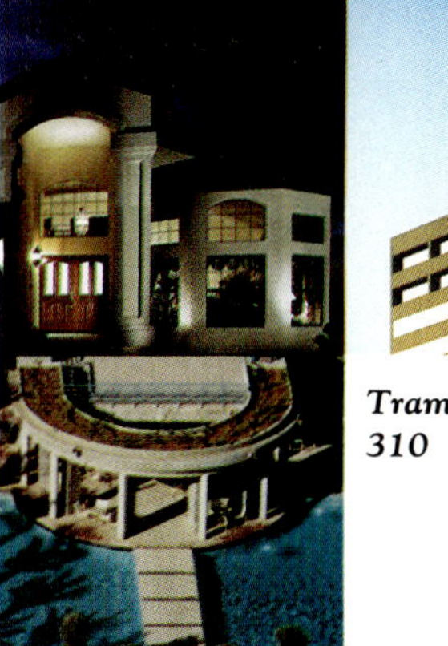

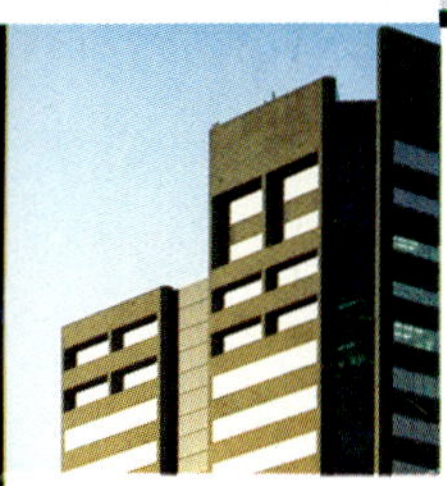

Photo by Don Stevenson

PARAGON GROUP

The 11th-largest diversified developer (office, industrial, retail, and apartment) in the United States, Paragon Group expanded to the Phoenix area in November 1984. By 1986 the company had built two major industrial complexes—the Scottsdale Business Center, totaling nearly 58,000 square feet, and the Paragon Business Center in Mesa with more than 76,000 square feet of floor space. Paragon Group was off to a fast start in the valley.

With a unique corporate structure behind it, Paragon Group operates as a coast-to-coast network of autonomous regional offices, each aggressively entrepreneurial. Yet, at the same time, the Dallas-headquartered operation acts as a major unified organization that successfully combines agility and local understanding of the entrepreneur with the strength and experience of a large national company.

The officers and partners in Paragon's various regions are local developers who understand well the market dynamics of their regions. Each team in each regional office is highly skilled in the development, marketing, and management of top-quality, profitable real estate assets. Consequently, the primary source of Paragon's development capability is the creative energy of these real estate professionals.

With complete capability in planning, financing, construction, investment strategies, operations, sales, and leasing, Paragon's expertise is both broad and deep. Standardized project information from all the regions served by Paragon Group provides the firm with accounting and management information that can be readily applied beyond the company to serve the needs of other property owners.

With a management style that is pragmatic and comprehensive, Paragon Group builds working partnerships with its tenants, who are regarded as valued clients. Success, to Paragon, depends upon a combination of quality development and quality tenants. Tenants range from individual apartment residents to small business people to more than half the corporations comprised in the *Fortune* 500.

Complementing its client commitment, Paragon Group is equally at-tuned to the communities where its developments are located. Key people in the firm contribute actively to community organizations. Striving to be a model of excellence in approach, in product, and in the results attained, Paragon Group is making a difference in Phoenix.

Paragon Group expanded to the Phoenix area in 1984 and by 1986 had built the Paragon Business Center (bottom) in Mesa and the Scottsdale Business Center (below).

Left: Paragon Center, Fort Lauderdale, Florida.

Below: Though national in scope, Paragon Group blends its individual projects into the local surroundings such as Crosse Pointe, shown here in Fayetteville, North Carolina.

COLE EQUITIES INCORPORATED

Ten years ago, when Christopher H. Cole founded Cole Equities Incorporated, he set his sights on Scottsdale. The young entrepreneur had determined that land in the area around that Phoenix suburb was both plentiful and significantly undervalued. Accordingly, Chris Cole organized Cole Equities Incorporated with the intent of assembling and selling land in the Scottsdale area.

The concept got off to a rapid and successful start. Within a relatively few years Cole had put together 32 properties, which he sold through limited partnerships. Land was offered both as individual sites and as assembled sites—with results that pleased investors. In the course of the next few years Cole Equities properties were sold with an average cash-on-cash return of 38 percent compounded annually.

As the firm continued to find and assemble prime land and attract a cadre of eager investors, the original concept was expanded. Soon Cole Equities was including infrastructure improvements in land plans, which further enhanced the value of these properties for both immediate and future development.

The rapid-fire success of Cole Equities during the years from 1979 to 1989 reflects well both on the quality of the land in the Phoenix metropolitan valley, and on the acumen of those leading this young and vibrant firm. Acutely aware that explosive growth has characterized Phoenix for the past 20 years, Cole Equities banked its future on future growth. A young and aggressive firm, Cole Equities determined to be a participant—not a spectator—in the Phoenix growth game. It quickly gained a reputation as a firm that could identify prime land and seize the opportunities to assemble and market it. Thus this dynamic firm both benefited from and contributed to the impressive growth record of the valley.

After concentrating on the outlying areas for six years, Cole Equities shifted its focus from the suburbs to the city. Once again Christopher Cole had recognized a heretofore unsung opportunity. The chairman and chief executive officer realized that land in the

Christopher H. Cole, founder, is the guiding force in making Cole Equities Incorporated the largest landowner in the central business district of Phoenix.

central business district of Phoenix was significantly undervalued relative to central business district land in other cities. What's more, this land was undervalued relative to its own income potential. Accordingly, Cole and his company set to work to acquire properties within the heart of the Phoenix business district—especially land with Central Avenue frontage.

"Once we obtain these properties," Cole explains, "we work with the city and other property owners and developers. Our goal is to make Central Avenue the grand boulevard that it has the potential to be."

To date, Cole's enthusiasm to garner investment money and interest on Central Avenue has been shared with hundreds of investors. Only a few years after putting this new policy into effect, Cole Equities Incorporated became the largest landowner in the central business district of Phoenix. While the firm is proud that its investors continue to share in its economic success, it is equally proud that it is helping to shape the heart of Phoenix.

EMERALD HOMES

Fulfilling the American dream is the business of Emerald Homes, a company that has led the way in helping generations of families find that perfect home.

In an industry that is highly competitive and constantly facing cyclical interest rates, Emerald Homes has remained one of Phoenix' most respected home builders. "We are, proudly, the first NYSE-traded, Phoenix-based public home-building company," says Philip J. Polich, president.

The firm also has operations in the San Francisco Bay Area in Northern California; in Houston, Texas; and in San Diego, California. It successfully designs, builds, and finances single-family homes on land it develops. Since 1970 Emerald has sold approximately 5,000 homes in the Phoenix metropolitan area and, since 1974, approximately 3,000 homes in the San Francisco area. Its principal market is move-up buyers of medium- to upper-price-range single-family detached homes. The firm also sells single-family attached homes, including patio homes and town homes. Currently Emerald is offering homes in 27 residential developments at prices ranging from $54,900 to $315,000.

Emerald's history dates back to 1970, when the company's predecessor, Ditz-Crane of Arizona, Inc., was founded. Emerald Homes was formed in September 1982, when the senior management of Ditz-Crane—Philip J. Polich, H. Arthur Nottingham, and Curtis J. Henderson, along with several partners—purchased the assets and operations of Ditz-Crane. Within a short time Emerald continued Ditz-Crane's profitable history in the Phoenix housing market. Today Phoenix is Emerald's largest market in terms of unit deliveries and ranks in the top five markets among metropolitan areas nationwide in terms of housing starts.

The firm's strong business philosophies have helped lay the foundation for its prosperous development. Emerald Homes believes, for example, that its experience in and knowledge of local housing markets enhances its ability to acquire land in desirable locations on favorable terms, and to monitor and respond to local customer preference.

"The way we manage the company is important," says Polich. "We have top-notch people and limit our management levels so we don't lose control."

The quality of its properties has made Emerald Homes a popular choice for Phoenix home owners during the 1970s and 1980s. Today the firm is looking ahead, designing homes that will meet the expectations of home buyers in the twenty-first century. Phoenix has long prided itself on being a livable city—one of sunny neighborhoods where the single-family private home is still the residence of choice. Happily, Emerald Homes has played a role in helping to create this unusual urban environment. Looking ahead toward the increasing population that will continue to pour into this hub of the Southwest, Emerald Homes will continue to maintain its leadership role in designing and building the Phoenix of the future.

Emerald Homes is helping to design and build the Phoenix of the future with its developments of single-family homes such as North Place in Glendale. Shown are the 2,200-square-foot, gray-brick Ruby model (below) and the elegant 3,300-square-foot Diamond model (bottom).

THE KOLL COMPANY

In less than a decade the Phoenix Division of The Koll Company, a diverse real estate development, construction, and asset management company, has firmly established itself in nearly all markets of metropolitan Phoenix.

Since making its entry into the Phoenix market in 1979, The Koll Company has pioneered quality industrial and office developments in the Northwest Valley, high-tech facilities in the East Valley, and large mixed-use developments in the Central Business Corridor.

In each case The Koll Company has been a leader of responsible development in Phoenix—sensitive to local planning issues, existing development, and the general condition of the local real estate market.

Headed by its division president, James N. Wentworth, The Koll Company has developed, acquired, or constructed an inventory of 3 million square feet of commercial office and industrial space in metropolitan Phoenix. The firm currently has another one-million square feet of commercial space on the drawing board.

A gregarious and approachable man, Wentworth sets the tone for The Koll Company's Phoenix office. "I'm always searching for new challenges that represent sound opportunities for Koll," says Wentworth. "As developers, we're not bound by traditional methods of doing business in a corporate environment. I try to tap our entrepreneurial qualities to create winning development concepts and better financial packages. Making those concepts come to life . . . breaking ground on a new development and seeing it through to completion, is what really makes this business exciting."

With an ability to find creative solutions to challenging situations, Wentworth and his staff have successfully projected the needs of an evolving marketplace and, in the process, have pioneered new locations and forms of office industrial developments.

Koll has also successfully structured a variety of financial packages with sophisticated partners in order to take advantage of exceptional develop-

Phoenix Tech Center, a 68-acre research and development park devoted exclusively to high-technology tenants, was developed by The Koll Company.

ment opportunities.

According to Wentworth, The Koll Company recently completed work on a joint venture redevelopment project in Scottsdale, a Phoenix suburb. Koll Plaza, a well-located office building, was stripped down to a shell and completely redesigned.

"At Koll Plaza, we utilized the broad range of development, construction, and property management skills for which The Koll Company is known. There aren't many real estate development companies capable of performing all of those jobs," says Wentworth.

From the start of its operations in Phoenix, The Koll Company has retained the skills of respected real estate experts to head up its development, construction, and asset management divisions.

With Wentworth's lead The Koll Company established the first high-quality office and industrial developments in Northwest Phoenix, the city's fastest-growing office and industrial market.

Koll Business Center Northwest, a 37-acre industrial/office park, has attracted more than 400,000 square feet of tenants, including Valley National Bank and Prudential Insurance Company.

The firm has also spearheaded the

The Phoenix Plaza.

James N. Wentworth, division president of The Koll Company.

integration of high-quality office and industrial space with such business parks as Koll Business Center Westech, a 24-acre business park in Phoenix, and Phoenix Tech Center, a 68-acre research and development park devoted exclusively to high-technology tenants.

The Koll Company, in a joint venture with BetaWest Properties, Inc., is also developing The Phoenix Plaza, a distinctive 1.7-million-square-foot mixed-use development on the Phoenix Central Business Corridor.

Wentworth's experience as an executive with Coldwell Banker Real Estate Services and his ties with the brokerage community have given him a unique perspective into both the development and tenant side of the real estate industry. "Of all cities where Koll operates, Phoenix is recognized as the strongest broker-oriented market," says Wentworth. "We interface daily with any one of the more than 400 brokers that bring us business.

"Because we understand what motivates them and how they prefer to work with developers, Koll has received more than its fair share of development and tenant opportunities in the marketplace."

While the Phoenix division is part of The Koll Company, based in Newport Beach, California, its organizational structure allows division offices to operate independently and under the direction of local professionals. "Individual markets have their own

little quirks and players," explains Wentworth. "When you have a lot of experience in a market, you develop a feel for what's right in the community. You develop a sensitivity to what is and isn't acceptable to the people in surrounding neighborhoods."

As a fully integrated real estate company with the in-house tools to create, build, and maintain long-term investments, The Koll Company is in complete control of product quality. At the inception of a proposed development project, comprehensive feasibility studies are performed. During the conceptual phase, The Koll Company hires architects that share the company's concern for harmony and commitment to excellence. With the expertise of Koll Construction Company, the project is built with quality, on time, and within budget. And while the design, construction, and initial leasing process of a property is completed in two or three years, how that property is managed during the ensuing 10 to 20 years will determine whether its full potential value is realized. With The Koll Company's own asset management di-

vision providing property management services for its developments, service to tenants and long-term profitability is ensured.

"The best tenant that you can get is the one you've already got," states Wentworth. "Each month we're communicating with nearly 500 tenants at Koll developments throughout metropolitan Phoenix." Those tenants are familiar with Koll's service, quality product, and asset management team, he added.

"We're in a strong position to grow with our tenants and continue to offer them new solutions or new product to meet their changing space requirements," says Wentworth. "We've recognized that the ability to meet the ongoing needs of our tenants is a major selling point for Koll developments. If we can evolve and grow with these companies, they will be free to concentrate on developing their businesses, and in that way, we both come out ahead."

Koll Business Center Northwest, Phase IV.

THE PHOENIX PLAZA

The Phoenix Plaza, the largest mixed-use project to break ground in Arizona, has become the archetypal mixed-use development for Phoenix.

The 1.7-million-square-foot project features a distinctive office environment set on a 10.6-acre site at Central Avenue and Thomas Road, a prestigious address in Phoenix' Central Business Corridor.

The Phoenix Plaza consists of twin 20-story office towers each totaling 400,000 square feet, a 25-story office tower totaling 585,000 square feet, a Hilton Suites hotel, a 35,000-square-foot retail pavilion, and a multilevel parking facility.

The development has attracted the attention of major accounting, financial, and law firms, including Brown & Bain, a leading Southwest law firm that is the anchor tenant for the first 20-story tower, and the national accounting firm of Touche Ross. The entire 25-story office tower, with more than 585,000 square feet of space, houses the new Arizona headquarters of US WEST Communications.

A project of such scope was conceived and brought to life through the financial strength and development expertise of two national real estate developers: BetaWest Properties, Inc., a wholly owned subsidiary of US West, Inc., and The Koll Company, a Newport Beach, California-based developer.

It's no surprise that the developers chose the Central Business Corridor site for the location of the development. The Phoenix Plaza's Central and Thomas location is at the heart of the financial district and is minutes from Sky Harbor International Airport and government offices. When construction is concluded on the nearby Papago Freeway Inner Loop, access to the Central Business Corridor from suburban areas of the valley will be complete.

Since The Phoenix Plaza is the first high-rise mixed-use development of its kind on the Central Business Corridor, the developers knew that the project would be under the scrutiny of the entire city. "Our plan is to create a mixed-use development that would exceed the expectations of the mayor, the city council, and the people of Phoenix," says Thomas W. Roberts, vice-president of development for The Phoenix Plaza. "We're creating Phoenix' first urban development in the Central Corridor that provides an all-encompassing office community for its tenants."

This aspect of the development, a key design element of the urban village concept advocated by the city's planning department, is the reason why The

Phoenix Plaza is considered a major development "in the right location," according to comments made by Phoenix Mayor Terry Goddard during the ground-breaking ceremony for the development. "The start of The Phoenix Plaza helps establish Phoenix as a major urban center of the Southwest," he added.

As a mixed-use project unique among high-rise projects in the city, The Phoenix Plaza is a self-contained environment offering its tenants a complementary mix of services, specialty shops, health club, and dining facilities. Shaded seating areas on a landscaped plaza, enhanced with sculptured water features and a multilevel retail pavilion, provide ample and usable public space. A 1.2-million-square-foot, multilevel parking facility, the largest single structure parking facility in the country, provides an abundance of parking space.

The 20-story towers feature exterior walls of double-pane, bronze reflective glass with horizontal bands of polished granite and stainless-steel accents; virtually column-free hexagonal floor plates each totaling 21,000 square feet; dramatic 18-foot-high main entry lobby of polished granite; nine-foot ceiling height on all floors; intelligent energy-management systems; single-card-access system and 24-hour security guard service; and an underground service level.

Another factor considered by the developers was the impact the project would have on the Phoenix skyline. "We studied the buildings along the Central Business Corridor before designing The Phoenix Plaza and found that Phoenix doesn't have a focal point for its skyline," explains architect Ernie Wilson of Langdon Wilson Mumper Architects and Planners, designer of The Phoenix Plaza. The Newport Beach-based architect designed pyramid-shape structures to top off the three high rises of The Phoenix Plaza, adding a degree of distinction to Phoenix' developing skyline.

Iliff, Thorn & Company is the exclusive leasing agent for The Phoenix Plaza.

Koll Construction Company, a wholly owned subsidiary of The Koll Company, is the construction manager and general contractor for The Phoenix Plaza.

The Phoenix Plaza features a distinctive office environment set on a 10.6-acre site in Phoenix' Central Business Corridor in the heart of the financial district.

UDC-UNIVERSAL DEVELOPMENT L.P.

Headquartered in Tempe, UDC-Universal Development L.P. (UDC Homes) is one of Arizona's largest and most successful home builders. Since the inception of UDC's home-building activities in 1976 in Mesa, the company has grown to become the largest builder of family move-up and retirement housing in the Phoenix area. More than 1,100 UDC homes were sold in the Phoenix area during 1987.

The firm currently has 23 active subdivisions under development in 11 different communities in the Phoenix area. With homes priced from $80,000 to more than $300,000, UDC offers a wide variety of product types to the move-up family and retirement buyer throughout the valley.

As the dominant builder of move-up housing, UDC offers homes predominantly in Phoenix, Scottsdale, and the East Valley cities of Tempe, Chandler, and Gilbert. Building single-family detached homes in planned-community environments has been a hallmark of UDC's success. UDC developments are generally part of large, master-planned communities that offer extensive natural and man-made amenities. Many UDC homes are designed around golf courses, lakes, and spectacular mountain views.

UDC's major retirement community, Westbrook Village, is a 1,200-acre planned community designed around 36 holes of championship golf, lakes, and generous open space. Upon completion the project will house approximately 10,000 adults. Property ownership at Westbrook Village required that one resident be older than 40 and no one be under 18. Located in Peoria adjacent to Sun City and offering homes from $80,000 to more than $200,000, Westbrook Village is one of the most successful adult communities in the Phoenix metropolitan area.

UDC is a publicly owned master limited partnership whose shares are traded on the New York Stock Exchange. In addition to its operations in Arizona, UDC builds in California, Georgia, Florida, and North and South Carolina. With 1987 sales of more than $250 million and profits in excess of $34 million, UDC is one of the largest, most profitable home builders in the country.

Clearly, with the Phoenix area as its largest market, UDC-Universal Development L.P. is committed to working toward continued quality growth and economic development of this exciting metropolitan marketplace.

UDC-Universal Development L.P. (UDC Homes) offers a wide variety of homes to the move-up family and retirement buyer throughout the valley.

GOSNELL BUILDERS

Project development is a complex process. Gosnell Builders has been successfully meeting the most stringent corporate requirements since it was founded in 1973.

With more than $2 billion in completed construction contracts, Gosnell Builders and its San Diego company, Pointe Builders, provide a full range of related construction services nationwide. From inception the firm incorporated and refined a highly efficient full-service team philosophy; planning, architecture, engineering, contracting, interior design, and property management are offered individually or as an integrated whole. Projects are ultimately reviewed by all functional departments to ensure that the final product is viable and desirable. The expert in-house resources necessary to apply this extensive feasibility audit are exclusive to Gosnell.

As Arizona's largest private company, this major contractor employs more than 3,600 people. But the impact that the firm has on the community extends far beyond sheer numbers, for during the past 16 years Gosnell Builders has literally changed the face of Phoenix.

Early on, the company began targeting and developing overlooked areas in the outlying regions of the city, turning them into highly desirable commercial and residential complexes by pioneering a total community concept. With its Camelhead Project encompassing 72 acres at 44th Street and Thomas, the firm has shifted its focus

to the central city. This project is the master-planned, mixed-use Urban Village Square, a vision for the finer Phoenix/Tempe/Scottsdale area. It is a unique cityscape with hospitality, retail, commercial, and residential uses linked by multilevel bridged walkways and open park areas.

Demonstrating both vision and viability, Gosnell Builders quickly achieved prominence as one of the most honored and respected building organizations in the Southwest. From site planning to construction, the company portfolio is hallmarked by integrity, reliability, and stability. All custom-designed business environments are of unprecedented quality and feature luxury amenities as well as a superior working atmosphere. This combination creates the ideal corporate destination.

In addition to its general contracting specialty, Gosnell owns and operates extensive prime commercial properties throughout Arizona and

Custom-designed business environments such as this building constructed for the Anheuser-Busch Hensley & Company are a Gosnell Builders hallmark.

Southern California. Completed projects include mid-rise office complexes, community shopping centers, regional shopping malls, health care structures, multiuse high-tech facilities, hotels, planned residential communities, and the celebrated 5-Star, 5-Diamond Pointe Resorts.

Reputation, performance, product, financial strength, and depth of management all set Gosnell Builders apart from its industry counterparts. With a unique conceptual approach and complete control over all project phases, Gosnell Builders will continue to realize today's needs and tomorrow's dreams.

The celebrated 5-Star, 5-Diamond Pointe Resorts are a creation of Gosnell Builders.

A Gosnell Builders superintendent raises the flag signaling the beginning of another day at Gosnell Builders.

TRAMMELL CROW

"Trammell Crow Company's philosophy and style are tremendously compatible with the Phoenix environment," according to area partner Paul Barker, who moved to Phoenix for the company in 1982. "Phoenix is a city of modern pioneers. This is a city where the fundamentals of cooperation and friendship make newcomers quickly feel part of the community. Our people came here from cities across the country seeking a life of opportunity in the vibrant Southwest. So we raise our families and our buildings with an eye to creating a great community."

Trammell Crow has a history with contemporary Phoenix. Beginning in 1948 with a single, speculative warehouse building, the company has grown to become one of the nation's largest and most diversified real estate entities. Forty years after its founding, this firm incorporates assets of more than $14 billion and includes more than 7,500 employees throughout the United States and various foreign markets.

One of the largest developers in metropolitan Phoenix, Trammell Crow projects include nearly 2 million square feet of industrial space, 2,000 apartment units, 180 single-family lots, and more than a half-million square feet of retail space. While these numbers are impressive, the firm is best recognized for its office profile.

Crown Central, on Central Ave-

Renaissance Square, Trammell Crow's signature project, is an ultracontemporary complex of two office towers in revitalized downtown Phoenix.

nue in the heart of Phoenix, boasts 400,000 square feet of office space in an office tower and two low-rise buildings. A second office tower, on the drawing board, will add an additional half-million square feet of class-A office space to this postmodern site. In Scottsdale, the firm has developed a European-style complex, The Forum, a 200,000-square-foot building on Scottsdale Road.

The company's signature project, Renaissance Square, is an ultracontemporary complex consisting of two office towers that provide nearly one million square feet of the valley's finest office space in a revitalized downtown Phoenix. "This project is an excellent example of public/private partnership working to enhance the city's quality of life," notes Paul Barker. "This was the first new project in downtown Phoenix in more than a decade, and with the assistance of the mayor, the city council, and the Central Phoenix Redevelopment Authority, the project has been tremendously successful. Downtown is

once again a vital commercial center." Renaissance Square is a unique mix of elegant offices, eye-catching retail units, delightful restaurants, athletic facilities, and open plazas—all of which add up to a vibrant downtown center.

Building a great new downtown is just one of the ways this firm actively works at creating a great community. Implicit in all projects is the company's philosophy, which stresses integrity, service, and quality.

Concludes Trammell Crow partner Bill Steinberg, "Our goal is to provide financially viable projects that will have a positive impact on our quality of life. As more people locate in the valley, we hope to provide them with better places to work and more enjoyable places to shop and have fun. We intend to create projects that will become focal points for all who live here."

Trammell Crow commissioned sculptor Trevor Southey to create Full Reach of Life *for the pedestrian mall of One Renaissance Square. The sculpture depicts "the human frailty and also the enormous potential for greatness that lies in the human being."*

CONTINENTAL HOMES

Continental Homes is the largest home builder, both in the metropolitan Phoenix market and throughout Arizona. Having sold homes to more than 20,000 satisfied buyers over the past 10 years, Continental recognizes that each family has a distinct life-style and, therefore, has special requirements for a home. There are, however, common characteristics that all Continental home owners share: a demand for functional, practical floor plans with plenty of closet space; quality appliances, carpeting, and fixtures throughout the home; and sound construction at an excellent price. It is Continental's commitment to value in every neighborhood and price range that has made this company number one throughout the valley.

For singles or young families looking for the unusually rare combination of spaciousness and affordability, Continental offers a wide range of single-family homes priced from $60,000. Built in desirable areas of the valley, close to schools, shopping areas, and business centers, these single-family homes are only slightly more expensive than town homes, yet they include such standard features as energy-efficient dual-pane windows, solid-block privacy fences, and all-stucco exteriors—features normally found in homes with much larger price tags. In addition, homes can be customized with options such as patios, fireplaces, upgraded flooring, and many other amenities.

For families ready to "move up" and build their dream home, Continental has an exciting range of mid- and upper-end semicustom homes, priced from $150,000 to $250,000. They include more than a variety of floor plans with luxuries such as cathedral ceilings, country kitchens connecting with large family rooms, fireplaces, separate oval tubs and shower stalls, and elegant master retreats. Options include upgraded flooring, cabinetry, fireplace facings, appliances, whirlpool tubs, and even a separate guest house for visitors.

Today Continental thrives on its reputation as a builder of quality homes at reasonable prices and as a profitable, well-managed, permanent corporation

that has been prominent since it began in 1969.

In addition to its Phoenix home-building activities, Continental Homes Holding Corporation, the parent company of Continental Homes, Inc., currently operates subdivisions in the Denver area, through its subsidiary, KDB Homes, Inc., and is a joint venture partner in several subdivisions in Southern California.

Another important subsidiary is Continental Homes Mortgage Company, which originates a substantial portion of loans for Continental-built homes. From ground breaking to move

in, Continental maintains high standards that ensure continued customer satisfaction through its customer service department.

Since design improvement is constant and new product development is ongoing at Continental, management is confident that Continental Homes will remain the local industry leader, continuing to provide desirable new locations, innovative new floor plans, and value in every home.

Continental offers an exciting range of homes, priced from $60,000 to more than $250,000.

SHASTA POOLS

Who can imagine Arizona without its swimming pools? Flying over Phoenix, one looks down upon a landscape studded with liquid turquoise gems—every size and shape imaginable. And no wonder, for the desert heat makes a swimming pool almost a necessity in Phoenix during those searing summer months. Then, too, where would Phoenix-area resorts be without fantasy pools rimmed with waterfalls and even trimmed with sandy beaches?

Thanks to Bob and Ed Ast, founders of Shasta Pools, Phoenix is synonymous with swimming pools. Since 1966 the Ast brothers' company has built more than 28,000 swimming pools in the Phoenix metropolitan area. This is a record that is unequaled by any other pool builder in the industry.

The two young brothers entered the pool business because their father had owned a small pool company. Today the firm generates revenues in excess of $35 million a year, has more than 350 skilled employees, and owns and operates more than $2 million in pool construction equipment.

In fact, the Shasta story is as dazzling as the pools it builds. Beginning with total sales of 28 pools in 1966, Shasta had become the number-one pool builder in the Phoenix area by 1969. Shasta is the only pool company to exceed 2,000 sales in one year and the only firm to hold that record for three consecutive years. In its more than 20 years in business, Shasta has averaged one out of every three pools built in the Phoenix metro area, selling an average of some eight pools every day. This kind of sales effort allowed the firm to build more pools in 1985, for instance, than the next five competitors combined did.

How does Shasta Pools maintain this high sales profile? "We do the majority of work on our pools ourselves with our own equipment and crews," says Bob Ast. "We meet deadlines and we maintain control. We are also able to attract the cream of the craftsmen and reward them accordingly."

Ast points out that Shasta has built its reputation on quality and adds that the company stays close to home, building only in the Phoenix metropolitan area. This means that every Shasta pool stays in sight of Ed Ast, president of the firm. Ed maintains his office in a totally equipped van that enables this involved executive to do personal on-site checks every day. "Our people never know which day Ed may show up on the construction job," says Bob Ast, "but they know that he will visit them during some phase of the project."

On-site inspection by the company president is just one example of how this firm has propelled itself to the forefront of the industry. Another is Shasta's well-positioned sales stance. In 1983, for example, Shasta created a Home Builder Division. That first year the division completed 20 pools for various builders. It grew steadily until it now builds pools for most of the leading home builders in Arizona—more than 40 builders in all and 600-plus pools per year. This division not only assures the new home owner of a quality pool, it also opens up some financial advantages for the home owner. By including the cost of the pool and/or spa in the first mortgage, pool owners can avoid a second loan at higher financing costs.

While its residential pools have received local distinction, Shasta is also

---

Turquoise gems dot the Phoenix landscape and blend with the desert surroundings. This Shasta pool, "Lifescapes by Patrick Duffy," is a local NSPI Silver Award winner.

known nationwide for award-winning design and innovation for commercial pools. In 1986 Shasta built the pool for the Hyatt Regency at Gainey Ranch in Scottsdale that achieved an international award for the pool company. This facility, which ranked in 1988 as one of the world's largest resort swimming pools, contains more than 26,000 square feet of surface area and more than one million gallons of water. In addition to its vast surface area, the pool also sports a variety of water features, including a clock tower slide and even a sandy beach for guests who want the feel of the ocean with all the advantages of the desert.

Until Shasta tackled this project, the largest pool it had constructed was in 1983 at LaPosada Resort, now Red Lion LaPosada. Longer than a football field, it contains more than a half-million gallons of water.

In addition to its complete pool-building capabilities, Shasta's six retail Swim N' Save stores keep its customers coming back. Conveniently and strategically placed, these stores offer such bonuses for Shasta clientele as ID cards that entitle customers to discounts on pool furniture and other items sold at the store. Tap water analysis is also available at these locations, and the pool stores offer systems for treating drinking water.

Finally, Shasta has built its reputation on innovation. "To the best of my knowledge," observes Bob Ast, "we are the only pool company with a complete research and development division. We manufacture the Quick Clean in-floor automatic cleaning system and the electric control panel that allows home owners to control pool lights or other

The unique pool at the Hyatt Regency, Scottsdale, is a Shasta Pool creation. Winner of the national NSPI Gold Award and the local NSPI Gold Award, the pool holds more than one million gallons of water and features a clock tower slide and a sandy beach.

pool accessories from inside the house." This is standard in the Shasta pool program, he adds. Shasta also developed a chlorine generator, notes Ast. "This is the latest innovation to pool maintenance that we have come up with. While it is an investment, pool owners soon realize that the chlorine generator quickly pays for itself."

Although the innovations in pool building and pool service add glamour, Bob Ast prefers to talk about service. He is proud that the company has 17 radio-controlled trucks to dispatch at a moment's notice. The company also

holds the world time record for completing a pool from start to finish—in just 7.5 hours. As the largest privately owned swimming pool construction company in the world, Shasta can do it all—from pool design to backyard beautification.

Neither Ed nor Bob Ast takes Shasta Pools' success for granted. Says Bob, "It is hard to make it in the pool business in Arizona because it is so competitive. But we have a good working climate and plenty of labor to choose from—and we keep our profits very tight." Because the firm has such faith in its product, Shasta offers a lifetime structural guarantee with every pool.

Faith is a driving force behind Shasta Pools. Explains Bob Ast, "I firmly believe that if we do a good job, it will come back to us. We are not likely to premeditatively take advantage of a customer. This means that we get a tremendous number of referrals—some 87 percent of our business is the result of direct or indirect referrals." While he credits hard work for much of the company's success, Ast looks to a higher source for inspiration. "My philosophy is to work like it all depended on you and pray like it all depended on God," he says.

This philosophy has enabled Shasta Pools to grow with integrity, maintaining a reputation for excellence and honesty and, above all, stability. "We are a credible company," affirms Bill Russ, general manager of Shasta Pools. "Our representatives can design pools and equipment—even suggest landscaping. We do the preliminary work without a contract, and if at that point the customer is ready to make a decision, then our representative can price the pool." This full-service approach has served Phoenix for 23 years, presenting Shasta Pool customers with value that is unprecedented in the industry.

Residential pools are a specialty of Shasta Pools, and each is an individual design blending into its surroundings. This mosaic-tile pool at the Cappellini residence is a national NSPI Silver Award and local NSPI Gold Award winner.

*Advanced Copy
Systems, Inc.,
318*

*American
Greyhound Racing,
Inc., 320*

*Famous
Restaurants
Inc., 319*

*Grand Canyon
Color Lab, 321*

*Service Control
Corporation, 322*

*Best Western
International, 323*

*Ramada Inc.,
324-325*

*Waste Management
of Phoenix, 327*

*ABCO Markets, Inc.,
326*

*Horizon Moving
Systems, Inc.,
328-329*

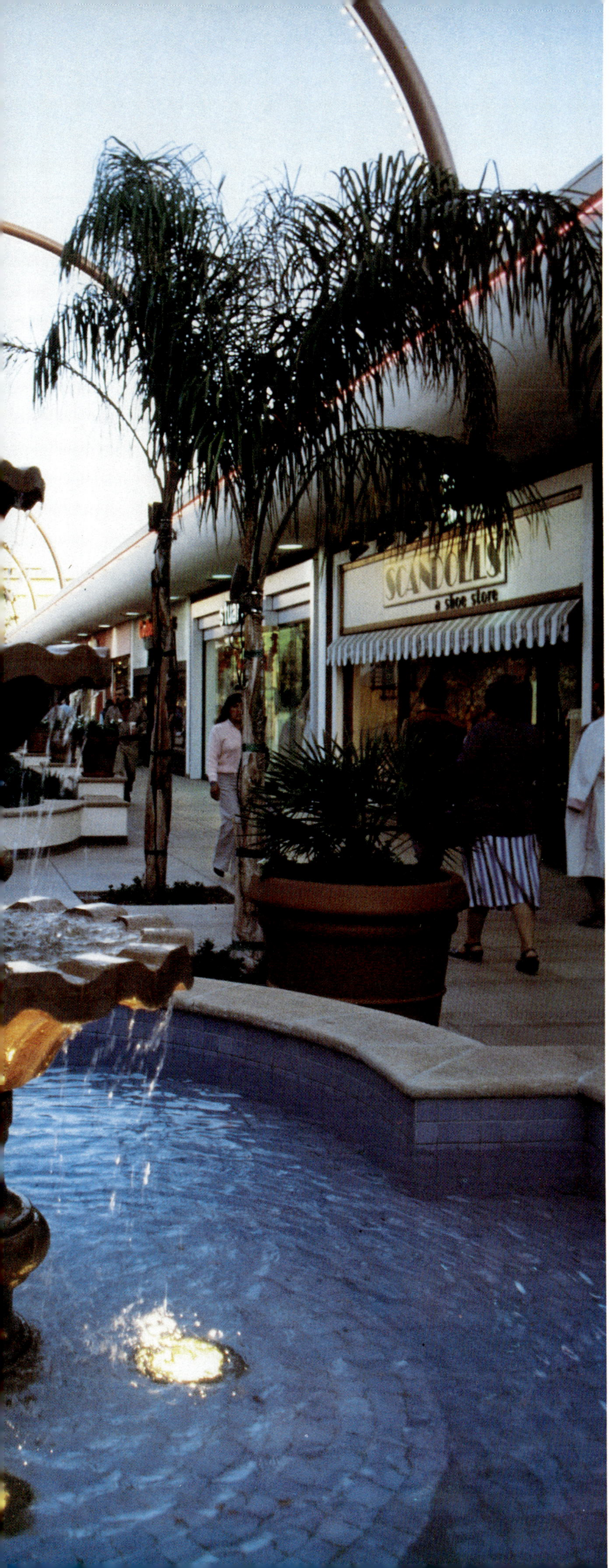

CHAPTER FIFTEEN

The Marketplace

The area's retail establishments, service industries, products, and sporting events are enjoyed by residents and visitors to the area.

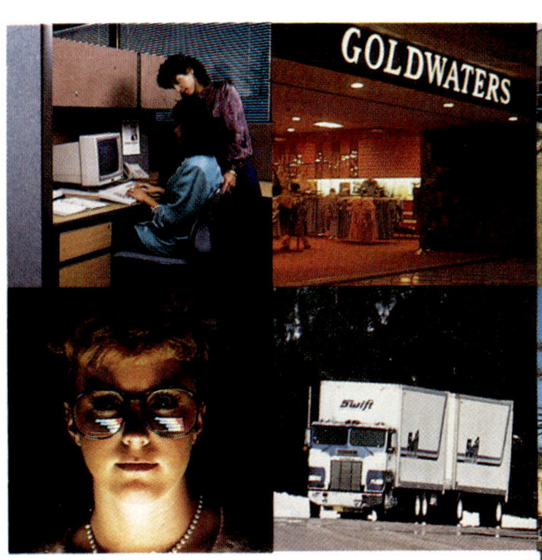

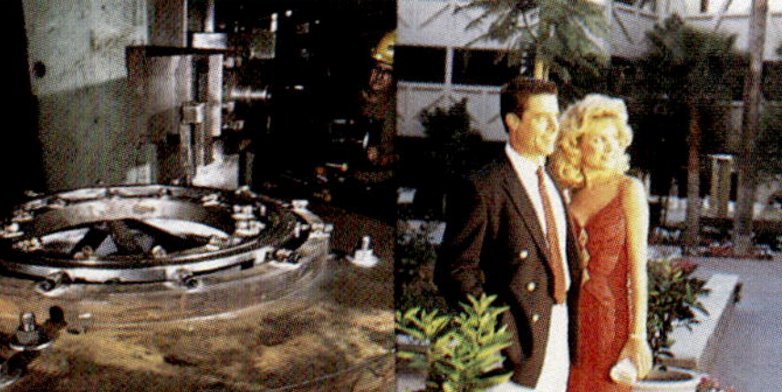

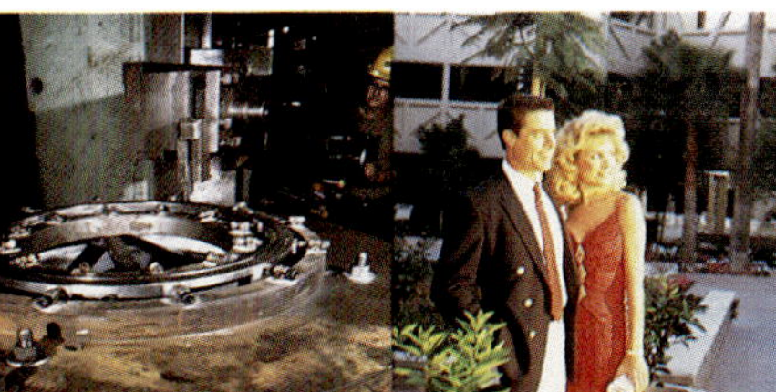

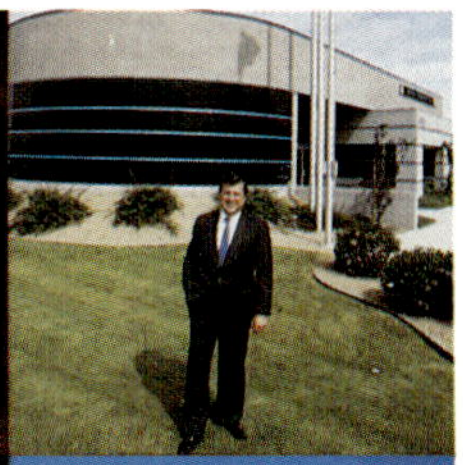

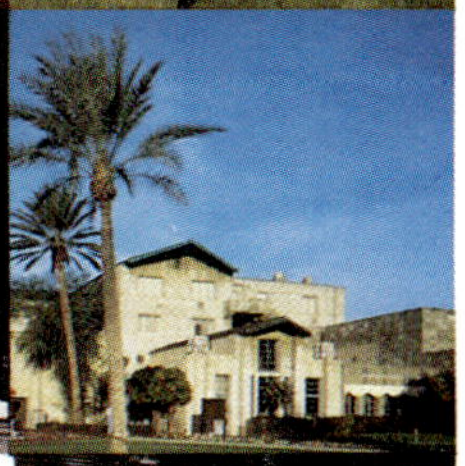
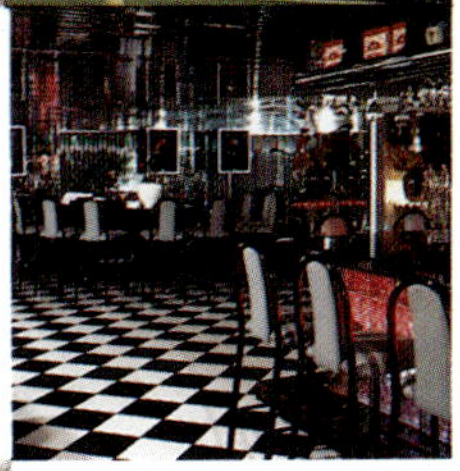

Photo by Bill Timmerman

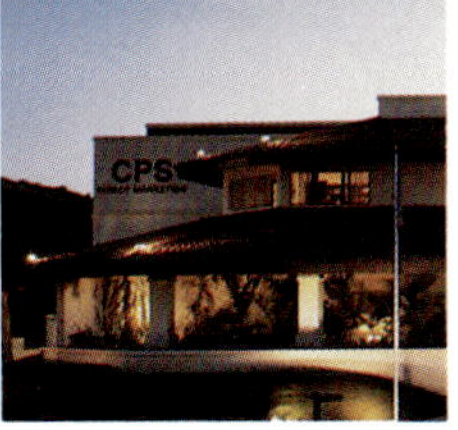

ADVANCED COPY SYSTEMS, INC.

When Robert Livingston decided to start a copy business, he knew what he was after—repeat customers. Accordingly, he was determined to build a firm that would stress customer service, the kind of old-fashioned, stand-behind-it service that wasn't seen much any more. Beginning with just three employees in 1978, Livingston made good on his word. Today he directs a staff of more than 70 employees. His business, Advanced Copy Systems, Inc., is already the oldest and largest fully authorized Canon Copier and Facsimile dealer in the state.

The firm sells the gamut of copiers from personal copy machines up through digital laser copiers. "We try to give the best value for the dollar," says Livingston. "We go in and assess the needs of our customers and recommend the equipment that will best serve them. If you do a good job, repeat business occurs. Our key is service, and all our technicians are Canon factory trained. Above all, we do what we say we will."

While sales and service are the wings of his business, innovation has helped it fly. Over the years Livingston instituted a number of unique features. With the purchase of an Advanced Copy Systems, Inc., service contract, customers receive a seven-year guarantee—in writing—that formally states the company policy: to stand behind its equipment for seven years. Livingston can make this promise because he knows his product. He also has a policy that every copier or FAX machine is checked out on the premises before being delivered to a customer.

Should service problems arise, Livingston responds with what he refers to as "a unique service trick." He devised this system to cut downtime. Basically he stocks an ample parts and supply inventory at all times, which virtually eliminates waiting for parts. Service not only means going that extra mile, it also means not damaging the customer's office walls or furniture in the process. To assure safe delivery, Livingston invented a special three-wheel delivery vehicle that allows one man to bring in and install a console

Advanced Copy Systems ensures its customers quality service with a seven-year guarantee to stand behind its products.

machine smoothly. Once the equipment is installed and operating, Advanced Copy Systems has one last extra to offer. The firm's service contract includes reinstruction to office personnel for the length of the contract. "We know that secretaries change," Livingston explains, "so our contract covers any reinstruction as needed."

Although Advanced Copy Systems, Inc., grew up in Phoenix, Livingston is looking toward the expanding valley. New offices are planned for Scottsdale and Mesa. With his daughter, Tracy, and his son, Kent, as active corporate officers, the firm appears headed for more success. Livingston agrees that innovations in equipment keep his company on the move. However, he credits his firm's support system for much of Advanced Copy Systems' success. "I looked at this business from a consumer standpoint," he says. "What would I want if I were buying a piece of equipment? How would I want to be treated? I knew that I would want a knowledgeable, professional person servicing me." So that's exactly what Advanced Copy Systems, Inc., produces.

In the quickly changing world of copiers and facsimile machines, the manufacturer and the dealer must be committed to the same goals: great products, great service, and, above all, caring. Advanced Copy Systems, Inc., offers all of these important ingredients and more.

Advanced Copy Systems, Inc., is the oldest and largest fully authorized Canon Copier and Facsimile dealer in Arizona.

FAMOUS RESTAURANTS INC.

When Julio and Olivia Garcia opened a restaurant in Phoenix in 1956, they had no idea they were starting a tradition that would ultimately stretch coast to coast. Remember, in the 1950s salsa had not yet taken the world by storm. Now, a little more than 30 years later, the name "Garcia's" says "excellence" in Mexican cuisine from Alaska to New Jersey. Although Julio and Olivia have since retired from the kitchen, diners are assured that all original dishes are faithfully prepared according to Olivia's recipes. And there's an ever-growing list of equally delicious and inventive new creations.

Today the Garcia's tradition is continued by Dennis Mullen, president of Famous Restaurants Inc.; Lowell Petrie, vice-president/marketing; Dan Anderson, vice-president/operations; Doyle Judd, vice-president/finance; and Geoff Zinke, vice-president/construction. "Our company's roots are here in Phoenix," Petrie says. "Our company grew because Arizonans love Mexican food."

The story really begins in 1979, when the Garcias joined with outside investors to expand their restaurants beyond Arizona. During the next three years Garcia's restaurants opened in Minneapolis, Des Moines, and Chicago. In 1981 Julio and Olivia sold their interest, the company went public, and an overly ambitious growth campaign was launched. By 1983 Garcia's of Scottsdale had grown from six to 29 restaurants. Says Petrie, "It was too many, too fast."

Enter Dennis Mullen, former president of Chart House and Cork & Cleaver and co-founder of a small regional chain of Mexican restaurants. For the next three years operations were streamlined, management solidified, and Famous Pacific Fish Company, a small California firm with restaurants in Santa Barbara, California, and Scottsdale, acquired. In 1985 Garcia's of Scottsdale became Famous Restaurants Inc.

Now with successful operations in California, Arizona, Nevada, New Jersey, Florida, Iowa, Colorado, Ohio, Tennessee, Washington, Oregon, South Carolina, and Alaska, and franchises in New York and Idaho, Famous Restaurants Inc. is expanding again. By 1988 Famous Restaurants Inc. included 47 restaurants. Mexican food remains the mainstay, but seafood and Caribbean specialties add diversity to the corporate menu.

While themes, locations, and specialties vary, the rationale holds fast. Each Famous Restaurant customer deserves the best-possible dining experience. This translates as quality food, courteous and friendly service, and great ambience at each location. The taste-and-tell program, for example, hires consumers to visit Famous Restaurants and rate them. "It's our best way to check up on our staff, food, and ambience," says Petrie. "The last question we ask is, 'Do you feel that the staff is genuinely concerned that you have a positive dining experience?'" Because staff excellence is amply rewarded, Famous Restaurants Inc. has one of the lowest employee turnover rates in the industry.

As for the future, Petrie assures that the whole enchilada has not been covered in Phoenix. "The valley is one of our main expansion markets," he says. "We have an established history here and a 12-month market, and we see growth coming."

A bountiful combination plate with a tempting margarita is typical Garcia's fare.

AMERICAN GREYHOUND RACING, INC.

With the opening in January 1988 of the new Phoenix Greyhound Park, racing took on a new dimension in Arizona. The $17-million clubhouse complex offers all the excitement of the sport and the ambience of fine art and architecture. Racing fans have never had it like this—not in the more than 30 years since greyhounds began chasing lures around Phoenix ovals.

The dogs and the fans have William Gresser to thank for their elegant surroundings. The energetic, dedicated president of American Greyhound Racing, Inc., is on the fast track, determined to improve the prestige and popularity of the sport and enhance the local name recognition of its parent, Delaware North Companies. Delaware North, a privately owned international holding company, is headquartered in Buffalo, New York.

In addition to his racing responsibilities, which include operations at the Phoenix, Apache Junction, and Yuma Greyhound parks, Gresser handles giant Park 'n' Swap flea markets held at various track locations and parks in Arizona, Tennessee, and Mississippi.

Gresser is a member of the Arizona Academy and a director of various organizations, including the Arizona Museum of Science and Technology, the Arizona Community Foundation, the Arizona Foundation for the Handicapped, the Boys Clubs of Metropolitan Phoenix, the National Conference of Christians and Jews, the Phoenix Symphony Association, and the Harvard Business School Club of Arizona.

While he takes pride in the expanded, improved racing facility, the president is especially proud of the Arizona Greyhound Foundation. "We give away a half-million dollars a year to charitable and civic causes," he points out.

Gresser notes that the foundation has donated a permanent exhibit at the Phoenix Children's Zoo, has donated considerable money to Arizona State University for scholarships in both fine arts and business, and is a primary sponsor of the Phoenix Boys Choir. "Between the foundation, our racing interests, and various other projects we

The $17-million Phoenix Greyhound Park, which opened in January 1988, offers not only the excitement of the sport but also the ambience of fine art and architecture.

have in this state, including APCOA, the largest parking company in the world, American Greyhound Racing and Delaware North Companies make a sizable economic impact in Phoenix.

"We have nine charity days a year, during which time we donate our profits to designated causes," Gresser continues. "We have always believed that if we live in a community, it's incumbent upon us to help that community in any way we can." He adds that he does everything in the name of American Greyhound Racing, Inc., "because it is imperative that we project a positive corporate presence in Arizona. We must let people know that we are contributing here, that success is a two-way street."

Thanks to the efforts of Gresser, his dedicated staff, and the policies of Delaware North Companies, Phoenix is the big winner.

William P. Gresser, president (left), and William Georgantos, vice-president and general manager of American Greyhound Racing, at the entrance to the terrace level/clubhouse.

GRAND CANYON COLOR LAB

"It is unusual for a lab that provides such a wide range of services to be so consumer oriented," observes Michael Aron of Grand Canyon Color Lab. But at Grand Canyon Color Lab the company thrives on its split image.

The wholesale arm of the firm concentrates on serving a variety of printing needs for Arizona, California, and Texas. The first lab to process color film in Arizona, it has continued to pioneer innovations. Today Grand Canyon Color Lab is one of just 13 in the country to process Kodachrome film. "Basically we are the only people who process this film between Los Angeles and Dallas," says Aron.

While the lab handles developing and printing requirements, the retail end of the company concentrates on selling service. Twenty stores help keep Grand Canyon Color Lab in touch with consumers. "Our store personnel is our strength," emphasizes Aron. "Our people behind the counters are more knowledgeable about the full range of services available. And if they have a question, each of them has access to our production manager."

Aron explains that part of his company's success can be traced to its policy of continually changing and diversifying to answer consumer needs. The firm has seven locations doing one-hour work, once considered an innovation in the industry. As more radical changes occur in the photo field, Aron anticipates that his lab will adapt

A Kodachrome film-processing machine. Grand Canyon Color Lab is one of just 13 in the country to process Kodachrome film.

Owner Michael Aron has kept Grand Canyon Color Lab in the forefront of color-film-processing techniques.

quickly to each new technology.

Professional service has been a hallmark of this company since 1957, when Michael Aron's father, Benjamin Aron, purchased the business. With less than a dozen employees, he opened up shop on Van Buren. Soon Aron moved his enterprise to Washington Street, and in 1969 the firm relocated to its present site on Seventh Avenue. Today two production facilities—a second one is located on Thomas Road—and the retail stores employ more than 130 people.

Although the size of the company and the sophistication of the equipment has changed over the past 30 years, the dedication to serving customers holds fast. "There is a correlation between having a lab on site and a store in the front," Aron says.

The firm is known for producing high-quality, high-volume work. "In the early days everything was done by hand," Aron says. "Now, of course, we use sophisticated film-processing machines that process film, and computerized color printers." However, he cautions, state-of-the-art equipment never replaces the skill of a sensitive eye and hand. Some work still must be done by hand at the lab. Moreover, each step of the process is overseen by professional technicians who are dedicated to assure customers the highest-quality photo product.

This double image—the combination of wide-ranging services and assured superior quality—has made Grand Canyon Color Lab a favorite in the Grand Canyon state.

SERVICE CONTROL CORPORATION

Service Control Corporation was founded in 1977 to acquire a local Phoenix textile-leasing facility that was grossing $1.8 million per year. Eleven years later Service Control Corporation boasts revenues of more than $100 million per year. Stretching across the Sunbelt from California to Florida, SCC employs some 2,500 people and is acknowledged in the textile-leasing industry as the leader in the Southwest.

The genius behind this amazing story is William Zacks, founder of Service Control Corporation and its leader until his untimely death in 1987. Zacks recognized that the nation was beginning to realize the benefits of personnel in uniform (professional image, safety), yet the textile-leasing industry remained a scattering of small, family-owned businesses. An imaginative entrepreneur, Zacks saw an opportunity to create a nationwide network of occupational textile-leasing companies throughout the Southwest, providing services to the hospitality, health, and industrial markets. With the Phoenix plant, Industrial Uniform Service, he began building his network

The dynamic thrust of this company continues under the leadership of George E. McFall, president and chief

Officers of the corporation (from left): Edward Tormey, vice-president and secretary/treasurer; George E. McFall, president and chief executive officer; and David Eisenberg, executive vice-president, who, with the board of directors, maintains the forward thrust of Service Control Corporation.

---

executive officer, who continued the forward momentum of SCC with a theme of Accelerate in '88. While still in an acquisition mode, SCC attributes much of its success to the customer-related service programs in effect.

William Zacks, founder of Service Control Corporation in 1977 and chairman and chief executive officer until July 1987. This man's vision and sense of urgency inspired his team to excellence.

One of these programs is a questionnaire called "How Do We Rate" that is periodically mailed to all customers. Each returned questionnaire is read by McFall and key executives of the company: David Eisenberg, executive vice-president, and Edward Tormey, vice-president. "We treat each customer as if he were our only customer," says Tormey. "Many customers write back to say that they are pleased as punch, but whenever there's a problem, we immediately get on it. After the problem is resolved, we check back with the customer to verify that the problem has been resolved satisfactorily. We work hard at customer relations."

"One of our most important assets," says McFall, "is the great team of people we have at SCC. We encourage suggestions from everyone on the team, and it gives me great pleasure to hear from so many of them."

Good customer relations, superior management, an unusual depth of inventory, and fine products all contribute to the fast-track record of Service Control Corporation. Growth is a given there. Whether viewed from a revenue, customer, or employee base, Service Control Corporation rates "uniformly" as a success.

BEST WESTERN INTERNATIONAL

Best Western International, the world's largest motel membership association, is headquartered in Phoenix. By 1993 the international headquarters will be reaching out to every corner of the globe.

"Earning the largest market share and then keeping it year after year is not something that happens simply by accident," says Ron Evans, chief executive officer of the world's largest lodging membership association. "It requires high-quality properties in the right places, offering the finest customer service at the right price."

Travelers the world over would agree. Today the Best Western sign translates as quality in any language. "We are only as good as the quality of our products and services we offer our guests," continues Evans. "Building market share requires that we provide consistent standards of quality wherever we display our name and logo."

In the next few years that name and logo will become even more familiar as Best Western International reaches out into the far corners of the globe. By 1993 it is anticipated that Best Western will add nearly 1,000 affiliates in 50 countries, bringing the total number of properties associated with the chain to 4,200. Targeted areas include Europe, the South Pacific, the Middle East, South America, and Africa, with a major push planned for Asia.

Merrill K. Guertin, a California hotelier of uncommon insight, decided to link independent properties 43 years ago. His idea was simple: to form a loose association of small business people who would band together to promote their individually owned lodging properties. Guertin, who had developed the concept of "auto camps" in 1923, reasoned that each would draw strength from the others without sacrificing individuality and independence. The next four decades proved Guertin's instinct prophetic.

"Referrals" meant that front-desk operators could call one another to make recommendations and place reservations. Travelers soon found out his system worked. By 1948 Guertin was publishing and distributing several millions of copies of a book listing the associated properties. *Best Western Motel (BWM) Guide* was a nationwide hit, and Guertin's organization was headed for the highway of success.

In 1966 Merrill Guertin retired. Best Western moved its headquarters from Long Beach, California, to Phoenix and soon announced a major expansion program. Over the next 15 years the association grew in size and sophistication, and in 1981 Best Western became the world's largest chain of independently owned and operated hotels.

Because Best Western is dedicated to making travel more comfortable and more convenient, its standards for quality have set the standard in the industry. The organization has led the way in improving the overall lodging experience. It has standardized and formalized international affiliate agreements and instituted computer reservations links to airlines and travel agents.

Today Best Western hotels, motels, and resorts are a world away from the auto camps Merrill Guertin developed. But the original concept of the association remains intact: to develop a network of unique, independent lodging facilities that serve travelers' needs.

In achieving this goal, Best Western has never wavered from its focus: to encourage and preserve ambience and charm throughout member properties. Consequently, whether heading for Tahiti or Tombstone, those who choose the independent Best Western route know that a pleasant surprise always awaits them.

Dedicated to making traveling more comfortable and convenient, Best Western's reservation system takes the worry out of travel.

RAMADA INC.

Marion Isbell, a retired Chicago restaurateur, and a group of investors started it all in the early 1950s with a simple idea: Why not build roadside hotels in convenient locations along the fast-growing interstate highway system? The first property opened in Flagstaff, Arizona, in 1954. By 1959 the group had adopted the Ramada name—Spanish for "shady resting place"—and sold its first franchise. The rest is hotel history. Now more than 30 years later Ramada Inc. is an international hospitality company playing host to guests in the lodging, gaming, and restaurant industries.

Headquartered in Phoenix, Ramada is organized into three divisions reflecting its three lines of business: the Ramada Hotel Group, the Gaming Group, and the Restaurant Group.

The Ramada Hotel Group owns, manages, franchises, or has contracts for more than 138,000 hotel rooms in some 800 properties worldwide. The company's hotel brands—Rodeway Inns, Ramada inns and hotels, and Renaissance hotels—span the economy to upscale markets. All three products offer outstanding accommodations, great service, and value, but have distinct differences and are targeted at specific segments of the lodging market.

The franchised Rodeway Inn properties, located primarily in the southern and southwestern United States, compete on value in the economy, limited service market. Ramada inns and hotels are the company's best-known and most widely represented lodging products. These two lodging products aim squarely at the mid-price lodging tier, offering convenient and attractive accommodations to business and leisure travelers. Renaissance hotels, introduced in 1982, are four-star-quality properties with luxury-level services and amenities at a more modest room rate.

In recent years Ramada's Hotel Group has been reshaping its operations through the sale of older, less appealing properties and the extensive refurbishment of its other hotels. The firm has tightened quality standards for franchised hotels and, most recently, made a major commitment to improving the quality of guest services systemwide with its You're Somebody Special program.

Internationally, Ramada has set its sights on increasing its representation in major cities within targeted regions of the world. Development projects are expanding Ramada's presence in the Asia-Pacific region, which includes Australia, as well as Europe, Canada, Mexico, and the Caribbean. Owing to this successful expansion activity, Ramada's collection of international hotels numbers more than 100 properties in 33 countries.

The Hotel Group also is moving to broaden domestic representation of its inns and hotels in primary and secondary markets alike. As part of that effort, the company has introduced a new Ramada Inn design to meet the needs of frequent business and leisure travelers. This new-style property offers larger, residential-style accommodations, downsize public spaces, and limited services at a reasonable value.

In addition to developing new Ramada inns for its own account, the firm has mounted an aggressive franchise sales push with a view toward achieving continued growth in the number of licensed properties in its product tiers in major U.S. markets.

Ramada's Gaming Group operates a portfolio of four themed gaming properties in the primary U.S. gaming markets: Las Vegas, Nevada; Atlantic City, New Jersey; Reno, Nevada; and Laughlin, Nevada.

The Las Vegas Tropicana Resort and Casino has emerged as a world-class destination resort and convention center following the completion of a $70-million expansion program in 1986. With its tropical island theme and growing reputation as an unmatched attraction in Las Vegas, the Tropicana is positioned to remain a strong, profitable operation for Ramada in the years to come.

Ramada's Atlantic City hotel casino is a luxurious gaming facility located on the city's famous Boardwalk. Recently Ramada completed a $200-million expansion that positioned the Tropicana, now known as TropWorld

This new Ramada Inn at Union Hills Drive and the Black Canyon Freeway (Interstate 17) in north Phoenix represents the new style of business-oriented Ramada properties.

Casino and Entertainment Resort, as one of the first of the new generation of gaming megafacilities in Atlantic City.

With about 90,000 square feet of casino floor space, TropWorld ranks as one of the largest casinos in the world. The most distinctive element of the property is an adult-oriented, two-acre indoor theme park showcasing Old Atlantic City and the Boardwalk's famous traditions. With its world theme,

the TropWorld megafacility offers day and overnight visitors to Atlantic City the widest range of gaming and entertainment options available in its market.

Eddie's Fabulous 50's Casino & Diner is the firm's 1950s-theme gaming property in Reno, Nevada. The 30,000-square-foot facility is located along Virginia Street, Reno's main casino thoroughfare.

Ramada's fourth gaming property is a railroad-theme hotel casino in Laughlin, Nevada, the country's fastest-growing gaming market. Known as Ramada Express Hotel and Casino, the Laughlin property targets drive-in customers from Los Angeles and Phoenix.

The Restaurant Group operates and franchises the Marie Callender's chain of mid-price, family-style restaurants located primarily in the western United States.

Today Marie Callender's is recognized as one of the country's finest family-style restaurant operations, known for its outstanding product quality and commitment to guest satisfaction. Ramada's growth objective for Marie Callender's, which was acquired in 1986, is to extend the chain's presence nationwide by the early 1990s.

Growth, Ramada style, manifests itself in a variety of ways in Phoenix. In 1988 the company moved its Ramada and Rodeway hotel reservations centers

from Omaha to Phoenix, creating more jobs and solidifying its corporate presence in the valley. Ramada also began building several new Ramada inns in the Phoenix metropolitan area—hotels that enhanced Ramada's local image. Marie Callender's is also enjoying growing representation in the valley. The recent opening of its newest location in Chandler gave Marie Callender's six restaurants in the area.

As the corporation looks to the 1990s, the homegrown "shady resting place" image of Ramada is a memory. Today Ramada Inc., rooted in the Arizona sunshine, is a dynamic, diverse, global corporation that serves the hospitality industry with excellence.

ABCO MARKETS, INC.

To the customers who shop ABCO and to the 6,000 employees who keep the 75 stores in the state of Arizona running, Ed Hill *is* ABCO Markets.

The president and chief executive officer seems to run the locally owned and managed chain of supermarkets effortlessly, or at least without getting winded. Since the leveraged buyout in October 1984, Hill has added ten new stores with four presently under construction. With the help of his two business partners, Les Knox as vice-president/marketing and Ed Gast as vice-president/finance, Hill has brought ABCO to the number-three position in the Phoenix market, and is working on being number one.

"We saw the Phoenix market as the place to do business," he says about the buyout from Alpha Beta Company of California. "We want to grow with Phoenix, and with the strength of our management people who are committed, aggressive, and alert, we'll do just

Phoenix is headquarters for the 75 ABCO Markets throughout Arizona, all of which are committed to close ties with the local community.

that."

People are what separate ABCO from the pack of retail supermarkets. It's obvious from the courtesy clerks to the executives that something's going on at ABCO—something that has to do with local commitment, close ties with the community, and an investment in employees who are the backbone of any retail, labor-intensive business.

"We got great cooperation from the development companies in Phoenix, from Fleming (Food Distributors), and from the Arizona Bank when we launched this company," says Hill of the birth of ABCO Markets, Inc. "Now our goal is to make Phoenix the headquarters for a regional chain, expanding into other markets but keeping our base here."

In the meantime ABCO is putting a lot of money into capital investments: building new stores, remodeling existing stores, and creating new jobs for some 600 people. Even with the challenge of overseeing the growth of a large retail chain, ABCO management keeps people at the top of the priority list.

"What separates us from the pack?

Ed Hill, president and chief executive officer of ABCO Markets.

It has to be people," says Hill, referring to the strength of his company. "People who work hard, who like other people, who enjoy their jobs—that's what differentiates us from our competitors."

WASTE MANAGEMENT OF PHOENIX

As the city grows so does the market for urban services. In Phoenix, commercial and residential customers look to Waste Management of Phoenix for this important task. The company, one of the largest divisions of the Oak Brook, Illinois-headquartered Waste Management, Inc., appeared on the Phoenix scene in 1970, when the parent firm bought Universal Waste Control. Acknowledged as a global leader in the field of solid waste management, the international firm generates revenues in excess of $2.8 billion annually and employs more than 31,000 people worldwide. All are trained professionals.

The key to the firm's success, says James D. Teter, general manager and vice-president of the Phoenix operation, is its personnel. He points out that more than 70 percent of the Phoenix employees have been with the company 15 years or more. This solid employee base has helped Waste Management, Inc., to grow more than 20 percent per year for the past 20 years.

Waste Management of Phoenix employs more than 200 people and operates in excess of 100 vehicles per day to dispose of 1,600 tons of solid waste daily. The firm focuses on commercial and residential collection services, waste-transfer systems, resource recovery, and disposal of solid waste. Nationally, the corporation is the industry leader in promoting and establishing curbside recycling through its RECYCLE AMERICA residential and commercial service.

In Phoenix the company operates the 27th Avenue landfill for the City of Phoenix and serves more than 12,000 commercial customers and 70,000-plus residential customers.

The recent development of a new 1,200-acre, environmentally sound waste-disposal site in southeast Maricopa County and a waste-transfer facility in Phoenix represents a significant investment for the parent firm. Although Waste Management, Inc., owns or operates more than 100 sanitary landfills nationwide, this represents the first privately owned and operated facility in Arizona. "It will solve the East Valley disposal problems for the next 50 years," says Teter.

Expansion in all areas keeps this New York Stock Exchange-listed corporation on the move. In 1987 the parent company established WMI Services. This division offers services other than solid waste management that are provided to commercial, governmental, and special events customers. In 1988 the Phoenix operation followed suit. Under WMI, the company provides Port-A-Let portable sanitation services, modular offices, construction trailers, storage containers, temporary fence rental, and pest control.

"The solid waste management field is just beginning to grow. We are the IBM of the 1980s." Teter emphasizes that ongoing research and development efforts are designed to support environmental concerns. "We do environmental audits on all of our customers because we want to know exactly what we are hauling and disposing." Not only is Waste Management of Phoenix addressing the environmental concerns in Phoenix, but, says Teter, "We are also committed to solve the environmental problems of Arizona."

Waste Management, Inc., is international in scope and the parent company of Waste Management of Phoenix, which addresses the environmental concerns of solid waste management for the local area.

HORIZON MOVING SYSTEMS, INC.

"We got into Phoenix at a time when there was so much opportunity," says Leonard F. Boyles, executive vice-president of Horizon Moving Systems, Inc., "and yet we see that so much more opportunity exists here. We are just now reaching out to attract new industry. I can see continued growth here over the next 20 years."

Boyles speaks from the comfortable perspective of a 65-year corporate history. Although the firm was founded in 1924 in Tucson, the explosive growth years began in 1970, the year Horizon Moving & Storage opened in Phoenix. Today the company has revenues in excess of $10 million and agencies in Phoenix, Tucson, Flagstaff, Yuma, and Sierra Vista. It is an acknowledged industry leader, one of the most progressive privately held firms in the moving and transportation field. Even the federally mandated events of the most recent years have not daunted this company. Says Boyles, "I believe that deregulation has forced us to be more sophisticated to survive."

Founded as City Van & Storage by C.R. Dusenberry, the company was originally set up to haul baggage and household goods from Tucson for residents who had cabins in Madera Canyon, 35 miles to the south. Dusenberry's family owned and operated the Santa Rita Lodge and Cabins in the canyon and provided moving help as a sideline. On the return trip Dusenberry hauled oak wood, which was sold in Tucson for fuel.

In the mid-1930s the family moved to Tucson, where it continued in the hauling business. City Van & Storage handled baggage, made deliveries for a large Tucson department store, and occasionally helped a family move to a new home.

By 1939 City Van & Storage had become an agent for the fledgling United Van Lines, an owner-operated consortium of national agents. Like other moving and storage firms, City Van & Storage became heavily involved in the war effort and responded to the increased demands on the moving industry that accompanied World War II.

By 1941 Bruce E. Dusenberry had joined his father in the business, which was operated out of the family home in Tucson. A decade later, in 1952, the elder Dusenberry sold the business to the children, Bruce and Lois. Although Lois maintains a financial interest, she retired from active management in the company after several years.

In 1965 Bruce and his wife, Katie, bought a 70-percent interest in a small moving company in Sierra Vista. Five years later, in 1970, they opened a third operation in Phoenix. To assure better statewide identity, they named this company Horizon Moving & Storage and moved Len Boyles from Tucson up to Phoenix to manage it. Within a few years the firm had added operations in Yuma and Flagstaff to round out its statewide profile.

Today Horizon Moving Systems serves not only Arizona and the nation but also the world. On the domestic front, the firm is fully equipped to handle all kinds of services—from moving household goods, cars, general commodities, and electronics to receiving, warehousing, and installing furniture and fixtures for model homes, hotels, motels, offices, and restaurants. In addition to its physical services, the company also offers emotional support through the Bette Malone relocation seminar and destination information center. For more than 30 years this service, which is a key department at United Van Lines, has helped take the uncertainty out of moving.

Boyles emphasizes that the firm has made a deliberate effort to diversify its services. "When we first moved into Phoenix, our market was primarily an inbound customer. Everything was coming into the Phoenix area, which meant that we had to go out to book these incoming moves. This caused us to offer relocation seminars and do turnkey moves. Before long word got out that we were experts at this."

On the international front, Horizon Moving Systems handles a variety of services to ease the trauma of overseas moves. Agents oversee moving or forwarding, packing and crating, domestic forwarding, warehousing and customs brokering, and complete door-

Horizon Moving Systems, Inc., is prepared to handle any phase of moving and storage domestically, and provides a variety of services to ease the trauma of overseas moves.

to-door shipping via land, sea, or air.

Explains Boyles, "We do a great deal of international moving. We help families relocate all over the world, and a large part of our business is factory relocation. We oversee moving both the people and the equipment for clients."

In addition to domestic and international moves, Horizon Moving Systems is also well known for its distribution expertise. "We are now the leader in hotel, motel, and restaurant turnkey

operations," acknowledges Boyles. "Not only do we store equipment and supplies in our warehouses, but we also deliver and install the stored items. The restaurant business has turned into a real specialty of ours," he concludes.

With 80 employees in Phoenix and some 175 people statewide, Horizon Moving Systems is today equipped to handle every moving need from packing and crating to distribution and warehousing. Much of the company's success can be traced to its innovative attitude. Horizon Moving Systems moves with the times. The firm pioneered a sophisticated computerized inventory-control system in which every piece that is handled is bar coded so it can be traced through every step of the moving process. "We can punch up our computer screens and see an inventory that shows what each of our customers has in our warehouse or in transit," Boyles notes. This extensive computer network provides an invaluable service to customers, management, and operating staff by providing updated tracing, monitoring, and status reports on each item handled by Horizon Moving Systems.

In addition to computerized inventory control, Horizon developed a specialty in moving highly delicate electronic equipment. Computers, medical and dental equipment, and scientific and laboratory machines all can be safely moved, stored, and installed when in the hands of Horizon Moving Systems. Delicate shipments are blanket-wrapped, secured, and moved on an air-ride suspension van—a precaution that reduces road shock and vibration by as much as 75 percent as compared to transport in a van with conventional spring suspension.

A total transportation company, Horizon Moving Systems, Inc., has come a long way from Madera Canyon; yet in some respects, the company has not changed at all. It is still a family-owned business staffed with managers who have a longtime commitment to the company and to the customer. It is this commitment to providing the best-possible moving experience that has secured a place at the top for Horizon Moving Systems, Inc.

NORTHAMERICAN PHARMACEUTICAL SERVICES, INC.

As insurers, major employers, and other benefit sponsors saw the cost of providing a prescription drug benefit program soar dramatically, Benjamin D. Ward, chief executive officer of National Vision Services and founder of Pharmaceutical Card System, Inc., had a better idea: Why not establish a managed pharmaceutical care program geared to respond to the needs of both the employer and the employee?

The result is NPS, a national prescription benefit services company. It is a flexible, affordable, drug benefit program that lets the employer control the cost, the use, and the quality of the services without falling prey to mediocrity or negatively impacting employee relations.

To deliver on this promise, NPS offers innovative benefit plan features as well as careful claims administration. This total service approach to managed pharmaceutical care is unique in that it allows NPS to design and implement a prescription drug program that creates powerful incentives for participants to purchase only necessary prescriptions, shop for competitive pricing, and request generic and mail-service drugs. Because it serves both the employer and the employee, NPS is dedicated to customer service—further assuring the highest level of quality. With these kinds of forces driving the plan, it comes as no surprise that this young, Phoenix-based firm is fast changing the way in which nationwide corporate management and employee groups handle prescription drug care.

A seasoned entrepreneur who specializes in innovative answers to pressing health care questions, Ward is accustomed to success. Still, no matter how innovative the idea, he credits his team of NPS professionals for converting his concept into a nationwide company.

Ward, chairman of NPS, heads up an expert staff of top executives. Company president Robert O. McLaughlin comes to NPS with blue-chip experience in health insurance, having held senior positions in several Blue Cross and Blue Shield plans.

The heart of NPS is its Managed

Prescriptions and their instructions are checked by two or more pharmacists before leaving the mail-order pharmacy.

Pharmaceutical Care program (MPC), which is a cost-effective alternative to other prescription drug coverage plans. Designed with flexible components, MPC helps to customize the prescription program for each client. For instance, a plan may be designed to encourage the use of generic drugs, or geared toward the integrated mail-service plan that is also offered by NPS. MPC may also be a stand-alone benefit or incorporated into an existing health benefits package. As Ward and his team emphasize, the choice is the sponsor's.

While individual choice is the hallmark of this benefit program, the professional staff at NPS agrees that a sound prescription drug plan can take advantage of substantial savings if an employer encourages the use of generic drugs and a mail-service program in the plan design. Today generic drugs have gained wide acceptance both from the FDA and the general public, notes Ward; the FDA has approved more

than 5,000 generics. What's more, it is estimated that generics can save consumers more than $250 million per year. As part of a health care plan, Ward notes, employers can save as much as 50 percent by incorporating generic drugs into the benefits package.

The backbone of the MPC program is a network of carefully selected participating network pharmacies. These providers have contracted with NPS to pass on special benefits to the employees and sponsors who subscribe to the innovative program.

When a patient visits a network pharmacy, a discount is passed back to the sponsoring group. The provider network offers a service that is unequaled in its rewards, says Ward.

To further maximize savings, NPS offers a mail-service pharmacy option

A highly skilled management team steers the growth of NPS.

NPS helps its clients get a grasp on their prescription drug costs.

that features a nationwide network of mail-order pharmaceutical houses. Ward adds that this component can be designed with all the flexibility that has been built into the direct reimbursement component. This feature of NPS allows sponsors the greatest savings on maintenance drugs, he points out. Even more important, the savings is matched by employee satisfaction.

In addition to designing a managed care plan and delivering prescription drugs to employees, NPS administers specific claims programs and provides monthly reports showing utilization and savings compared to other prescription drug programs. Because NPS takes a unique position, serving both the employer and the employee, customer service remains its strength.

As part of the total package the plan distributes employee information kits, ID cards, payroll stuffers, and a toll-free number for customer service. Employees benefit from smart, cost-conscious purchasing as well as convenience in both obtaining prescription drugs and being reimbursed for them. Reimbursement is both efficient and easy with the MPC ID card and NPS claim forms that are provided to each employee. If the employee does not have an NPS claim form readily available, the pharmacist can use alternative

forms. The employee only has to mail the prescription drug claim signed by the pharmacist to NPS, which in turn reimburses the employee.

On the employer side of the ledger, NPS allows broad flexibility in program design, emphasizes cost containment, eases administrative responsibilities, provides management reports and unique customer service at no additional cost, and maintains employee benefit records. Monthly Decision-Maker reports detail utilization and show the savings accrued from the plan.

Above all NPS, with its MPC and mail-service pharmacy features, enables each client to be in control of his/her

A sophisticated state-of-the-art computer system is the backbone of the NPS claims-processing program.

own prescription drug program. As a result of this goal, NPS Managed Pharmaceutical Care is the most cost-effective and flexible alternative to both major medical and traditional plastic card programs.

A spin-off of National Vision Services, Inc., NPS is already making its mark in the world of managed health care. Although Ward calls his concept a "common-sense alternative," it may better be called a revolutionary approach.

Thanks to Ben Ward's ingenuity, excellence in specific areas of health care—delivered at an affordable price—is fast becoming a reality.

NATIONAL VISION SERVICES, INC.

Ben Ward is a man with ideas who admits that he likes starting things more than finishing them. With National Vision Services, Inc., the company he started from a single idea, Ward need not worry. The end is nowhere in sight.

National Vision Services is a Preferred Provider Organization offering managed care for primary vision needs. Currently serving 27 states, the plan is included in most Blue Cross and Blue Shield of Arizona products. Comparatively young, NVS traces its origins to an operation Ward founded in 1978 called National Optical Services, Inc. By 1986 the Arizona entrepreneur had taken his company public with an initial stock offering of 880,000 shares and had carved an impressive niche for himself.

Today NVS markets and administers vision benefit plans that enable card-holding members to obtain vision examinations, eyeglass frames and lenses, and contact lenses at the lowest-possible cost through a network of carefully selected optometrists and other vision professionals. That network is the heart of NVS. Every NVS provider is personally visited and evaluated by Ward's organization before becoming part of the network. The selection of each doctor by NVS is based upon specific criteria: technical abilities, quality and selection of eyewear, appointment availability, staff interaction, office layout, equipment, accessibility, and fee schedules. Ward explains that by hand-picking the professionals with whom they choose to work, "We are assured that we are spending dollars wisely."

Cost reductions are promoted through a strict system of pricing that dramatically reduces members' costs. Because providers see more patients, they are able to reduce their prices yet still make a good profit.

NVS looks upon its programs as not only an attractive benefit but also a way for employers to ease the problems associated with redesigning other medical and dental benefits for cost containment. "A vision-care system can help compensate for the loss of other coverage that results from these cost-shifting measures," Ward adds.

Although hundreds of PPOs are in existence today, NVS may be the only one devoted exclusively to providing vision services—and vision is big business. According to the National Center for Health Statistics, vision impairment ranks third behind heart disease and arthritis among chronic conditions that restrict accuracy and efficiency. Says Ward, "Most people, for example, don't realize that 72 percent of the working population requires corrective lenses." What's more, he adds, most employers are unaware that approximately one in five employees not wearing corrective lenses needs them.

Because NVS is experienced in dealing with the diversities of employee benefits as well as the complexities of the optical industry, the company is able to incorporate the necessary skills,

NVS has a vision of the future of eye-care benefits. Today 72 percent of the working population requires corrective eyewear, and the demand is growing.

A carefully screened network of optometrists and other vision-care professionals make up the backbone of the NVS system.

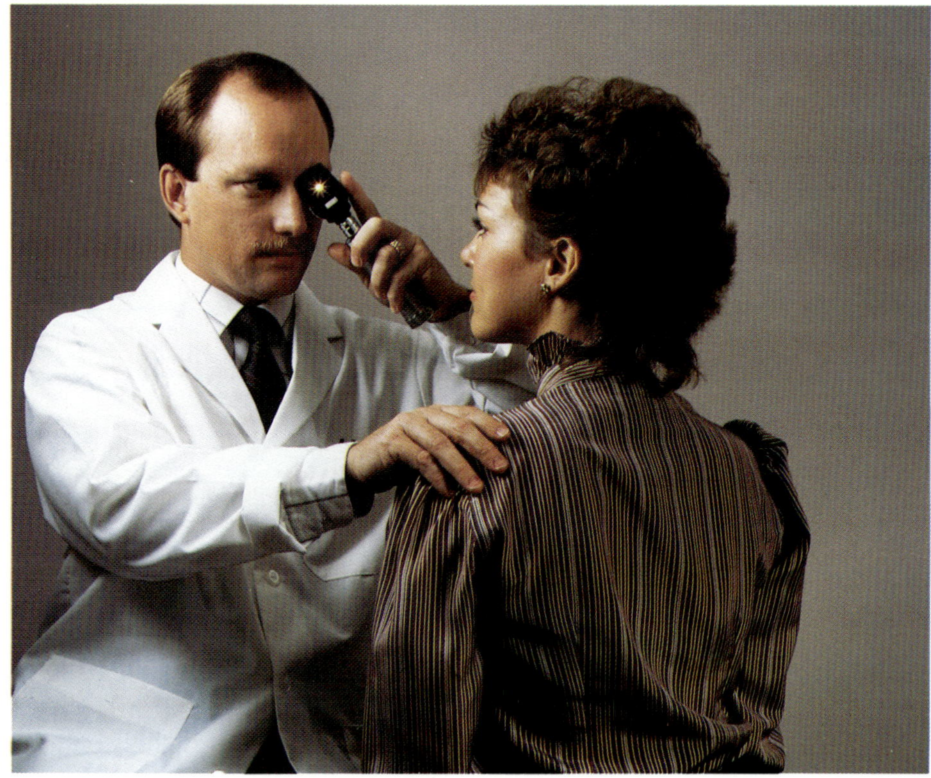

expertise, and insight to build a strong relationship with providers, clients, and individuals involved in all aspects of the optical industry. However, spotting a need does not guarantee a firm's success. Ben Ward admits that the company is growing so fast that it is difficult to cite statistics. However, revenues in 1989 are expected to top $5 million.

NVS assures its members of the best in optical supplies and the finest in professional services. The firm includes an unconditional guarantee on frames and eyeglass lenses for one year against defective materials and/or workmanship and also guarantees its pricing. If a member can purchase an identical pair of eyeglasses at a lower retail price within 30 days, the cost difference will be refunded.

A native of Tucson, Ward is a hands-on chief executive officer. "I've always taken an active role," he explains, "whether in my business or civic dealings." At NVS, his participation includes his personally interviewing every employee—from the receptionist on up. Ward is interested in employees' business skills as well as their hobbies and interests, and he requests that employees include this kind of information as standard data when they are interviewing for a job. He makes it his business to get to know each member of his team.

Ward explains his personalized approach by pointing out that it is only possible to build successful businesses through good people. "All my companies are service-oriented operations," he says. "You can't do this without good service-oriented people."

His interest in his employees' welfare extends beyond the norm. "We are trying to invest more money into our own people," says Ward. "One of my goals is to do something about child care for our employees. It is our intention to build the best-possible environment for people who work at NVS."

By any standard NVS is a clear winner; yet Ward takes his success in stride. He admits that when he gets restless, he starts a new business. NVS currently has four sister companies, National Card Services, Inc., National Dental Services, Inc., National Hearing Services, Inc., and Northamerican Pharmaceutical Services, Inc. However, he says candidly, it was not always a plus for an entrepreneur to be located in Phoenix. "When I first started a company in Phoenix in 1968 and went east to talk about it, many people thought we still had cowboys and Indians out here. Now all that has changed. Today Phoenix has arrived. Everyone wants to come out here to talk. Being located in Phoenix has now become an asset, since it is a place where we can both entertain visitors and conduct business."

Inset: Benjamin D. Ward, president and chief executive officer, is a hands-on leader who gets to know each member of his team.

NVS thrives in Phoenix. Marketing management easily entices prospective business to visit its central Phoenix headquarters.

GOLDWATERS

Goldwaters is a true Arizona story. From its pioneer beginnings to its present-day prominence, the name has always been synonymous with Arizona.

Says chief executive officer Howard Lehrer, "Our phenomenal growth story can be traced directly to Morris Goldwater, whose slogan was 'the best always.' In every department, we still stand for this motto. We are uniquely known for our collection of southwestern gifts. Customers look to us for merchandise and home accessories that are tailored to the Southwest. We also have a wonderful art collection of regional artists. Through the posters that we produce, we bring southwestern art to the public at affordable prices. We've continued this program every year since 1980."

With its newly remodeled and expanded showcase store at Scottsdale's Fashion Square and eight other stores located in Arizona, Albuquerque, and Las Vegas, Goldwaters might seem a

By 1876 the Goldwaters were doing business in Prescott in this impressive brick structure that defined them as Dealers in General Merchandise.

world away from the Old West origins. Yet this contemporary, fast-paced organization, a division of The May Department Stores Company since 1986, is keenly aware of its frontier beginnings. In some respects, it's as if founder Mike Goldwater never left.

When Michael Goldwater arrived in Arizona in 1860, only a few scattered settlements existed along the southern wagon road that led to the goldfields near present-day Yuma. The intrepid retailer recognized an exceptional opportunity. He opened his first traveling store, using pack animals and a buckboard to deliver supplies to weary miners. A few years later, when gold was discovered at La Paz on the Colorado River, he and his brother, Joseph, opened the first permanent Goldwater store. They sold it all there—everything from oysters to gunpowder, whiskey to boots.

Seven years later the La Paz boom ran out. When the miners departed for richer fields, the brothers followed suit. They abandoned that store, but opened a new one in the new boom town, Ehrenberg. To stock this shop, Mike Goldwater had merchandise shipped in from San Francisco via the Colorado River.

Although the Goldwaters had attempted a Phoenix location in 1887, that fledgling community could not support their venture. So when the route of the new Southern Pacific Railroad spelled the demise of Ehrenberg, the brothers looked north to Prescott. By 1876 they were doing business in an impressive brick structure that bore the name Goldwaters—"Dealers in General Merchandise."

Eventually Mike and Joseph agreed to disagree. Joseph sold out his interest

Goldwaters' Metro Center store in Phoenix. Goldwaters has been synonymous with Arizona history and a part of the Phoenix business community since the late 1800s.

to his brother and moved south to Bisbee to go into partnership with Miguel Castenada. That Goldwater & Castenada store became famous as the site of the Bisbee Massacre, an event that lives in Old West history, second only to the Gunfight at O.K. Corral.

By 1885 Mike Goldwater had served as Prescott's first mayor, but he decided to return to San Francisco. Accordingly he turned the store over to his sons, Morris and Baron, and headed west. By 1895 Baron believed that it was time to give Phoenix a second chance. Morris resisted. To settle the debate, the brothers played Casino. Baron won. That year Goldwaters opened in Phoenix at 31 First Street.

Morris, who had a keen interest in civic endeavors, brought the first telegraph line to Phoenix. As the premier operator, he remained on the line just long enough to send a historic message, "Get the hell off the line."

This time Phoenix was ready for Goldwaters. The store soon developed a reputation for superb service—even if that meant purchasing merchandise for a customer from another store, even an out-of-state department store. Through wholesale purchase and mass distribution, Goldwaters started the first branch merchandising operation in Arizona. From the outset, however, all these stores resisted a "chain" approach. Instead, Goldwaters adopted a philosophy of always serving the individual needs of more than one community at a time.

As Goldwaters' reputation flourished, so did its impressive list of firsts. The Phoenix store had the first passen-

ger elevator in Arizona and the first central cashier station. It also sponsored the first fashion show in the state. It became a tradition that has been an annual benefit event since 1929.

By the 1930s Baron had turned the business over to his two sons, Robert and Barry. Again, as was true of their predecessors, both men had plenty of ideas for business. Surely the most successful was their branding-iron design, a pattern of authentic Arizona cattle brands hand-screened on fabric. More than one million yards of this fabric were processed, and mail orders for it poured in from around the globe. Another hot item was the store's sterling silver swizzle sticks in the shape of branding irons that were offered through ads in *The New Yorker*.

Ultimately, Bob took over as president of Goldwaters. While Barry remained peripherally involved, as his uncle Morris did, he was drawn more to civic than business concerns.

When Associated Dry Goods bought Goldwaters in 1962, the three Goldwaters stores posted revenues of $8 million per year. Eight years later those figures had grown to $10 million. By 1988, under the ownership of The

Goldwaters' newly remodeled and expanded showcase store is located in Scottsdale's Fashion Square.

May Department Stores Company since 1986 and the leadership of Howard Lehrer, president and chief executive officer, the nine Goldwaters stores employed 2,500 and produced revenues of $170 million annually.

"We're growing with the spirit of the Southwest," says Lehrer. "We are aggressive, and we are benefiting from the significant dollars that our parent company is investing in this community. Above all, we are committed to 'excellence in retailing.'"

If "excellence in retailing" sounds a lot like "the best always" paraphrased, that's fine with Goldwaters. Tradition is important there. Over the years this company has maintained close ties to each community it serves. In Phoenix, this means being directly involved in nearly every major civic cause from the Phoenix Symphony to the Phoenix Zoo.

In fact, excellence is more than a slogan—it is a pervasive spirit, a way of corporate life. Excellence extends to all facets of this retail operation, from target markets to emphasis on innovation. Above all, the mission statement stresses, superior customer service is Goldwaters' strength and highest priority. Consequently, every Goldwaters employee is urged to have a passion for satisfying customer needs. This is both its challenge and mission as Goldwaters heads into the 1990s.

SWIFT TRANSPORTATION COMPANY, INC.

Jerry Moyes is a man on the move. Starting with one truck in 1966, Moyes has built a motor carrier business that today numbers more than 900 power units, employs 1,250 people, and serves the country with nine offices nationwide. "We are a full-service carrier based in Arizona, providing specialized service both in scope of operation and in types of equipment," acknowledges Moyes, president of Swift Transportation Company, in his quick, assertive fashion.

In a highly competitive business Swift Transportation has rolled up an enviable record both in revenues and performance. Beginning in 1977 with revenues of $5 million per year, the firm has grown at a phenomenal rate of more than 25 percent per year. This dynamic and youthful organization realized more than $50 million in annual revenues in 1987. Swift recently purchased Cooper Motor Lines in Greenville, South Carolina. With this acquisition, the company's revenues approached $100 million in 1988.

Its track record illustrates that this creative organization does not know the meaning of the word "complacent." Rather, Swift is always on the move, discovering new and better ways to serve its nationwide clientele.

Asked to comment on the company's remarkable success, Jerry Moyes credits the caliber of his employees for the firm's achievements. His executive team consists of Gary Knight, Bill Riley, Kevin Knight, and Clark Jenkins, all of whom are young, aggressive, and committed to the service and reliability that are the motivating forces behind this organization.

Innovation is what drives Swift Transportation. The computer linkup is one example of this state-of-the-art operation. Moyes explains that each tractor is equipped with a Rockwell Tripmaster that monitors driver adherence to company policy regarding speed limitations, operating efficiency, and

Swift Transportation Company, Inc.'s, corporate headquarters is located in Phoenix. The company also maintains eight additional terminals in key locations nationwide.

Photo by Tom Campbell

stops in transit. "Our computers enable us to keep track of every load we have on the road," says Moyes.

Equipment is another key part of the success equation. "Our special type of equipment means that we can serve every customer need. We are large enough that we can handle heavy loads, and we have the flexibility to move large volumes of equipment on a short period of notice," Moyes observes.

Noting that Swift has the capacity to haul 56,000 pounds of equipment with its flatbed trucks, the president points out that the company fleet includes high-cube doubles and special, 57-foot rollerbed carriers. "Although 25 percent of our loads originate in Phoenix, we haul all over the country," Moyes points out, emphasizing that

Top: Swift flatbed trucks have the capacity to haul 56,000 pounds of freight and are just part of the specialized equipment of this full-service carrier.

Above: The dynamic executive team at Swift (seated, from left): Gary Knight, vice-president; Jerry Moyes, president; and Clark Jenkins, vice-president. Standing (from left) are Bill Riley, vice-president, and Kevin Knight, vice-president.

Swift Transportation is a national corporation.

Listening to Jerry Moyes it's clear that professionalism is a hallmark of the firm. "It is unusual for a carrier to have so many different kinds of equipment geared to specific needs," Moyes agrees. "When we can't find the right trailer for the job, we design one. This perfectly exemplifies our service attitude."

In addition to designing equipment when needed, the president adds that it is company policy to replace tractors every three years to guarantee that only the latest equipment is on the road. Moyes is equally proud of Swift's warehouse facilities. "Our Los Angeles location is especially set up for import-export activities," he adds.

Swift drivers undergo the same kind of scrutiny as does all Swift equipment. "We screen and qualify all our drivers," says Moyes, noting that drivers must pass a complete training and education program to hone their skills before they take over Swift equipment. "If we are safe, we make it. If we aren't, we won't," he adds succinctly.

In an effort to promote more and better drivers for the company, Swift recently pioneered another innovation in the Phoenix area. The firm joined with Rio Salado Community College to produce a Drivers' Training School. Moyes estimates that there are fewer than a half-dozen such programs in existence nationwide and believes that this educational pairing will provide Swift with 200 drivers per year who are well trained and well equipped to handle this demanding profession.

With a 16,000-square-foot office building on 40 acres, Swift Transportation Company, Inc., makes an impressive mark on the southwestern desert landscape. "We keep 500 trucks based here," says Moyes, looking over the vast West Phoenix property. He adds that the Phoenix headquarters is also home to the company's maintenance department. Certified mechanics are on duty 24 hours a day, seven days a week to perform all required repair and maintenance services right on the premises. Keeping equipment in top shape minimizes downtime and increases operating efficiency, thereby helping to hold the line on costs.

Swift's customers have come to appreciate this attention to detail. Today, of the firm's 25 largest customers, 15 are listed in the *Fortune* 500. Says Moyes, "During the early 1970s our ability to meet delivery deadlines earned us a very favorable reputation within the grocery-warehouse industry, and our relationship with these customers is now one of our greatest assets. They know that Swift doesn't make commitments it can't meet."

On highways crowded with competitors, this Phoenix-headquartered nationwide firm has secured a position as an industry leader. Thanks to the caliber of its employees, equipment, and customers, Swift Transportation Company, Inc., will continue to grow—even faster than the West itself.

BUSINESS EQUIPMENT INC.

Within 18 months after moving into a brand-new, contemporary, high-tech building, Joseph B. Udvare's Business Equipment Inc. was already bursting at the seams. But this doesn't phase Udvare, who is accustomed to explosive growth. Within six years of starting Business Equipment Inc., the company expanded from 13 to more than 70 employees. By 1989 his operation is expected to number 120 employees, with branches in both New Mexico and Southern California, and gross annual sales exceeding $13 million.

"Our first year in business we did $1.2 million in sales," recalls Udvare. "And for the past five years we have increased sales by 30 percent per year each year." As for his space problems, Udvare anticipated such growth and has plenty of space to add on.

Asked to explain his success, this aggressive businessman credits a number of fortuitous factors. "First, we are the exclusive Minolta office automation dealer for Maricopa and Pinal counties," he explains. "Minolta is dedicated to its products. It is a pioneer in innovations in office equipment. Then, too, we were in the right place at the right time. The economy of Phoenix is excellent for our business. And finally, we have a great team of employees. It is this team that enabled us to be named Dealer of the Year in 1988—a national award that is selected from some 300 Minolta dealers."

His staff, he continues, is notable both for its talents and its dedication. "Our combined efforts in marketing are under the direction of Phillip Blake, vice-president/marketing and sales. Bradley Clark is supply division manager, and John Brigham is vice-president/ technical support," Udvare concludes. "It is this combination of three key individuals that has helped to propel us to our present position." Each of these executives has been with Udvare almost since the company's inception and has added an impressive measure of stability to a fast-growing concern.

A franchised Minolta Copier Dealership, Business Equipment Inc. was incorporated on July 8, 1980. Although Minolta cameras are almost household

Joseph B. Udvare, owner and president, outside Business Equipment Inc. headquarters at 3118 East McDowell Road, Phoenix.

words, Udvare quickly points out that the business equipment division is becoming almost equally as well known. This division continues to apply the company's advanced optical, chemical, electronic, and precision instrumentation know-how to the design and manufacture of advanced business equipment. New products produced by this Japanese firm continue to revolutionize the way office procedures and information are communicated, managed, and monitored.

Not only is Minolta long on quality, it is also fast on the draw. This company was the first to introduce the Reduction copier, the Enlargement copier, the Variable Zoom mid-volume copier, and pioneered the combination of a typewriter, word processor, and computer into one piece of equipment—to name but a few important Minolta innovations.

As the exclusive Minolta franchise in the Phoenix area, Business Equipment Inc. has quickly established a leading position for itself in the valley. Not only does it sell and lease an outstanding product, but through its sales force and well-trained field technicians, Business Equipment Inc. can assure its customers complete service both before and after purchase. To facilitate this ex-

Business Equipment Inc. was named Minolta Dealer of the Year in 1988 through an able group of employees and the executive management team of (from left) Phillip Blake, vice-president/ sales; John Brigham, vice-president/technical support; Joseph Udvare, president; and Bradley Clark, supply division manager.

perience, Udvare has put into place an intensive recruitment and training program featuring hands-on managerial supervision to keep his staff current on the latest innovations in Minolta equipment—not an easy task in light of the numerous new products that are introduced each year.

Today Business Equipment Inc. puts forward an impressive face in the Phoenix community. The well-designed facility on McDowell Road incorporates administrative offices, showrooms, and maintenance and storage facilities. Clients can come down to the showroom to see products demonstrated or have Business Equipment Inc. take the business machines out into the business community. As dedicated to his staff as he is to his cus-

tomers, Udvare has also installed a Nautilus workout room for his employees on the premises.

Udvare is justifiably proud of what his company has accomplished in such a short time. "Our business is a young man's business," says the youthful entrepreneur. "You have to keep learning with this. That's why I brought a training instructor on board to help keep us up to date with all the new equipment." Not only does Business Equipment Inc. handle all the Minolta business equipment, but Udvare adds, "We are also an authorized test center for Minolta, which means that we try out new machines anywhere from three to six months. We are testing new equipment for reliability and serviceability."

Reliability and service characterize Business Equipment Inc. as well. But these qualities are only part of the success story. Udvare is an unabashed civic promoter, a man who takes pleasure in giving back to the community. "We support all the chambers of commerce," he explains, adding that his firm also works on the East McDowell

Civic Association and that he serves as a member of the Phoenix Economic Growth Council. In addition, the corporation supports numerous athletic endeavors, including the Phoenix Suns, Arizona State Sun Devils, and the Phoenix Open golf tournament.

Sports are a particular favorite for this Phoenix executive. "I spend a minimum of four hours a week on civic activities—most of them having to do with kids and sports," Udvare says. "I work with basketball, baseball, and soccer teams through my capacity as a board member for the Madison Meadows School. I think that there are a lot of boys and girls out there who have to rely on organized activities to stay out of trouble. I get my company involved with me in this because I think that such civic involvement gives everyone a chance to feel that they are helping out and making a difference."

By any measure, Business Equipment Inc. has made a big difference in the Phoenix community. And, if the past is any indication, there's more to come.

ARIZONA BILTMORE

Cecil Ravenswood, general manager of the Arizona Biltmore, looks as though he came from Central Casting. The Aussie-turned Arizonan embodies the flair and easy elegance long associated with this resort. But don't for a moment suppose that Ravenswood takes the Biltmore's success casually: This is a man who enjoys competing hard—and plays to win. An anomaly in a business where frequent moves are the norm, Ravenswood, after more than a decade at the helm, appears permanent. Like the famous "Biltmore blocks," Maynard Dixon and Edith Hamlin tapestries, and Charles McArthur-Frank Lloyd Wright architectural controversy, Ravenswood adds to the Arizona Biltmore mystique.

Few resorts conjure up the immediate name recognition of the Arizona Biltmore. Owned by Rostland Corporation, a Canadian consortium, this resort has established the standard for excellence in the industry. It is, for example, this country's longest continuously awarded recipient of the prestigious *Mobil Travel Guide's* Five Star recognition. Although ownership and

Tourists and business people alike are attracted to the Arizona Biltmore for its central location and proximity to the airport.

management have changed during its 60-year history, the elegance, ambience, and service that define this hotel never have wavered.

However, the past isn't what Cecil Ravenswood wants to talk about. "I want to emphasize that while the Arizona Biltmore retains its history and its mystique, we have a totally new facility here," he says. "With the completion of the renovation in 1987, all of our rooms are the newest of any major resort in this valley. We've redone all our shops and added a new Southwest gallery created for us by valley entrepreneur Pam Del Duca." But new doesn't necessarily mean different, he cautions. "All our public rooms retain their traditional flavor."

Tradition is important to this resort. Monday-night cocktail parties are hosted by Ravenswood, and afternoon teas are open to all guests during the high season. Tradition is what keeps social guests such as Henry Foreman re-

turning each season—for nearly 60 years. It's what inspired the hotel to name the mezzanine history library and the drive west of the Conference Center for Howard Godown, head houseman from 1933 to 1973, zookeeper, and what Candice St. Jacques Miles in her history of the resort calls, "a seemingly omnipresent embodiment of Biltmore service." Tradition is not taken lightly at the Biltmore.

All of which makes this hotel's dynamic, progressive posture all the more remarkable. Observes Ravenswood, "We are a traditional hotel that is trying to address new markets while retaining the charm of the old. While we retain all that one associates with the Arizona Biltmore, we are also looking to capture the business market. We have so much to offer. We have 2 PGA championship golf courses, 17 tennis courts, 3 swimming pools, a magnificent setting, and an abundance of other features. Not only are we a full resort in the heart of town, but of all the major resorts in the country we are in the best proximity to a major airport. This is an extremely important feature to meeting-planners."

If position and proximity contribute to its success, physical improvements guarantee it. Within the past 15 years the Arizona Biltmore has undergone a total renovation. In 1975 the Paradise Wing was added. Four years later the Valley Wing and Conference Center were built. In 1982 the Terrace Court appeared on the grounds. The following year all the cottages were gutted, then modernized and given new, enlarged bathrooms. Finally, in the summer of 1987, the main building was rebuilt from the inside out. "This building had never been designed to accommodate air conditioning," Ravenswood points out. "Although air conditioning was added in 1963, it had never been energy efficient. In addition, the main building needed to be soundproofed to assure our guests a first-class experience in their rooms."

What changes have all this construction effected? Ravenswood smiles. While the hotel has doubled in size and quadrupled in meeting capacity, basically the Biltmore is as it always was. This is no small accomplishment. The hotel caters to the social and the business guest, pleasing both is a remarkable feat of physical planning and internal management. Outwardly, little has changed. The lobby and the Orangerie look just the same, Ravenswood says. Wrightian influences are what guests expect, and Westin Hotels & Resorts, the longtime management firm, appreciates the spirit that lives in the place.

By all accounts the spirit of the Biltmore is special. From its inception the hotel and estate area were planned in concert with the environment. The official history of the hotel states that the Arizona Biltmore was to have been part of the Bowman Biltmore Hotels, a chain of 14 elite operations. As developers Charles and Warren McArthur envisioned it in 1927, this particular project would come in at one million dollars. Plans included a resort built on 200 acres of citrus orchard in the foothills of Squaw Peak; the adjacent 400 acres were to become a residential park. Even by contemporary standards theirs was an exciting and visionary dream. Within a year, however, the brothers had to revise their cost estimates to $2 million as dreams became reality.

From the outset no expense was spared. A private water system was developed with a reservoir and on-site treatment plant. The area was the first to boast underground electrical facilities; roads and homes were positioned to accommodate water runoff and scenic views. A full mile of the canal crossing the property was incorporated into the master plan, and even a nursery was established to produce vegetables and fruits for the resort guests.

The hotel was to be the crown jewel. The McArthurs invited their brother, architect Albert Chase McArthur, to design the gemstone of the development. Albert McArthur, who had studied at the Armour Institute of Technology in Chicago and at Harvard, had worked as an apprentice draftsman to Frank Lloyd Wright and considered Wright his mentor. Indeed McArthur's faithful adherence to Wright principles, and his choice of textures and materials contribute to the long-disputed confusion over "authorship" of the hotel.

The famous gardens bloom in every season.

The Arizona Biltmore breathes elegance from every angle.

In the history of the Arizona Biltmore, St. Jacques Miles writes that McArthur designed the hotel. She notes that Wright was involved; he served in the unlikely capacity of construction supervisor for a short time. McArthur had requested permission to use the ornamental concrete block system that the master architect had devised, and Wright had agreed on the condition that he be invited to assist in the construction. Frank Lloyd Wright and his family stayed at the hotel for a few months, a time that the author refers to as "fraught with tension and disagreement."

From the outset rumors flew that Wright was really the project architect. McArthur anticipated this problem, and he asked Wright for a statement of record. Wright complied with a statement dated June 2, 1930:

To Whom It May Concern: All I have done in connection with the building of the Arizona Biltmore, near Phoenix, I have done for Albert McArthur himself at his sole request, and for none other. Albert McArthur is the architect of that building—all attempts to take the credit for that performance from him are gratuitous and beside the mark. But for him, Phoenix would have had nothing like the Biltmore, and it is my hope that he may be enabled to give Phoenix many more beautiful buildings as I believe him entirely capable of doing so.

Officially the Biltmore opened on February 23, 1929—hardly an auspicious year for the luxury business. Six weeks after the gold key was dropped from an airplane to the waiting crowd

Cecil Ravenswood, general manager.

342

(it actually landed on the roof), the season ended and the resort closed for the summer. Before the hotel could reopen for the winter season, the stock market crashed. When the hotel opened on schedule November 10, 1929, majority investor William Wrigley, Jr., found that he owned the hotel in reality if not in name.

The Wrigley association continued until Talley Industries purchased the resort and estate property—including the Wrigley mansion—from William's son, Philip, on June 6, 1973, for $21.5 million. Just two weeks later the Talley investment literally went up in smoke. Workmen were installing a sprinkler system when a spark from a welder's torch ignited insulation. The grand lady of the desert suffered serious burns, some $2.5 million worth of damage. Immediately Talley Industries hired the Frank Lloyd Wright Foundation at Taliesin West to redesign and refurbish the hotel, allotting 82 days for completion of the job.

When the hotel opened that season—on time—the new look garnered raves. Taliesin had found inspiration in Frank Lloyd Wright. A glass mural that had been designed by Wright in the 1920s graced the main entrance. Bolder colors, more in keeping with Wright's desert vision, now brightened the public areas.

Today it is difficult to imagine the Phoenix metropolitan valley without the gracious presence of the Biltmore. Its signature facade and green lawns are hallmarks of elegance. History glitters there. The gold room with its world-famous gold-leaf ceiling echoes with whispers of an era when "dressing for dinner" meant formal gowns and dinner jackets. The guest list is rich with names such as Nancy and Ronald Reagan, who honeymooned at the Biltmore, and Edna Ferber, who penned novels there. Henry Kissinger rested from shuttle diplomacy, Clark Gable played golf, and Irving Berlin became a regular—all at the Biltmore. Jimmy Durante, President Gerald Ford, Elizabeth Taylor, the Duke and Duchess of Windsor, Clare Booth Luce, and George Burns and Gracie Allen—the jewel of the desert beckoned the great and the famous to Phoenix.

It also attracts a healthy conference and meeting business. "One of the things we do best is that we can hold a meeting for 40 to 1,000 people without interruptions to our leisure guests," says Ravenswood. "Our conference center was designed to be separate, and it works better than even we expected." The National Football League, the Arizona Bankers, the Aerospace Industry Association, and Price Waterhouse are just a few of the longtime regulars and repeaters who return to the Biltmore year after year. "We have an innovative conference service team," the general manager continues. "We believe it is one of the best in the country."

Being one of the best in the country is what the Arizona Biltmore is all about. Asked how he maintains that edge, Ravenswood does not hesitate. "Our greatest asset is the people of this hotel," he replies. "We have a longtime staff, who are extremely dedicated. Our building superintendent, Roger Keltgen, retired after 30 years. Our housekeeper, Ellen Galland-Burkel, has more than 20 years of service with Westin Hotels. Our food and beverage director has been here more than 10 years. I can honestly say that I have never been blessed with a better crew."

The newly renovated main building retains its traditional charm.

AVANTI

The story has the ingredients for a screenplay; the players are straight out of Central Casting; even the ending is happy-ever-after perfect.

Four handsome young European waiters meet in Bermuda in 1964. They travel on to the Bahamas, where they continue to work together at a hotel. After seven years they decide to open their own restaurant. Accordingly, Ramon Vives from Barcelona, Angelo Livi from Florence, Benito Mellino from Capri, and Franco Ferrandi from Milano open Portofino in Barcelona in 1972. A second restaurant soon follows.

Two years later Franco and Ramon arrive in Arizona. Unabashed sunlovers, they see a golden opportunity in the desert city. On January 1, 1975, Franco and Ramon open Avanti, a sophisticated restaurant featuring northern Italian cuisine. Avanti takes off immediately. Angelo and Benito join Avanti and open the second restaurant in Scottsdale.

In 1976 they open Ibiza, which offers the cuisine of Spain. Although the Scottsdale location is a hit, the menu is ahead of its time; Arizona isn't ready for *tapas.* It becomes Avanti of Scottsdale and adopts the northern Italian menu.

Success follows success for the four. In 1984 they open Prego, "a casual Avanti," in Phoenix and expand to California with Avanti of LaJolla. But will success spoil Ramon, Angelo,

Piano bar.

Top: *Pasta bar.*

Above: *Dining room.*

Benito, and Franco? "We've been partners for 20 years," says Ramon. "While we each brought our own specialties to the restaurant business, we each take care of our own restaurants."

"Avanti means 'go forward,'" he continues, speaking to this partnership's remarkable longevity. He suggests that consistency is the key to Avanti's story. Not only have the four partners remained intact, but, he points out, the staff is stable. "We have the same waiters and busboys for years," Ramon says. "Our chefs have been with us for years and years. Consistency is the main reason we have been successful."

Although now employing 125, the owners still greet customers at the door. "We have no manager; we always take care of our places," Ramon continues.

This combination of personal attention, exquisite interiors, and outstanding food has made Avanti Restaurants Phoenix favorites. In addition to attracting area residents and winter visitors, Avanti is a perennial favorite of celebrities. Julio Iglesias has been known to entertain spontaneously after enjoying a leisurely dinner.

At Avanti there's always a tempting array of elegant appetizers and outstanding entrées such as delicately prepared fresh fish, paella, specialty veal dishes, *osso buco,* and *saltimbocca fiorentina.* A fresh pasta bar and desserts complete the dining experience. And catering is available from the Scottsdale location.

"I definitely believe that Italian food is the best food," concludes Ramon. "It offers the most variety." Whether it's Benito salad, Ramon steak tartare, chicken breast Angelo, filet mignon à la Franco, or a Cappuccino Avanti, the menu bears him out.

CAMELVIEW-A RADISSON RESORT

Anyone who visits the Phoenix metropolitan valley leaves with an indelible vision: Blue skies. Towering mountains. Intriguing deserts. Add to this a sophisticated urban area that is young, vibrant, and second to none—and it is clear why the Phoenix area is a favorite tourist destination.

At Camelview-A Radisson Resort, all this and more awaits both the pleasure and the business traveler. There, business and pleasure are elevated to a new art.

Located on 35 lushly landscaped acres in the heart of an elegant Phoenix suburb, the property includes 200 beautifully appointed guest rooms with 17 one- and two-bedroom suites. All rooms have every convenience—cable, clock radios, and breathtaking views. Suites are equipped with stereos, video cassette players, and free movies. In addition to these accommodations, Camelview will offer guests a choice of luxury town house suites at the Courtyards in the near future.

Dining at the Camelview is an exciting gourmet experience. At The Café on the Lakes Restaurant, serving breakfast, lunch, and dinner, specialties include slow-roasted prime rib, creative pastas, and fresh seafood. Gracious and

A recent $3.5-million renovation of guest rooms, lobby, and restaurant reflects the natural color and beauty of the Southwest in a striking, contemporary setting.

attentive service complement the chef's cuisine. For a more secluded atmosphere, guests may prefer the private dining room.

As for casual entertainment, Camelview can satisfy every mood. The Café Lounge boasts specialty wines or cocktails in an intimate setting; the Lobby Lounge features premium wines and champagnes by the glass, complimentary hors d'oeuvres six nights per week, and nightly movies and current sporting events on a big screen television. The Fountain Courtyard offers cocktail service to take advantage of the famous Phoenix weather. Finally, the Pool Bar serves light snacks and refreshments during the day. Of course, room service is just a phone call away.

Successful meetings are the rule at Camelview. Meeting planners can choose from more than 15,000 square feet of meeting space, and 11 major gathering rooms are designed to provide flexible accommodations in terms of size, acoustics, and decor. In addition, three executive business suites for up to 14 people and 14 one-bedroom suites perfect for hospitality functions or VIP accommodations make Camelview a superior choice.

In planning meetings this resort makes it a policy to pay special attention to outdoor and prefunction areas. Not only does this allow groups more flexibility, but it enables those who attend the meeting to enjoy the great Arizona weather. At the Camelview, Phoenix-area friendliness means that no detail is too small for the staff. Every function, from a welcoming reception to a formal, elaborate banquet is efficiently and happily handled.

Finally, this premier resort is full service when it comes to fun. Lighted tennis courts and a heated swimming pool are on the property, and golf and horseback riding are nearby. Shopping, desert jeep excursions, and the cultural facilities of the Phoenix metropolitan area can fill every vacationing hour.

Outstanding meetings and unforgettable memories make Camelview a Phoenix favorite.

Camelview provides an elegant setting close to recreation and shopping, yet away from the hectic pace.

KARLSON MACHINE WORKS, INC.

"When I welcome new employees aboard, I make sure that they start off with a solid footing," says Gail E. Houser, general manager of Karlson Machine Works, Inc. Karlson employees are made aware that the firm emerged after several years of struggle. "It took dedication, hard work, and sacrifice to build this company, and we want our employees to share in our pride," concludes Houser.

With virtually no money and very little credit, the Karlson family carved a successful enterprise from what started as a backyard business. In 1932 Andrew J. and Marie C. Karlson set up shop in the rear of their Phoenix home, providing commercial and industrial refrigeration installation and service repair work for produce, meat packing, and dairy stores. This small venture, born during the height of the Great Depression, has blossomed and grown into one of the largest independently owned and operated job repair machine shops in the southwestern portion of the United States.

"The company was built slow but steady by adding one new piece of equipment each year," says Houser. Decisions such as gradually shifting the firm's marketing emphasis away from the refrigeration business and toward providing repair services to the mining and construction industries in Arizona ultimately created explosive growth for

Karlson Machine Works, Inc., is the acknowledged expert in heavy industrial job service repair, serving the construction, mining, manufacturing, timber, utility, and service industries in the Southwest.

the corporation. In the 1970s sales increased an average of 33 percent each year through the end of the decade.

To better serve its many Arizona mining customers, Karlson Machine Works acquired another well-established machine shop, J.G. Biggs and Sons, in 1978. This proved to be very prosperous, enabling the company's Tucson plant to completely pay for itself two years ahead of schedule.

The dramatic fall of "King Copper" in the early 1980s prompted the firm to reestablish its goals. Karlson expanded its sales and marketing efforts, promoting the organization as the acknowledged expert in heavy industrial job service repair, serving the construction, mining, manufacturing, timber, utility, and service industries in the Southwest. Along with the marketing changes the company suffered some setbacks, such as the 1986 closing of Industrial Design and Machine, Inc., a Tempe prototype shop that it purchased in 1984. Reorganization continued through 1987, at which time the Tucson division was closed to further consolidate operations and continue to cut overhead and operational costs.

Responding to a changing market, the organization made smart business judgments. The closure of some of its facilities, disposal of nonprofitable assets, and the continual monitoring of daily expenses, job costs, and operational efficiencies have kept Karlson Machine Works in the forefront in a growing city.

Karlson's strong belief in customer satisfaction is part of the firm's recipe for success. "Providing high-quality service entails more than just being available 24 hours a day," says Houser. "Karlson Machine Works believes that when our customers have a problem, we have an obligation to completely satisfy that problem.

"Along with the massive influx of people and business into Phoenix, our commitment to high-quality and expedient delivery continues to grow," says Houser. "The company policy of aggressive yet stable growth will ensure a rewarding, profitable, and secure future for many years to come."

CPS DIRECT MARKETING

CPS Direct Marketing has a direct line to success. With 600 full-time employees, the firm projects revenues in 1989 in excess of $150 million. For the past few years the compounded growth rate has exceeded 20 percent. These numbers tell a major marketing story and are a long way from the organizer wallet developed in 1961 by Canadians Joy and Murray Hall.

That wallet evolved into Ambassador Leather, which relocated to Phoenix in 1969. During the 1970s the company was purchased by an investment group, and in 1980 it became part of the MacDonald Companies. In 1984 Carson Pirie Scott and Company, headquartered in Chicago, acquired the organization, bringing new energy, the dream to become a major catalog marketer, and a new name—CPS Direct Marketing.

While Ambassador Leather remains integral to the line, CPS emerged, within five years, as a leading multiproduct organization with an ever-growing impact on direct-to-the-consumer catalog marketing. Cur-

Nearly all aspects of the CPS Direct Marketing operation are carried out at the South Mountain Phoenix facility.

rently CPS catalogs include Ambassador, Easy Living, Chris-Craft, Jewelry Values, Beauty Collection, Compartment Store, Private Edition, Clothes to Home, and Appointments—and there's more to come. The syndication division, Arizona National Marketing, Inc., markets products to the credit customers of major oil firms, retailers, and travel companies.

The CPS philosophy is succinct: be customer driven and bring the store to the people. Merchandise is developed by an in-house group that shops the world, working with fabric designers and fabricators to assure that fashions are current and unique. Catalogs are designed for immediate reader attention. Superior customer service is emphasized in all phases of selection and shopping.

From creating catalogs to researching products, from purchasing to shipping to customer service, CPS calls Arizona home. Nearly all aspects of the operation are carried out at the South Mountain Phoenix facility, with the exception of catalog printing, some of which is done by Meredith/Burda at its Casa Grande plant. From fashions to generated revenues, CPS Direct Marketing has a direct, positive impact on Phoenix.

CPS has become a major contender in direct-to-the-consumer catalog marketing.

Phoenix: Shining Star

Time has shown us that great cities are not born but built. They are more than brick and mortar; they are the result of commitment of leadership, recognition of opportunity, and application of valuable resources. Virtually all cities are in competition for these resources, whether they take the form of investment capital, people, or jobs. Garnering these resources and helping to focus them on opportunities that make positive contributions to the future health of the city is the motivating force that led to the creation of the Phoenix Economic Growth Corporation.

Judgments about the future of Phoenix require an understanding of what we are today and what our options for to-

This view of Phoenix was shot from the balcony of the Governor's Office at the state capitol. The copper on the dome was donated by Arizona mining companies; the white figure atop the dome is called "Winged Victory." Photo by Nyle Leatham

With careful water management, Phoenix will remain a vibrant oasis. Photo by Nyle Leatham

morrow can be. These questions were the focal point of a strategic economic development plan completed in 1986 in concert with The Fantus Company. The plan serves as Phoenix' economic blueprint for tomorrow.

Today, Phoenix stands as one of the nation's fastest growing major cities. This growth is fueling Phoenix's emergence as the regional commercial center for the entire Southwest; it also trumpets the challenge to build not only a big, but also a better,

city for all who live and work here. The foundation to meet this challenge has already been created with the passage, in 1988, of a $1.1-billion quality of life bond issue.

The city's economic performance over the past two decades has been stellar. This performance, along with the determination and pride of the Western spirit, will carry Phoenix to new heights in the twenty-first century.

PATRONS

The following individuals, companies, and organizations have made a valuable commitment to the quality of this publication. Windsor Publications and the Phoenix Economic Growth Corporation gratefully acknowledge their participation in *Phoenix: America's Shining Star: A Contemporary Portrait.*

ABCO Markets, Inc.*
Advanced Copy Systems, Inc.*
Allied-Signal Aerospace
    Company*
American Greyhound
    Racing, Inc.*
Ameron Southwest Concrete
    Pipe Division*
Arizona Biltmore*
Arizona Central Credit Union*
Arizona Public Service Company*
Avanti*
Balmer Architectural Group,
    Inc.*
Best Western International*
Blue Cross and Blue Shield
    of Arizona*
Brown & Bain*
Business Equipment Inc.*
Callahan Mining Corporation*
Camelview-A Radisson Resort*
John Carollo Engineers*
Carroon & Black/Olliver Pilcher*
Chase Bank of Arizona*

Cole Equities Incorporated*
Continental Homes*
Coopers & Lybrand*
CPS Direct Marketing*
CyCare Systems*
Digital Equipment Corporation*
DWL Architects+Planners, Inc.*
Emerald Homes*
Evans, Kitchel & Jenckes*
Exodyne, Inc.*
Famous Restaurants Inc.*
Fennemore Craig*
Franzoy Corey Engineers &
    Architects*
Fujitsu Business
    Communication Systems*
Goldwaters*
W.L. Gore & Associates*
Gosnell Builders*
Grand Canyon Color Lab*
GTE Communication Systems
    Corporation*
Phyllis Hawkins & Associates*
Horizon Moving Systems, Inc.*
IBM Corporation*
Johnson & Higgins of
    Arizona, Inc.*
KAMJ Radio*
Karlson Machine Works, Inc.*
The Koll Company*
KPHO*
Lewis and Roca*
M&D Electrical Parts*
MCI*
MechTronics of Arizona, Inc.*

Meyer, Hendricks, Victor,
    Osborn & Maledon*
MicroAge, Inc.*
National Vision Services, Inc.*
North American Pharmaceutical
    Services, Inc.*
Paragon Group*
Phelps Dodge Corporation*
The Phoenix Plaza*
Ramada, Inc.*
Roberson and Company*
Salt River Project*
Service Control Corporation*
SGS-THOMSON Micro-
    electronics*
Shasta Pools*
Snell & Wilmer
Southwest Gas Corporation*
Storey & Ross*
Sunbelt Holdings, Inc.*
Sun State Savings*
Superlite*
Swift Transportation
    Company, Inc.*
Talley Industries, Inc.*
Trammell Crow*
UDC-Universal
    Development L.P.*
Valley National Bank of Arizona*
Waste Management of Phoenix*
Young, Smith & Peacock, Inc.*

*Participants in Part Two: "Phoenix' Enterprises." The stories of these companies and organizations appear throughout the book.

BIBLIOGRAPHY

Annual Report. Phoenix: Phoenix Aviation Department, 1984.

Annual Valley Progress Report. Phoenix: *Metro Phoenix* magazine, 1974-1988.

Arizona. Phoenix: Arizona Department of Commerce and the State of Arizona, U.S.A. Asian-Pacific Trade Office, 1988.

Arizona: 1987 Economic Profile. Phoenix: Business and Trade Program, Arizona Department of Commerce, 1988.

Arizona Business. Tempe: Arizona State University College of Business Center for Business Research, 1987 and 1988.

Arizona's Changing Economy, Trends and Prospects. Phoenix: Arizona Department of Commerce, 1986.

Arizona Exports. U.S. Department of Commerce, August 1984.

Arizona Labor Market Information Newsletter. Phoenix: Arizona Department of Economic Security, 1986 and 1987.

Arizona 1986-87 Directory of Exporters. Phoenix: Arizona Department of Commerce, October 1986.

Arizona Occupational Profiles. Phoenix: Arizona Department of Economic Security, 1986-1988.

The *Arizona Republic.* Articles. 1987 and 1988.

Arizona's Industrial Structure. Tempe: Center for Business Research, College of Business, Arizona State University, September 1986.

Arizona's Statistical Review. 42nd and 43rd Annual Editions. Phoenix: Valley National Bank of Arizona, September 1986 and September 1987.

"Arizona's Suburbs of the Sun." *National Geographic* magazine. Vol. 152, No. 4, October 1977.

Arizona Trend magazine. 1987 and 1988.

Arizona Waterline. Phoenix: Salt River Project, 1984-1988.

Bartlett, Michael H.; Kolaz, Thomas M.; and Gregory, David A. *Archaeology in the City: A Hohokam Village in Phoenix, Arizona.* Tucson: University of Arizona Press, 1986.

Buchanan, James E. *Phoenix: A Chronological and Documentary History, 1865-1976.* Dobbs Ferry, NY: Oceana, 1978.

Business Formation: 1981-1986; Impact on Metro Phoenix. Phoenix: Phoenix Metropolitan Chamber of Commerce Economic Research Group, 1987.

Christensen, Anne Driggs; Lambert, Linda Quimby; and Sikes, Diane Owens. *Phoenix: A Guide to Phoenix, Scottsdale and the Valley.* 6th edition. Phoenix: Valley Publishing Company, 1986.

Cities Are People. Phoenix: Phoenix Metrogroup; the Chambers of Commerce of Metropolitan Phoenix, 1987.

Coffer, William E. *Decline and Rebirth of the Indian People.* New York: Van Nostrand Reinhold, 1979.

Davis, Arthur Powell. *Water Storage on the Salt River.* Arizona Department of Interior, 1903.

Dutton, Allen A. *Phoenix Then and Now.* Phoenix: First Interstate Bank, 1984.

Economic Assets of Metropolitan Phoenix. Phoenix: Salt River Project, 1987.

Evans, Edna H. *Arizona: The Story of Our State.* Cave Creek: Black Mountain Press, 1980.

Forecast 1987. Phoenix: Western Savings and Loan Association, 1988.

"Growing Places: The Best (and Worst) Business Climates in America." *Inc.* magazine. October 1986.

Hello Phoenix! Phoenix: Phoenix Arts Coming Together, March 27-28, 1982.

Horizons Yesterday— Tomorrow. Salt River Project, n.d.

"Hot Spots." *Inc.* magazine. April 1987.

Inside Phoenix. Phoenix: Phoenix Newspapers, Inc., Marketing Department, 1980-1988.

Johnson, G. Wesley Jr. *Phoenix: Valley of the Sun.* Tulsa, OK: Continental Heritage Press, 1982.

MAG *Regional Development Summary, 1987.* Phoenix: Maricopa Association of Governments, 1987.

"Managing Change." *Arizona Capitol Times.* May 20, 1987.

McPheters, Lee R. *High Technology Manufacturing.* Tempe: Bureau of Business and Economic Research, College of Business Administration, Arizona State University, 1986.

Metropolitan Profiles. Phoenix: Metropolitan Phoenix, 1987.

"Phoenix." *Metro Phoenix* magazine. November 1986.

Phoenix: A Blue Print for Growth. Phoenix Economic Growth Corporation and the Fantus Company of Chicago, April 1986.

Phoenix Area Manpower Review. Phoenix: Employment Security Commission, 1968-1988.

Phoenix, Arizona: Location Opportunities in Telecommunications. Phoenix: Phoenix Economic Growth Corporation, October 1987.

The *Phoenix Gazette.* Articles. 1987 and 1988.

Pulliam, Russell. *Publisher Gene Pulliam: Last of the Newspaper Titans.* Ottawa, IL: Jameson Books, 1984.

"Selling the Valley." *Arizona Capitol Times,* September 23, 1987.

Seventy-fourth Annual Report of the Director of Insurance. State of Arizona, December 31, 1986.

Sky Harbor Center Redevelopment Area Plan. April 24, 1985.

Smith, Karen L. *The Magnificent Experience.* The University of Arizona Press, 1986.

"Taking Measure of Metro Phoenix." *America West Airlines Magazine.* September 1986.

Trimble, Marshall. *A Panoramic History of a Frontier State.* Garden City, NY: Doubleday & Company, Inc., 1977.

Update of the Population and Socioeconomic Database for Maricopa County. Mountain West: Maricopa Association of Governments, May 1987.

"Urban Land Institute 1985 Fall Meeting Project Brochure: Phoenix Metropolitan Area . . . Today." Phoenix, 1985.

Visitor's Guide. Phoenix: Phoenix and Valley of the Sun Convention and Visitor's Bureau, Fall/Winter 1987.

Wyllys, Rufus K. *Arizona: The History of a Frontier State.* Phoenix: Hobson and Herr, 1950.

Zarbin, Earl. *The Swilling Legacy.* Salt River Project, June 3, 1980.

INDEX

General Index

Italics indicate illustrations.
Bold type indicates sidebars.